Late Stone Age Hunters of the British Isles

Christoph

ROUTLEDGE

London and New York

First published 1992
by Routledge
11 New Fetter Lane, London EC4P 4EE

Simultaneously published in the USA and Canada
by Routledge
29 West 35th Street, New York, NY 10001

Reprinted 1997

Set in 10/12pt Times by Florencetype Ltd, Stoodleigh, Devon
Printed in Great Britain by T.J. International Ltd, Padstow, Cornwall

British Library Cataloguing in Publication Data
Smith, Christopher
    Late Stone Age hunters of the British Isles.
    I. Title
    930.12

Library of Congress Cataloguing in Publication Data
Smith, Christopher.
    Late Stone Age hunters of the British Isles / Christopher Smith.
        p. cm.
    Includes bibliographical references and index.
    1. Palaeolithic period – Great Britain. 2. Mesolithic period – Great Britain. 3.
Tools, Prehistoric – Great Britain. 4. Animal remains (Archaeology) – Great
Britain. 5. Palaeoecology – Great Britain. 6. Great Britain – Antiquities. I.
Title.
GN772.22.G7S65 1992
936.1 – dc20 91–23152

ISBN 0–415–07202–6

Printed on paper manufactured in accordance with the proposed ANSI/NISO Z
39.48–199X and ANSI Z 39.48–1984

Contents

Preface

A book about the Stone Age which has comparatively little to say about stone tools calls for some explanation. The origins of this work lie in a public lecture entitled 'The Red Deer, the Seal and the Limpet' given at the University of Newcastle on 5 October 1987, and an undergraduate course taught since 1983 in the Archaeology Department of the same institution. In both the lecture and the course I sought to shift the emphasis away from the study of stone tools, which has been the traditional approach to the archaeology of the Stone Age, and towards the environmental context within which Stone Age people lived their lives. My reasons for adopting this approach are twofold.

Having been trained in both archaeology and geography, my interests have always lain within the area in which these two subjects overlap. The issue which has interested me most is that of the relationships which exist between people and their environment, on both the small scale of the individual site and on the larger scale of the settlement pattern as a whole. Only very rarely have I become involved in the study of stone tools and claim no expertise in this field. There are numerous works dealing with this topic, and if they are out of date there are others far more competent than me to undertake their revision.

The study of stone tools has made important contributions to our knowledge of the past in two respects, however. First, insofar as we can learn how these tools were made and used, they have much to tell us about human behaviour. This aspect of stone tool studies makes an important contribution to the approach I have followed. Second, the way stone tools changed over time has been used to provide a chronological framework and, indeed, this lies behind the concept of a 'Stone Age' which antedated ages of bronze and iron. This method of establishing a chronological framework for the past always had its difficulties. Stone-tool types did not obligingly change at regular intervals and new discoveries, by showing that a particular type was in use earlier, later or for longer than had hitherto been supposed, led to a need for constant revision. The development and widespread application of the technique of radiocarbon dating is rendering chronologies based on stone tool typologies obsolete. Over

300 dates are available for the period covered by this book and the chronological framework I have used is based exclusively on that provided by radiocarbon dating.

While I hope this book will be of interest to archaeologists, and be of some use to students of the subject, I also hope colleagues and students in the natural sciences and geography will find it helpful to have the archaeological evidence from this period summarized within a framework they should find familiar. The period in question, from 13,000 to 5000 BP, is known to archaeologists as the late Upper Palaeolithic and Mesolithic, though I shall have little occasion to use these terms. Natural scientists and geographers will know it as part of the Lateglacial and the early Postglacial.

The book begins with an introduction to the approach that I have adopted. There follow two chapters in which the hunter-gatherer way of life and the archaeological traces it leaves are examined. Readers not very interested in methodology may prefer to skip these chapters and proceed straight to chapter 4, which offers a summary of the main issues raised in chapters 2 and 3, presented in the form of a framework within which the archaeological evidence for the Late Stone Age hunters of the British Isles may be reviewed. We then proceed to a summary of the environmental conditions prevailing during the period in question, and the ways in which they changed. The next three chapters consist of case studies in which a range of archaeological discoveries is reviewed. The case studies concentrate attention at the level of the individual site, while in the final chapter the scale of observation is increased to that of the region as a whole.

A work of synthesis is based primarily on the work of others. I make few claims for originality and my debt to colleagues will be obvious to all who are familiar with the subject. Each chapter concludes with an 'Additional reading' section in which I have cited the main works used. Readers who wish to pursue particular topics further may do so via these references.

A string of radiocarbon dates can make an untidy mess of even the most well-honed paragraph and within the text each date is quoted in approximate terms only. All dates used are in Radiocarbon Years Before Present (BP) and are listed in full in an appendix. Archaeological sites are referred to by their most commonly used name, but the first time a site is mentioned its National Grid Reference (NGR, or INGR for sites in Ireland) is also given. Similarly, I have used the common English names for plants and animals but quote the full scientific name the first time each occurs.

Like all subjects, archaeology has developed its own specialist terminology, otherwise known as jargon. I have done my best to avoid using unfamiliar terms, or familiar terms in an unfamiliar way, but sometimes this is unavoidable. Where any term is used in a specialized sense a definition is provided. When it is used subsequently this definition can be found via the index.

This preface began with some words of explanation about part of the title and I will conclude with some remarks about the rest. The geographical expression the 'British Isles' is unambiguous and I hope uncontroversial. But in these days of widespread vegetarianism some readers may blanch at the reference to 'hunters', rather than hunter-gatherers, or hunter-fishers, or even hunter-fisher-gatherers, all of which are used regularly. No offence is intended. In spite of attempts by some to promote the role of plant foods in the diet of pre-farming peoples the fact remains that in middle latitudes, such as those occupied by the British Isles, it would be impossible to subsist on wild plant foods alone for more than a short period. The people of the Late Stone Age had to hunt to survive. It is also the case that the collection and consumption of plant foods leaves little or no archaeological trace and most of the available evidence relates to hunting, both in terms of equipment and the victims of the hunt. Plant foods could undoubtedly be important but the evidence is such that this book is mainly about Late Stone Age hunting. Hence the title.

NOTE TO THE 1997 PRINTING

Apart from a few minor corrections, the main text is the same as that published in 1992. I have, however, taken the opportunity of making a number of changes to the 'Additional Reading' sections found at the end of each chapter. This has been to take account of new work published in substantive form since the original text was completed in the summer of 1990. It has been necessary to undertake these revisions within the existing pagination of the volume. In some cases where new material has to be referred to this has been at the expense of references to earlier work. I hope readers will continue to find these sections of the book useful. The updating of the 'Additional Reading' sections has, of course, also necessitated changes to the bibliography.

Acknowledgements

I am most grateful to the following friends and colleagues who have read and commented on sections of the text in draft: Clive Bonsall, John Chapman, Pat Lynch, John Manley, Professor Sean McGrail, Tony Smith, Myra Tolan, Richard Willis and Rob Young. They made many helpful suggestions and in all cases where I followed their advice the text has been improved. I accept the blame for whatever shortcomings remain.

With the exception of figure 1.2, all the line drawings have been drafted by Sandra Hooper, the illustrator in the Department of Archaeology, Newcastle University. The book has been greatly enhanced by Sandra's skilful realization of my often rather vague notions about the visual presentation of archaeological data. I also thank her for her patience and forbearance in the face of my unreasonable attitude to deadlines.

This book could not have been written without the support of my colleagues in the Department of Archaeology who made it possible for me to take a substantial period of study leave in 1990 during which the text was completed. My thanks to them all, and especially to Kevin Greene for encouragement and guidance through the pitfalls of book production. As I explained in the preface this book has grown out of a lecture course and I am grateful to several generations of students for their comments and for their blank, uncomprehending expressions which encouraged me to try to explain things better. I hope that some will feel that I have succeeded.

Lastly, the following organizations and individuals are to be thanked for agreeing to the reproduction of photographs: Lindsay Allason-Jones and the Museum of Antiquities of the University of Newcastle upon Tyne, Clive Bonsall, The British Library, The British Museum, Bodil Bratlund and Archäologisches Landesmuseum Schleswig, Cambridge University Committee for Aerial Photography, Canadian Museum of Civilization, Margaret Deith, Hans Kruuk, Paul Mellars, Museum of Mankind, Royal Museum of Scotland, Royal Ontario Museum, Sue Stallibrass, University of Newcastle upon Tyne Library and Audio-Visual Centre, Derek Upton, W. A. B. van der Sanden and Drents Museum, Richard Willis, and Peter Woodman.

1 Introduction

Captain William Hawkins was not only one of the great navigators of the Age of Discovery, he also had a taste for the curious and an eye for the sensational. When he returned to London in 1532 from a voyage to the South Atlantic, in addition to the surviving members of his crew, he had on board a Brazilian 'chieftain' whom he presented to Henry VIII 'at the sight of whom the King and all the nobilitie did not a little marvelle, and not without cause'. Illustrations of such 'alien' beings had been circulating in Europe since the early years of the century, but not until towards its end did it occur to anyone to suggest that comparably 'savage' peoples might once have lived in Britain. In 1585 John White, a highly talented artist, joined Sir Walter Raleigh's expedition to Virginia and, in addition to Indians, he drew a series of ancient Britons and Picts, giving them many characteristics in common with the indigenous peoples of the eastern seaboard of America. Many others followed suit, and American Indians were soon being used as sources of analogy in the interpretation of stone tools, and as points of reference for the reconstruction of ancient British society. According to John Aubrey, writing in 1659, the ancient British of Wiltshire 'were 2 or 3 degrees, I suppose, less savage than the Americans'.

This fascination with people of an alien way of life has remained with us, and hardly a week passes when groups of hunter-gatherers in tropical or sub-polar regions cannot be watched on television or read about in the more serious newspapers and supplements. There are many reasons for this interest, and at various times such societies have been seen as 'savage' (but noble), 'primitive' as opposed to 'advanced', and 'simple' as opposed to 'complex'. They are certainly much 'greener' than anyone else, and, living their lives in harmony with the natural world, they provide an example for us all. Recently, to this fascination has been added real concern over the future of surviving indigenous peoples in the face of development and habitat loss. It is to be hoped that this sympathy can be effectively mobilized in their support, and in this respect I believe archaeology has an important part to play.

Ten thousand years ago the world was inhabited by hunter-gatherers.

From the emergence of the first humans, perhaps 3 or 4 million years ago, people had lived exclusively by scavenging, gathering and hunting. Compared with this immense span of time, the last few millennia when food production or farming has become predominant form a very brief part of the cumulative human experience. In the long term, that experience has been one of hunting and gathering and for the great majority of that time the only evidence available is that provided by archaeology. By documenting aspects of the past which are common to all, archaeology makes an important contribution to the study of human life in general, and in all its diversity. An increasing awareness of that diversity may perhaps lead to an appreciation of its value and a will to maintain it.

In the intellectual climate of the seventeenth century, which viewed world history in terms of the Old Testament, the savage ancient Britons of Aubrey and his contemporaries were thought to have lived in the period immediately preceding the Roman conquest. It was not until the revolution in natural science in the middle years of the nineteenth century that the full antiquity of the human species became established. Present evidence suggests that the first humans to reach the British Isles arrived about half a million years ago during the period known to archaeologists as the Palaeolithic or Old Stone Age. This term was first used by Sir John Lubbock along with the term Neolithic, or New Stone Age, in his book *Prehistoric Times as Illustrated by Ancient Remains and the Manners and Customs of Modern Savages*, published in 1865. Since then archaeologists have subdivided the Palaeolithic into Lower, Middle and Upper stages, and added a Mesolithic between the Upper Palaeolithic and Neolithic, while further subdivisions such as late Upper Palaeolithic add to the potential for confusion. At one time it was believed that the advent of the Neolithic coincided with the adoption of farming, and while this remains generally true, the transition was rarely clear-cut or simultaneous. To avoid the arbitrariness of such schemes, the period covered by this book is defined in geomorphological and economic, rather than archaeological, terms.

At the height of the last glaciation, about 18,000 years ago, the British Isles were devoid of human settlement. People did not start to return until about 13,000 years ago when the amelioration of the climate was well under way, and this book begins with this re-establishment of human settlement after a lapse of several thousand years. It ends with the widespread establishment of farming 8,000 years later. Throughout this period we are dealing with the activities of *Homo sapiens sapiens*, a creature to all intents and purposes biologically indistinguishable from modern humans. This would not necessarily have been the case had this study been extended into earlier periods. The time covered spans the late Upper Palaeolithic and Mesolithic and stops with the onset of the Neolithic. I find it simpler to refer to all these episodes as the Late Stone Age.

TYPOLOGY AND CULTURE HISTORY

The systematic study of this period in Britain can be said to have begun with the publication of Dorothy Garrod's *The Upper Palaeolithic Age in Britain* in 1926 and *The Mesolithic Age in Britain* by J. G. D. Clark in 1932. Both are essentially treatises on the development of stone tool typology and as such set the tone for most subsequent work. In the days before radiocarbon dating, the classification of stone tools, leading to the delineation of 'cultures' and 'technocomplexes' (see chapter 3 for a further explanation of these terms) provided one of the few ways in which archaeological sites could be dated, and the concentration of most early work on this aspect of the subject is hardly surprising. Less easy to understand is the amount of attention still given to this topic, when radiocarbon dating has provided an independent, objective temporal framework.

As I have mentioned in the preface, it is not my intention to deal in any detail with the topic of typology, and readers seeking further details are referred to the works cited in the 'Additional reading' section at the end of this chapter. However, since so much written on the period has been presented within the terms of the traditional typological framework, readers may find it helpful to have the main outlines of the conventional scheme summarized here. I have attempted to do this mainly in the form of two diagrams (figs 1.1 and 1.2). Examples of virtually all the 'diagnostic' types are also illustrated elsewhere in the book.

It has been the practice in the typological, or culture history, approach to place most British late Upper Palaeolithic material in a single 'culture' or 'technocomplex' known as the *Creswellian*, which takes its name from the group of sites at Creswell Crags in Derbyshire. This Creswellian group appears to have technological affinities in neighbouring parts of Europe, especially with the *Federmesser* and *Hamburgian* groups of the Low Countries and northern Germany, and these in turn may be regarded as aspects of the *Magdalenian*, the latest of the major technocomplexes of the Upper Palaeolithic in western Europe. These technological links are not surprising, given that the resettlement of the British Isles amounted to little more than an extension of the existing pattern of settlement on the North European Plain. Stone artefacts regarded as diagnostic of the Creswellian in Britain consist of a range of points made on blades (fig. 1.1b–e), usually regarded as the tips of spears or arrows, though this need not necessarily always have been the case. Significant differences are believed to occur in the extent to which these items were retouched and in the provision made for hafting.

The Creswellian group remained dominant through the late Upper Palaeolithic in Britain, though occasionally new forms appeared which may indicate a continuing spread of people or ideas from the Continent while there remained land bridges. The best examples are *Brommian* and *Ahrensburgian* points (fig. 1.1f and g), both of which are common in northern Germany and southern Scandinavia and occur in small numbers

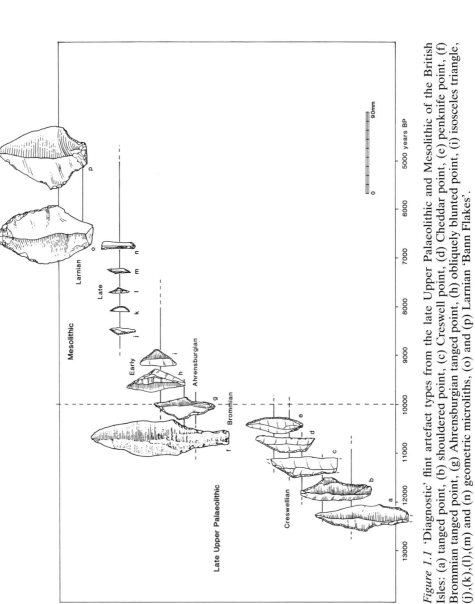

Figure 1.1 'Diagnostic' flint artefact types from the late Upper Palaeolithic and Mesolithic of the British Isles: (a) tanged point, (b) shouldered point, (c) Creswell point, (d) Cheddar point, (e) penknife point, (f) Brommian tanged point, (g) Ahrensburgian tanged point, (h) obliquely blunted point, (i) isosceles triangle, (j),(k),(l),(m) and (n) geometric microliths, (o) and (p) Larnian 'Bann Flakes'.

mainly in southern and eastern Britain. They were presumably in widespread use across the North Sea Lowlands, which may have been one of the most densely occupied areas of northern Europe at the time.

The Mesolithic period conventionally begins with the onset of the Postglacial, but late Upper Palaeolithic assemblages continue to be found with rather later dates while the earliest Mesolithic assemblages antedate the end of the Lateglacial. The diagnostic artefact of Mesolithic assemblages is the microlith; microliths may be divided into two main categories according to whether they have been manufactured on broad or narrow blades. Assemblages with broad-blade microliths are held to be typical of the earlier Mesolithic (fig. 1.1h and i), while later Mesolithic assemblages consist of narrow blade microliths, often of markedly geometric form (fig. 1.1j–n).

At one time it was the practice to relate British Mesolithic assemblages to well-established Continental groups, the *Maglemosian* of southern Scandinavia and northern Germany in the case of the broad-blade group, and the *Sauveterrian* of France in the case of narrow-blade assemblages. This practice has largely been discontinued. The distinction between broad- and narrow-blade assemblages is an oversimplification, in that broad-blade microliths are often a component in so-called narrow-blade assemblages. What do change are the proportions of the different types found and their sizes. The earliest narrow blade assemblages occur simultaneously in north-eastern England and northern Ireland early in the ninth millennium BP, hardly more than a few generations before the land bridges with the Continent were inundated. The initiation of the technique of making geometric microliths on narrow blades may mark the last input, of people or ideas, to Britain from the Continent until the initiation of farming over 3,000 years later. From the mid-ninth millennium BP technological development in the British Isles was an insular affair.

It is characteristic of societies in large islands that have substantial populations isolated from other groups that they develop rather idiosyncratic responses to social, economic and technological issues. The later Mesolithic of Ireland provides an excellent illustration of this in the technological field. Whereas throughout the rest of the British Isles later Mesolithic assemblages are typified by narrow-blade microliths which become increasingly smaller and more geometric in shape, in Ireland the reverse is the case. The characteristic artefacts of Irish later Mesolithic assemblages are broad, rather leaf-shaped flakes, the butts of which are often lightly trimmed ('Bann Flakes'), and in some cases formed into a tang (fig. 1.1o–p). This was presumably to facilitate hafting or holding. At one time the entire Irish later Mesolithic was referred to as the *Larnian*, after a series of sites investigated around Lough Larne, but it is better to reserve this term to describe the technique of producing the broad flakes, which appears to have involved the application of direct percussion with a stone hammer to cores with a single striking platform. This is one of the

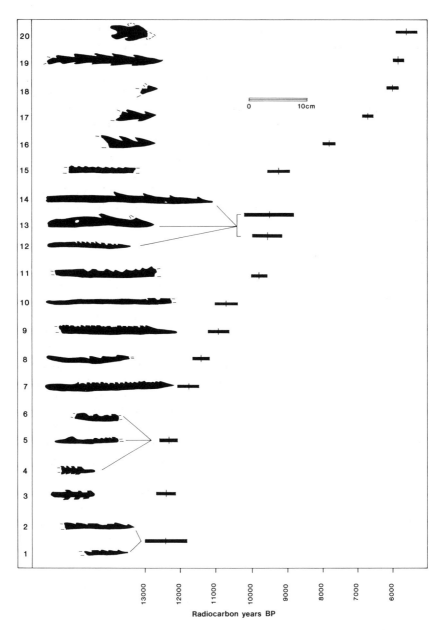

Figure 1.2 Radiocarbon-dated barbed points of bone and antler: (1) and (2) Poulton (OxA–150), (3) Aveline's Hole (OxA–1121), (4),(5) and (6) Kent's Cavern (OxA–1789), (7) Leman and Ower (OxA–1950), (8) Porth y Waen (OxA–1946), (9) Sproughton 1 (OxA–517), (10) Sproughton 2 (OxA–518), (11) Waltham Abbey (OxA–1427), (12),(13) and (14) Star Carr (Q–14 and C–353), (15) Earl's Barton (OxA–500), (16) Druimvargie Rock Shelter (OxA–1948), (17) MacArthur Cave (OxA–1949), (18) Risga (OxA–2023), (19) Shewalton (OxA–1947), (20) Cnoc Sligeach (Birm–465). NB: Except for OxA–150 (12,400 ± 300) and C–353 (9488 ± 350) all dates are listed in the appendix.

most elementary, but effective, ways of producing flakes of a standard size and shape and was presumably a response to the good-quality and widely available Antrim flint.

The *Obanian* culture or technocomplex of western Scotland is defined not by diagnostic flint tools, which are usually lacking from Obanian assemblages, but by a set of bone and antler artefacts, chiefly harpoons and mattocks (fig. 8.7). The Obanian, like the Larnian, belongs to the final stages of the Mesolithic, though its antecedents span several millennia.

An alternative to this scheme based on the typology of stone tools is beginning to be provided by the direct radiocarbon dating of artefacts made from bone and antler. The principle involved is described more fully in chapter 4, but figure 1.2 illustrates the typological sequence of barbed projectile points established by direct dating.

ECONOMY AND ECOLOGY

If the typological or cultural history approach can be said to represent one school of thought in Palaeolithic and Mesolithic studies, another can be described as the economic approach, the leading proponent of which was Grahame Clark. This seeks to look beyond the typological status of arte-facts to see them in terms of the behaviour they represent, and this has led to an acceptance of the importance of the environment and context within which this behaviour took place. However, it would be unfair to classify archaeologists conducting research into these periods as either cultural historians or economic prehistorians, for many have tried to take account of the possibilities of both approaches. Examples of this are provided by John Campbell's (1977) and Andrew Myers' (1989) respective studies of the British Upper Palaeolithic and Mesolithic, though the extent to which either was able to integrate the two approaches is debatable.

This book owes more to Professor Clark's economic approach than to typology and culture history. Preferring to see human beings as part of the ecosystem rather than as actors performing on a stage provided by the environment, my approach might be found more ecological than simply economic. This may lead some to regard this work as an example of environmental determinism. I hope not, for this is not what I intend. All forms of determinism – environmental, social or whatever – are of dubious validity and a balanced view can only be obtained from a balanced approach. However, it remains a fact that at the most basic level of human experience – and dealing with events in the remote past it is often at this level that we have to operate – the environment sets the rules and estab-lishes what is possible. I should like to hear critics of this view trying to convince an Alaskan Eskimo or a Cree Indian that the environment does not have an important bearing on their lives. But it also remains the case that, within the broad parameters set by the environment, individuals and groups have many opportunities of making choices, and such choices are often mediated by what are called social factors. Nevertheless, when we remember that probably the most important single element in any individual's environment is other people, even such social factors take on an ecological tinge.

In this book I have concentrated on the ecological relationships of Late Stone Age hunter-gatherer settlement in the British Isles. I have deliberately selected sites which have better than average ecological data, and the regional synthesis in chapter 9 is presented within a broadly ecological framework. I hope I never lose sight of the role of social factors, but these very rarely leave any archaeological trace.

EVIDENCE AND SPECULATION, PROCESS AND CONTEXT

In dealing with remote periods in which unequivocal evidence is often hard to come by, the archaeologist is always tempted to indulge in speculation, perhaps based on ethnographic analogy or ecological theory. I shall have more to say on this topic in the next chapter, but I feel this is a temptation which should be resisted. It has been one of my aims in writing this book to state the evidence in simple terms without confusing the issues by excessive speculation.

If we place the emphasis on the evidence rather than speculation, it is reasonable that a good deal of attention should be devoted to what the evidence actually means in behavioural terms. By what processes have episodes of human behaviour come to be represented by the physical traces uncovered by archaeologists? Consideration of such issues has become known as *processual* archaeology, and chapter 3 is undeniably processual in approach.

Processual archaeology has made a major contribution to our understanding of the past by enumerating some of the many factors that need to be taken into account in assessing the meaning of the archaeological record. It has introduced a welcome element of objectivity which was hitherto lacking, but any claim to levels of objectivity comparable to those found in science is unreasonable. Such a quasi-scientific stance has led to a *post-processual* backlash which points out the subjective nature of all historical enquiry and the need always to be conscious of the context, both of the events which are the subject of enquiry and of the enquiry itself.

Again, a balanced approach is called for. The evidence must be examined rigorously, and as objectively as possible, while the basic subjectivity of the enquiry is acknowledged. After all, I have chosen the data to investigate and the questions to ask, and I shall be happy if readers wish to bear in mind that this book has been written by a middle-aged, middle-class academic with interests in bird watching and astronomy!

FRAMEWORKS

In chapter 2 I have set out to delimit the broad parameters which constrain hunter-gatherer behaviour while in chapter 3 I have considered ways in which that behaviour may manifest itself in the archaeological record. Consideration of these two topics makes it possible to devise a framework within which the evidence from the British Isles may be viewed and tentatively interpreted. This framework is set out in chapter 4.

The ecological perspective adopted means that careful consideration must be given to the environment within which the Late Stone Age hunters and gatherers of the British Isles found themselves. This was an environment which was at times changing rapidly, and I have tried to present the evidence for these changes in terms which underline their significance for the human population. Similarly, those other components of the biomass, the plants and animals, are also viewed mainly from the viewpoint of their impact on human behaviour and their utility as economic resources.

SITE AND REGION

The data available for the period covered by this book are considerable, and I have not attempted a comprehensive synthesis. While expediency is part of the reason for this, there is simply too much to cover in a relatively small book; a great deal is in any case of only marginal relevance to our enquiry. The great bulk of material dating from the Late Stone Age in the British Isles consists of assemblages of stone artefacts, either collected from the present ground surface or recovered during poorly recorded and methodologically inadequate excavations, often undertaken over a century ago. This can tell us little about the ecological relations of the people responsible for the assemblages. It is also the case that most of this material cannot be precisely dated.

I have chosen instead to examine a few sites in detail, selection being determined in most cases by the availability of good biological, in addition to archaeological, evidence and radiocarbon dates. Inevitably there will be some bias in this selection towards sites where conditions of preservation are good, such as caves and waterlogged deposits, but I firmly believe that this handful of informative sites can tell us more about the life of the Late Stone Age hunter-gatherers of the British Isles than many hundreds of flint scatters.

The twelve case studies presented in chapters 6, 7 and 8 enable us to draw a picture of life in the Late Stone Age which is often surprisingly detailed. But by themselves these sites, and the few others mentioned in more summary fashion, do not provide an adequate picture of the region as a whole. This I have attempted to do in chapter 9 by reviewing the settlement pattern throughout the British Isles and within the broad environmental categories established in chapter 5. Given that one of the main points of interest at the regional scale is the date at which the various parts of the British Isles came to be occupied, this part of the study is presented in terms of a geographical analysis of radiocarbon dates. The rationale behind this approach is more fully discussed in chapter 9, but the key question has to be 'Are the results convincing?' I believe they are and that they offer a number of useful insights into the life of the Late Stone Age hunter-gatherers of the British Isles. Readers may decide for themselves whether they agree.

ADDITIONAL READING

Most general books on British prehistory provide some coverage of these periods but the main summaries of the Upper Palaeolithic in Britain remain those of Campbell (1997) and Jacobi (1980) to which should now be added Barton's review of the period in the Hengistbury Head excavation report (1992) and papers by Cook and Jacobi (1995) and Barton and Roberts (1996). Jacobi's 1976 paper remains the most recently published survey of the Mesolithic of mainland Britain though Woodman has dealt with Ireland (1978) and Scotland (1990) while the latter is also extensively treated in Caroline Wickham-Jones' *Scotland's First Settlers* (1994) and a volume of conference papers edited by Pollard and Morrison (1996). Brief general syntheses of the British evidence in a European context will be found in Gamble (1986) and Price (1983, 1987). Important accounts of specific categories of artefact are provided by Radley and Mellars (1964), Radley *et al.* (1974), Pitts and Jacobi (1979), Myers (1989) and Smith and Bonsall (1991). Much information on the European Upper Palaeolithic and Mesolithic, of both a typological and economic kind, will be found in volumes edited by Mellars (1978a), Bonsall (1989), Vermeersch and van Peer (1990), Barton *et al.* (1991), Fischer (1995) and Larsson (1996).

Clark's 'economic' approach is fully developed in *Prehistoric Europe: The Economic Basis* (1952) and was applied in his work at Star Carr (1971, 1972). The most explicit demonstration of the 'ecological' approach followed here will be found in I. G. Simmons' *The Environmental Impact of Later Mesolithic Cultures* (1996). I am pleased to acknowledge the influence on my own approach of L. P. Louwe Kooijmans' *Sporen in het land: De Netherlandse delta in de prehistorie* published in 1985 while Erwin Cziesla's *Jager und Sammler: Die mittlere Steinzeit im Landkreis Pirmasens* (1992) offers a comparative study from another region of Europe.

For processual archaeology see Schiffer (1976, 1989) and Binford (1980, 1981, 1983, 1989). Useful assessments of the environmental and ecological approaches and their status in relation to processual and post-processual archaeology have been provided by Mithen (1989) and Simmons (1996) while Bintliff (1991) has provided a stimulating review of the debate between the two competing paradigms.

2 Hunters and gatherers in action

Hunting and gathering ceased to be a full-time occupation for the majority of the population of the British Isles over forty centuries ago and attempts to reconstruct such an alien way of life from the meagre traces it has left are fraught with difficulty. The reconstruction of life among early farmers is rather easier. Not only did they generally leave more evidence for the archaeologist to study, but their experiences have more in common with our own and those of the recent past. For all but a few of us, the contemporary experience of hunting and gathering is limited to the annual collection of blackberries!

Hunter-gatherers still live in some parts of the world and in many others they survived long enough to be recorded in detail by explorers, travellers and ethnographers, who were usually of European origin. Such studies provide a basis for an understanding of the hunter-gatherer way of life, and a number of writers have proposed models of hunter-gatherer behaviour, derived partly from ethnographic analogy and partly from what are considered to be general ecological principles. While such studies often provide fascinating insights into the ways in which hunter-gatherers adapt to their environment, they are beset by too many uncertainties to be useful as explanations of archaeological data. The archaeological record is usually insufficient for a full ecological reconstruction and it becomes necessary to draw analogies with contemporary environments which are often not very analogous. In addition, the ethnographic record provides the only way of testing such models. Given that this same ethnographic record is used in the construction of the model, an obvious circularity is present from the outset. I have not followed such an approach. Instead, ecological considerations are used to delineate the basic constraints placed on hunter-gatherer behaviour by the environment while the ethnographic record is referred to for examples of hunter-gatherer social organization, an aspect of behaviour which leaves few unambiguous archaeological traces.

HUNTER-GATHERERS AND ECOLOGY

The prime biological goal of human beings, like all living things, is to reproduce themselves and ensure that their offspring survive long enough to do likewise. To accomplish this they have to secure adequate supplies of energy for maintenance and growth. People, like other animals and plants, obtain the supplies of energy they need from the sun, albeit indirectly. The distribution of solar energy in forms in which humans can use it, such as plant and animal tissue, is uneven, and this unevenness has had a fundamental influence on the evolution of human behaviour over the past 3 to 4 million years. Human behaviour, like other aspects of the ecosystem, is composed of a complex web of interrelationships, and to consider any aspect in isolation is artificial. However, for the sake of simplicity a broad distinction between (a) the growth, density and distribution of population on the one hand, and (b) the practicalities of resource extraction on the other, is useful.

Population growth, density and distribution

It is a self-evident truth that humans have a great capacity for reproduction. In some parts of the world annual growth rates of 2 to 3 per cent are common. This is a recent phenomenon. Even at a rate of 0.05 per cent the current world population of approximately 5 billion could have been attained in a few thousands of years whereas human evolution is measured in millions. Actual growth during most of the Stone Age must have been very slow, perhaps as low as 0.001 per cent (1:100,000), but may have risen as high as 0.1 per cent (1:1,000) towards the end of the period. Low or negligible growth rates are a fact of hunter-gatherer life. While it is not entirely clear why this is so, given the enormous biotic potential of human beings, it seems likely that prolonged lactation leading to suppressed fertility may have played an important part. In the mobile existence of most hunter-gatherers, having more than a single infant to carry would be a distinct disadvantage. Keeping each child at the breast until it was able to walk may have helped avoid this problem by suppressing fertility.

While growth rates were undoubtedly low, groups of hunter-gatherers were usually successful in reproducing themselves, although local extinctions no doubt occurred from time to time. For reproduction to be successful in the long term it is necessary to avoid inbreeding and this poses special problems for people living at low densities and in small groups. Individuals choose their mates from the surrounding population and in order to avoid inbreeding it is necessary for an individual to have access to between 200 and 500 potential mates. Such potential relationships provide the basis for what biologists call breeding networks. These occur in two forms: open or closed. In an open, or *exogamous*, network all individuals are in effect at the centre of their own networks and draw their mates from within the surrounding populations. The network for each member is slightly different (fig. 2.1a). Open networks are typical of people living at very low densities, as has been the case with most hunter-gatherers. In a closed, or *endogamous* network, all the members take their mates from within the same group, the effect of which is that individuals living near the bound-

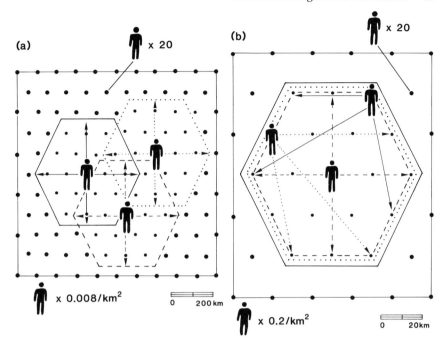

Figure 2.1 Breeding networks: two hypothetical cases. In each case individuals live in groups of twenty but must select partners from a population of about 400, and cannot travel more than 200 km to do so. In the low-density case (a) population is thinly scattered and open, or exogamous, networks form, whereas in case (b) population density is sufficient for closed, or endogamous, networks to emerge.

aries have to travel up to 60 per cent further than those in the centre in order to gain access to potential mates from the whole network (fig. 2.1b). Typically, closed networks are a feature of relatively high population densities and it has been estimated that densities of over 0.1 person per km^2 need to be reached before such networks emerge.

Population density is ultimately controlled by the net primary productivity of the environment, which itself is a reflection of geology, latitude and climate. Net primary productivity is very variable but broad orders of magnitude are well established:

tundra	100–400 grams/m^2/year
boreal forest	400–2,000 grams/m^2/year
deciduous woodland	600–2,500 grams/m^2/year

However, before the development of farming most of this productivity was in forms that humans could not utilize directly – chiefly wood and unpalatable leaves. Even in the deciduous woodlands, which were rich in nuts, berries and tubers, animal products must still have been of major importance and it is the productivity of the animal biomass which has more bearing on population levels than net primary productivity. Although hunters typically regard virtually everything that moves as potential prey, it was the biomass of the grazing and browsing ungulates such as reindeer, horse, red deer and wild cattle, that was critically important in the Stone Age.

It is difficult to estimate the ungulate biomass for the Lateglacial and early Postglacial environments of the British Isles because these environments have no precise modern analogies. However, the following ranges give a broad indication of the orders of magnitude:

tundra	440–800 kg/km^2
boreal forests	80–600 kg/km^2
deciduous woodland	1,000–2,000 kg/km^2

It should be noted that, although the net primary productivity of the boreal forests is greater than that of the tundra, the ungulate biomass is considerably smaller, suggesting that the birch forests of early Postglacial Britain may have been less fruitful hunting grounds than the Lateglacial tundras.

Such values provide an indication of the potential of a given environment, but of more relevance in human terms is the yield that it will sustain. This is the maximum amount of energy that can be removed from the system without impairing its ability to replenish itself, and is referred to as the *critical carrying capacity*. From the human point of view, the yield that can be extracted from ungulate prey should not exceed about 5 per cent, in order to allow for the natural replenishment of stock lost through age, disease or other predators. It should also be remembered that in most cases only about 50 per cent of an ungulate carcass has any food value. This is often referred to as the 'meat weight' but includes other delicacies such as offal, marrow and fat. Taking these factors into account the ranges quoted above can be used to calculate maximum sustainable yields:

tundra	11–20kg/km^2/year
boreal forest	2–16kg/km^2/year
deciduous woodland	25–50kg/km^2/year

Humans use approximately 2,200 calories a day, though this varies depending on the age, sex and work load of the individual in question. It also varies according to climate and latitude. The figure for Eskimos, for example, is considerably higher, at 3,100 calories per day. One kilogram of cooked meat provides about 2,700 calories and it is possible to suggest, in very general terms, the population densities that different areas were capable of supporting.

For example, on the figures quoted, 1 km^2 of tundra might yield up to about 20 kilograms of meat in a year. This is about 54,000 calories. If an active human in a tundra environment uses about 2,900 calories a day, 1 km^2 can sustain someone for about eighteen days a year. Put another way, this is a potential population density of about 0.05 people per km^2. Calculated on the same basis but taking the daily calorific requirement as 2,200 the upper value quoted for boreal forest also works out at 0.05 people per km^2 while that for deciduous woodland is 0.16 people per km^2.

However, dietary problems arise if more than 300 grams of the daily calorific intake is in the form of protein. Carbohydrates – usually, in the case of hunters, animal fats – are a vital part of a healthy diet and the fat component of a carcass varies between seasons. Red deer stags and reindeer bulls, for example, put on fat up to the beginning of the rutting season in autumn, but thereafter lose it rapidly. If protein should not contribute more than about a third of the diet it will be necessary to kill more animals during the lean season than at times when their fat stocks are high. The potential population figures quoted above need to be adjusted downwards to allow for this, by perhaps as much as a half or even two-thirds.

Few groups have a diet composed exclusively of ungulates and many, where the opportunities present themselves, exploit a wide range of both terrestrial and marine animals and almost all harvest wild plant foods. This must be taken into account in trying to reach a realistic estimate of potential population density. A group of hunters in Britain during the Lateglacial Interstadial may have had a diet which comprised 80 per cent ungulate meat, the remainder being made up of small game such as hares, water fowl and fish, while wild fruits such as crowberries may have been important at certain times of the year. If allowance is made for the dietary problems that arise from an imbalance between protein and carbohydrate intake, the potential population density for a tundra environment based on ungulate biomass is about 0.025 person per km^2. But if ungulates provide only 80 per cent of the diet, this figure can be raised slightly to 0.03 person per km^2 to allow for the contribution of the remainder.

These values give some idea of the maximum population densities that various areas are capable of supporting, but a population adjusted to the carrying capacity of an area is vulnerable to the risk of starvation due to short-term, random fluctuations in resources. The *optimum population* is determined by the quantity of nutritionally critical foods at the time of least abundance. Among hunter-gatherers the optimum population seems to be typically set at between 20 per cent and 60 per cent of the theoretical maximum. In the example quoted above for Britain during the Lateglacial Interstadial, the final range is from 0.006 to 0.02 persons per km^2 (fig. 2.2).

The calculations presented above give an indication of the principal ecological factors influencing the density of hunter-gatherer populations. They cannot be used as a basis for calculating the actual population in any environment at any particular time. They merely indicate what factors it is necessary to take into account in trying to make such an assessment. However, it is abundantly clear that low population densities are a feature of the hunter-gatherer way of life. In practice the factors which determine the density of population an area can support are very complex and include social as well as environmental considerations. But such simple calculations do

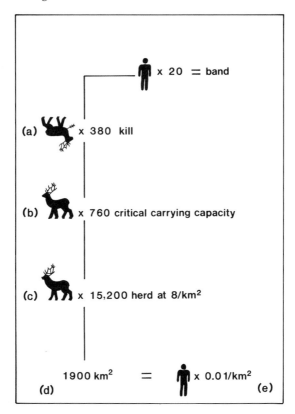

Figure 2.2 Hypothetical density calculation for a band of twenty basing 80 per cent of their subsistence on reindeer: (a) 380 animals must be killed each year to provide protein and carbohydrate while allowing for waste and fat imbalance; this should be 50 per cent of the critical carrying capacity (b), which should be about 5 per cent of the total herd (c). With a stocking density of eight reindeer per km² the size of the territory (d) and population density can be estimated (e).

enable orders of magnitude to be established, and the results compare well with the ethnographically derived figure of 0.012/km².

From the preceding paragraphs we see that it is typical of hunter-gatherer populations to have very low growth rates, participate in open, or exogamous, breeding networks, and live at very low densities. Some favoured areas may permit densities in excess of 0.1 persons/km², in which circumstances a closed, or endogamous, breeding network may emerge.

Resource extraction

If net primary productivity sets the broad limits of population density, at the regional and local scale this is influenced more by the character of the resources being exploited and the hunting and gathering strategies adopted by the groups involved. At one extreme, resources, chiefly plants and animals, are found evenly distributed across the landscape in numbers that do not vary greatly between areas or from year to year. Such environments, of which the deciduous woodlands are a good example, can be seen in human terms to be stable and predictable. At the other extreme, resources are found to occur in clumps, may be subject to wide annual fluctuations and are relatively unpredictable. The mid-latitude tundras, with their herds of migratory ungulates, were typically of this kind. Stable environments of the former type, although high in primary productivity, can be low in resources useful to humans, though the range is often wide. The less stable environments may have lower primary productivity but the resources of value to humans are often abundant for short periods.

These examples lie at the two ends of a continuum. It would be a mistake to expect to find environments which can be rigidly classified in such terms. Most situations in which hunter-gatherers find themselves have elements of both patterns but there is usually a tendency towards one or the other.

The manner in which resources are distributed across the landscape obviously has a bearing on the hunting and gathering strategies employed by the humans who live there. Two broad strategies can be recognized. In one, virtually the whole group is regularly involved in hunting or gathering within the area around the camp. When resources become depleted the group moves on and the process begins again. This is often known as *residential foraging*, in that activity rarely takes place very far from the home base and is typically the strategy adopted where a wide range of resources is fairly evenly scattered. In the alternative strategy, most hunting and gathering is undertaken by specialist task groups who may have to travel considerable distances to secure supplies. This is known as *logistic foraging* and is the policy adopted in environments where resources are found in widely scattered concentrations, such as herds of migrating reindeer. In such cases the main group may move relatively infrequently, while task groups range widely. In practice few hunter-gatherers conform rigidly to either strategy but adopt elements of both (fig. 2.3a and b).

Various forms of storage offer partial alternatives to moving camp once resources become depleted, but the extent to which this is a viable option depends on whether the technology is available, as well as on the nature of the product to be stored. Hazel-nuts can be stored in a secure container or pit for long periods, but while it may have been possible to freeze joints of horse and reindeer during the Lateglacial winters, storage of meat at other times must have involved smoking or drying, and even then shelf-life would have been limited.

Within each general pattern the actual process of hunting and gathering can be seen to consist of a number of distinct activities which vary according to the resources targeted. Both hunting and gathering involve time spent searching for prey to kill or plants to collect, while hunting will often also involve time spent in pursuit. Time has also to be spent in extracting

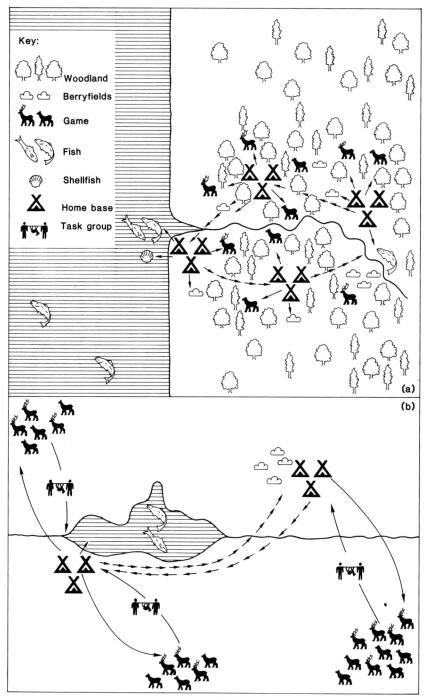

Key:

- Woodland
- Berryfields
- Game
- Fish
- Shellfish
- Home base
- Task group

(a)

(b)

Figure 2.3 Foraging strategies: In case (a) the band hunts and gathers around its residential home base and makes frequent moves as resources are depleted. In case (b) foraging is undertaken logistically by task groups ranging widely from the home base, which is moved only infrequently.

the resources: butchery in the case of most animal prey or collection in the case of plants or shellfish. Although some consumption may take place at the butchery or collection site, some of the meat or plant foods may need to be taken back to the main group if not everybody participated in the hunting or gathering. Some foods need to be cooked or otherwise processed before they can be consumed.

The activities of search, pursuit, butchery or collection, retrieval and processing all involve the expenditure of time and energy. For example, one hour spent in the search for prey involves the hunter in an expenditure of about 200 calories. Obviously the amount of energy invested in such an activity must be expected to yield at least an equivalent amount in return. The yield from a large animal such as a reindeer (50 kilograms of meat or 135,000 calories) is worth the investment of a considerable amount of energy, perhaps on the part of several hunters, whereas the return from small game such as hares is very low and not worth the trouble unless they can be caught in large numbers. The gathering of nuts or shellfish may entail a lot of time spent in searching but once supplies have been located pursuit costs are minimal! However, foods which occur in small units or are of low nutrient value need to be collected in large numbers and a lot of time must be spent in gathering. Many such items also need processing.

Hunting and gathering activities can therefore be assessed in terms of a cost:benefit analysis in which the energy costs are set against the gains in calories. This approach is known among ecologists as *optimal foraging theory* and assumes that animals, including humans, always seek to optimize the results of their hunting and gathering activities, producing a maximum yield for a minimum effort. This is suspiciously reminiscent of modern economic theory and it might be doubted whether it is really applicable in the very different world of Late Stone Age hunter-gatherers. From a biological point of view it is more appropriate to think of people adopting patterns of behaviour designed to satisfy their needs, which does not necessarily involve pursuing optimum goals or maximizing production. However, many animal species do follow broadly optimizing strategies and it is reasonable to assume that humans have tended to do likewise. In the human case the term 'optimal' may include benefits other than simply the immediate maximum calorific yield. For example, the social cohesion of a group may benefit from its members participating in group activities such as hunting and collecting, even though individual activities could fulfil basic calorific requirements just as efficiently. Food sharing is a common manifestation of such cohesion and the development of a pattern of reciprocal obligations within the group is of obvious benefit in times of scarcity. Accordingly, individuals may collect more food than is required to satisfy their own needs in order to have a surplus to share: a kind of social investment. Similarly, in order to optimize hunting or gathering efficiency it is necessary to have reliable information as to where prey or plant resources are to be found. Activities which increase the availability of

information, such as social contact with other groups, are clearly benefi-
cial, even though such contacts may have been made at the expense of time
spent actively hunting.

From considerations such as these it is possible to delineate a number of
characteristics of hunter-gatherer behaviour that we might expect to find in
virtually any such group:

1 Hunter-gatherers live at very low densities, usually considerably below
  0.1 person/km^2. Even where the distribution of resources is such as to
  encourage the formation of population aggregations the overall density
  of population remains low and aggregations are widely spaced.
2 Hunter-gatherer populations have very low growth rates, usually of the
  order of 0.001 per cent, though in exceptional circumstances rates of up
  to 0.1 per cent may have been attained. Such low growth rates will tend
  to lead to periods of long demographic stability.
3 Because of their low population densities, the need to draw marriage
  partners from a sufficiently large population to avoid inbreeding, and a
  reluctance to travel unnecessary distances, hunter-gatherers usually participate in open, or exogamous, breeding networks. The effect of this is
  that populations are biologically homogeneous over wide areas.
4 As population densities rise, distances between potential marriage partners diminish and closed, or endogamous, breeding networks emerge. It
  is difficult to know what the critical threshold is but endogamy is not
  usually found where population densities lie below 0.1 person/km^2.

These biological characteristics may also have social and cultural manifestations. Low growth rates and open breeding networks can be expected to
lead to a high degree of temporal and spatial uniformity in the realm of
material culture, and social organization remains relatively simple.
Conversely, as population density increases and the closing of breeding
networks leads to the emergence of more complex levels of social organization, we can expect this uniformity to start to break down as groups begin
to express their identity through such things as dress, ornaments and
weapons.

5 Hunter-gatherer populations are adjusted considerably below the critical
  carrying capacity of an area to allow for bad years.
6 Hunter-gatherers distribute themselves across the landscape according
  to the distribution of resources. Where resources are evenly distributed
  hunter-gatherers will be found in small evenly spaced groups, but where
  resources are clumped, aggregations of population may be expected.
7 Hunter-gatherers will tend to seek the nutritionally most valuable foods
  that can be obtained for the least effort. Exceptions to this proposition
  occur when other benefits, perhaps of a social kind, can be obtained by
  following a strategy which does not maximize calorific return.

The fact that hunter-gatherers still survive in some parts of the world provides a means of assessing the validity of these expectations. If they are not met among contemporary or recent groups they may well not have been met in the more remote past either. Although few groups conform to all the expectations, most exhibit a range of behaviour that could be predicted from a consideration of the environmental constraints with which they have had to cope. But hunter-gatherer ethnography provides more than just a testing ground for ecological hypotheses. It is also both a source of potential behavioural analogies, illustrating the variety of responses which can occur in a given situation, and it is virtually our only source of information about hunter-gatherer social organization.

THE HUNTER-GATHERERS IN THE ETHNOGRAPHIC RECORD

Less than 0.001 per cent of the world's population are hunter-gatherers yet these small groups, often living in remote areas, have been a focus of interest among ethnographers for more than a century. Prodigious quantities of scientific data have been published on the subsistence patterns and social structures of Eskimos and Aleuts, Aborigines and Bushmen, while the mass media have brought images of the hunting and gathering way of life into the homes of all of us. Part of this fascination arises from the view that they are the last remnants of a formerly much more widespread way of life, and prehistorians, in seeking to interpret hunter-gatherer sites, make frequent reference to modern groups. While modern hunter-gatherers have much of interest to tell us, making direct comparisons between the present and the past is in practice very difficult.

To begin with, today's hunter-gatherers live in marginal, atypical environments, and it seems questionable to use the deserts of southern Africa and central Australia or the circumpolar zone as a source of analogy for temperate, mid-latitude Europe. North America is a more appropriate source of analogy but the hunter-gatherers of this region have been subject to several centuries of influence from settled, farming societies of both American and European origin. Except for the final few centuries of the period covered by this book, the Late Stone Age hunter-gatherers of the British Isles lived in a hunter-gatherer world where the question of such influences does not arise.

Perhaps the most serious limitation on the use of ethnographic analogy in prehistory is the very atypicality of contemporary hunter-gatherers. Most of the world's population has, over the past 10,000 years, adopted a food producing, or farming, way of life. Those groups that have remained as hunter-gatherers are certainly not typical of the world's population as a whole and we may ask whether they ever were. By using such groups as a source of reference we run the risk of not recognizing ways of life and patterns of behaviour which have no modern analogy. The mid-latitude tundras and boreal forests of Lateglacial and early Postglacial Britain have no precise modern parallels and it follows from this that nowhere in the world do hunter-gatherers live under conditions the same as those in Britain between about 13,000 and 5,000 years ago.

In spite of these caveats, ethnographic data can be useful to prehistorians in a number of ways. Although no individual group is typical of the hunter-gatherer way of life in general, features that are common to several groups may be. Such common traits, when seen in the context of the ecological constraints described in the first part of this chapter, can be used to suggest ways in which hunter-gatherers cope with a range of problems. In particular, ethnographic data can provide information on the social organization of hunter-gatherers, an aspect of behaviour which can be barely perceived in the archaeological record.

At the time of their first contact with Europeans, from the seventeenth century onwards, many North American Indians were living in mid-latitude areas and following a wholly or partly hunting and gathering way of life. Accordingly, they offer some of the best sources of analogy for Late Stone Age hunting and gathering in the British Isles (plates I and II). But it is still necessary to remember that at the time of European settlement mid-latitude North America had not recently emerged from an ice age and its greater continentality means that its climate has always been rather different from that of western Europe.

The Indians of North America and their Eskimo, Aleut and Inuit contemporaries in Alaska, Greenland and the circumpolar zone have been intensively studied by ethnographers and anthropologists for centuries. Many groups were described in detail before the full impact of contact with Europeans had taken effect and these early accounts are especially useful.

In addition to their low population densities and slow rates of demographic growth, hunter-gatherers have tended to evolve similar social structures. A recent study of 256 North American Indian societies has identified a tiered social structure (fig. 2.4).

The basic biological unit was the *family* comprising adults and children of several generations. Families were found to be relatively short-lived as distinct entities, rarely surviving more than about fifty years.

The basic working unit identified was the *task group*. Such groups hunted and gathered together, and might consist of parts of several families or just one as the circumstances demanded (plate ii). It is the activities of task groups that are most often reflected in the archaeological record.

Several families were grouped together to form a *band* (plate i), which was usually associated with a specific territory and often known by it. Bands recognized leaders, but only on the basis of their experience and personal prestige. Leaders emerged to organize specific activities such as hunting expeditions or war parties. Their power was not permanent and not hereditary. The size of bands was enormously varied, ranging between less than 50 and over 2,000, with an average of about 300. The size of the territories occupied by bands varied by a similar order of magnitude, as did population densities, though the average works out at 0.15 persons/km^2.

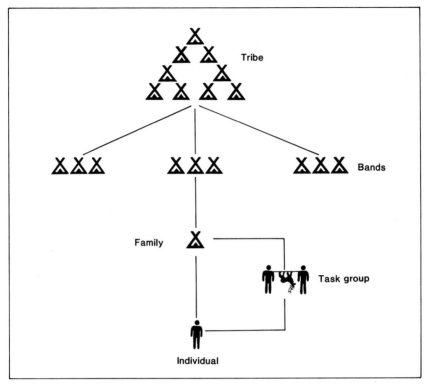

Figure 2.4 The social structure of a hypothetical band, based on the North American data.

The band was the principal residential unit for most groups and bands were found to move on average two to three times a year according to the seasonal availability of resources. While territories were generally quite stable, the area exploited could vary from year to year or over a group of years, and during a lifetime an individual might visit a much wider territory than during the course of a single twelve-month span (fig. 2.5). Bands could survive as distinct social entities for several centuries.

Bands were generally exogamous, and members had to seek marriage partners from other bands. Bands in the same mating network formed a *tribe*, sometimes known as a dialectic tribe because its members all spoke a common dialect. Like families and bands, tribes had a common name and participated in a common culture. The tribes studied had populations varying from a few hundred to several thousand, the average being about 900. The average number of bands per tribe was found to be four and where settlement was dispersed the bands of a tribe might come together several times a year for ceremonial purposes when resources were sufficient to support a large aggregation of people. Tribes could survive as distinct units for about a millennium.

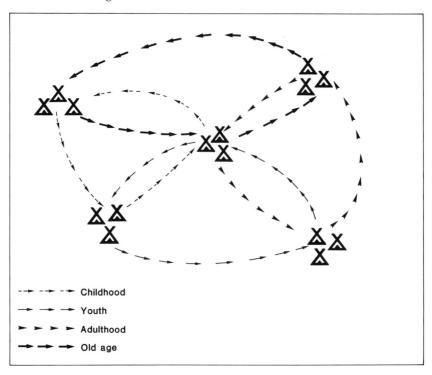

Figure 2.5 Annual and life-time territories. During the course of an individual's life the territory visited by the band in its annual cycle of movements may vary considerably in response to ecological or social pressures.

The data used were drawn from early ethnographic accounts which were often compiled some time after the first European contacts with the groups in question. European influence frequently had an effect in advance of the arrival of the Europeans themselves when trading contacts with intervening groups led to economic disruption and the spread of disease. Farming had begun in Mexico by 7000 BP and within 2,000 years had spread to the southern part of North America. Many of the hunter-gatherer groups studied would have had direct or indirect contact with farming groups and it is difficult to gauge the effect this had on their way of life. We can see that the results of this survey are subject to many of the limitations which affect the use of ethnographic data and it is hard to know how representative they are of hunter-gatherer life in North America. The average population density recorded among North American Indians may be higher than expected, but being an average figure has been disproportionally influenced by a few cases with very high densities. Commonly, densities were a good deal lower than the 0.15 persons/km² quoted.

This study drew on data from groups living throughout North America and its results are unlikely to be typical of any particular area. The hunter-gatherers of North America inhabited a number of environments, some of which are analogous in some respects to environments found in Lateglacial and early Postglacial Britain. These are the arctic deserts of Alaska, Greenland and the circumpolar zone, the high-latitude tundras and boreal forests of Canada, the Pacific coast north of about latitude 40°N, and the temperate woodlands of the eastern United States. The stereotyped Indian of Western films was a denizen of the plains of the Midwest and other groups were to be found further south, while Central and South America have their own hunter-gatherers. None of these latter groups are relevant to the study of Lateglacial and early Postglacial Britain.

The Arctic offers some potential analogies with Lateglacial western Europe, notwithstanding the latitudinal differences, and the Greenland icecap still extends as far south as the latitude of Shetland. However, there is little evidence that these areas were inhabited at all before the emergence of the *Arctic small tool tradition* about 5,000 years ago. It seems probable that the adaptation to a fully arctic environment may have been accomplished by *Homo sapiens sapiens* only relatively recently, and that the Inuit way of life had no counterpart in Lateglacial western Europe.

The main areas of relevance must be the tundras, and the boreal forests of Canada. Environments of these types were to be found in the British Isles between 13,000 BP when the area began to be occupied and about 8,000 BP when the land bridge to Europe was finally inundated. By this time much of Britain had developed a mantle of deciduous woodland. Although analogous conditions existed in recent times in the eastern United States, many of the Indian groups inhabiting these woodlands had made farming part of their way of life before the first Europeans arrived. The Pacific coast provides examples of the kind of subsistence strategies that can emerge when resources are relatively abundant and predictable, as may have been the case along the coasts of western Britain after about 9000 BP when present-day patterns of oceanic circulation became established. Many of the Pacific coast groups provide useful sources of analogy for hunter-gatherers in the British Isles.

ADDITIONAL READING

Ecological models of hunter-gatherer behaviour are frequently encountered in the literature and I. G. Simmons' *The Environmental Impact of Later Mesolithic Cultures* (1996) provides an excellent example of this approach in a British context. Breeding networks have been considered by Wobst (1974, 1976). For an examination of primary productivity see Lieth and Whittaker (1975). The ecological relations of hunter-gatherer subsistence in general have been studied by Bettinger (1991), Cohen (1977), Hassan (1979) and Wing and Brown (1979), while their social and cultural manifestations have been considered in papers edited by Price and Brown (1985). The ungulate biomass values quoted in this chapter are adapted from various sources while the classification of hunting and gathering strategies is derived from the work of Binford (1981, 1983). The ideas of optimal foraging theory as applied in a human context are most fully set out in papers in Winterhalder and Smith (1981). Details of North American hunter-gatherer social organization are taken from the studies of Newell and Constandse-Westermann (1986) and Constandse-Westermann and Newell (1989). More recently, Houtsma *et al.* (1996) have published a wealth of data from seventy Arctic and sub-Arctic hunter-gatherer societies in North America as an aid to understanding the archaeological record of the Lateglacial communities of the North European Plain.

3 Hunters and gatherers in the archaeological record

INTRODUCTION

Today hunting is very much a minority pursuit but many of us from time to time become collectors, perhaps of blackberries or hazel-nuts in the hedgerows or shellfish on the foreshore. We can recall the satisfaction at finding a bush laden with fruit, or a well-stocked bed of mussels, but after we have taken our fill or become overwhelmed with boredom what trace of our collecting activity remains? Perhaps no more than a few squashed berries or footprints in the sand (plate va), all of which are likely to disappear totally within a few days. Most shellfish need to be processed before consumption and this might take place on the beach as part of a picnic, the mussels or cockles being baked on an open fire or amongst hot stones. The following day, if the picnic site is above the high-tide mark, it might still be recognizable but some special circumstances are required, such as burial by blown sand, for it to survive more than few days (plate vc). Having a picnic is a casual affair and chance is the principal factor which determines whether any trace of such behaviour will survive. Among groups for whom the collection of shellfish is an important activity, collecting is more carefully organized. Chance still plays a decisive role in preserving traces of such activity but other factors, such as the size of the group, the duration of the collecting episode and the number of times it is repeated also influence whether any trace of the activity survives.

Archaeology may be defined as the reconstruction of past human behaviour from its material remains, but the nature of the evidence imposes strict limitations on such reconstructions. Many aspects of human behaviour leave no physical traces and, of those that do, only some traces will survive the passage of time. Even fewer will be found by archaeologists and not all of these will be understood. Archaeologists are interested in the totality of past human behaviour but their view is severely limited.

The material remains of past behaviour form the *archaeological record*, and that of hunters and gatherers is more limited than the record of most other societies. They rarely make use of substantial buildings and do not often indulge in the construction of large communal ritual centres or elaborate tombs – all features often recognized in the archaeological record of early farmers. However, at a basic level there are similarities in the remains left by most societies and several clear categories of evidence are found in all. These categories consist of discarded or lost artefacts and the waste associated with their manufacture and maintenance, organic refuse such as plant and animal remains, and abandoned facilities ranging in scale from the remains of complex structures such as buildings to the simple fireplace of a hunter's camp. Burials do not require a category of their own. A grave may be regarded as a facility and its contents as a form of organic refuse.

The previous paragraph listed the principal categories of evidence that comprise the archaeological record. This record is immensely varied and variability within and between categories of evidence provides the archaeologist with a valuable key to understanding the tangible residues of past behaviour. At all scales of analysis this variability is both spatial and temporal and arises from two main sources: variability in the behaviour of groups responsible for the remains and variability in the processes which affect those remains once they have become part of the archaeological record. These latter, post-depositional processes, will be considered further below, after we have looked at variability arising from human behaviour. Three scales of analysis may be employed: the region, the assemblage and the individual artefact.

VARIABILITY AT THE REGIONAL LEVEL

Archaeologists tend to view their data in terms of 'sites'. The concept of an 'archaeological site' is a difficult one to define and fraught with ambiguity. It is used to include everything from a major Palaeolithic cave with thousands of artefacts and tens of thousands of animal bones to a handful of flints eroding from a sand dune or even a single flint or bone tool picked up from the surface of a ploughed field.

Hunter-gatherers use a range of different types of site (fig. 3.1). The most important, but not necessarily the most conspicuous, is the *home base*, a centre of activity where most of the group spend part of their time. Home bases tend to be divided into a residential area and a peripheral zone (fig. 3.2). The concentration of activities at a home base could be expected to be reflected in an accumulation of discarded rubbish, but the density and duration of occupation might lead to a policy of organized rubbish disposal. The peripheral zone would be the scene of certain specialist activities such as butchery and flint knapping and may also include accumulations of rubbish in middens. Hunting and gathering is undertaken by specialist task groups and their activities give rise to two further types of site: the *kill, butchery* or *collecting site*, and, where such activity takes place at a distance from the home base, the *field camp*. The amount of rubbish discarded at a field camp is likely to be less than at a home base, and may be specific to the task group's activity. Home bases, field camps and kill,

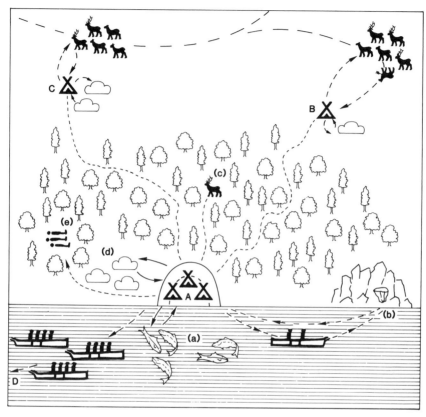

Figure 3.1 A home base (A), with its residential and peripheral areas, is situated beside a lake while various activities take place in the immediate vicinity: fishing (a), collecting flint for knapping (b), hunting (c), gathering (d) and funerary rites at the traditional burial ground (e). Other hunting is based on field camps (B and C), but after a time the band moves on (D), perhaps further around the lake. Each activity may be represented in the archaeological record by discarded artefacts or faunal remains, and abandoned facilities (for the key see fig. 2.3, p. 18).

butchery or collecting sites are linked by a network of paths, and occasionally items might be lost or discarded in transit. Many groups also have sites which are reserved for ritual purposes, such as disposal of the dead.

VARIABILITY IN ARCHAEOLOGICAL ASSEMBLAGES

Accumulations of lost or discarded artefacts are referred to as assemblages and the same term can also be used to describe accumulations of animal bones and plant remains. Assemblages of archaeological material are generated by the interplay of several factors including the range of activities carried out at the location in question, the number of times each activity is performed there and the way the group involved disposes of its

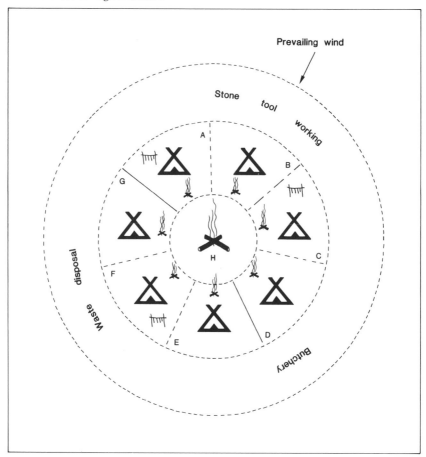

Figure 3.2 Schematic functional organization of a home base: Each one of seven families (A to G) occupies a sector of the residential area in which will be found its shelter, domestic hearth, and perhaps some storage facilities, such as drying racks. The focus of the residential area is a communal hearth (H). Some activities which produce a lot of debris or waste are confined to the peripheral area and, if they are likely to be smelly, are placed downwind.

rubbish. For archaeologists the last factor, known as *discard behaviour*, is the most important, for this has to be taken into account before any attempt is made to reconstruct the original activity at the site.

Most discard behaviour is deliberate and occurs at the time when something is thrown away or abandoned. This may be waste, or material that has become obsolete, perhaps through breakage. This kind of behaviour may be organized according to the status of the site, and a home base may be kept cleaner than a temporarily occupied field camp. The prevailing technology may also play a part. A group with an *expedient* technology, that is one in which equipment is made as needed and discarded on completion of the task, will leave a different set of remains from one following a more *curative* policy, in which equipment is made in advance of need and maintained for subsequent reuse. However, some material enters the archaeological record fortuitously through loss or by accident.

Consideration of discard behaviour is where the archaeologist should start in assessing the archaeological record, but, as we have seen, this is only one of the factors involved in the formation of archaeological assemblages. The other factors relate specifically to the tasks undertaken and the manner in which they are carried out.

Activity at a site usually revolves around the use of fixed facilities such as hearths or shelters, and areas dedicated to specific tasks such as flint knapping or butchery, or rubbish disposal, all linked by a network of paths. The archaeological assemblage which results from the way in which the site is organized is determined by many factors – physiological, social, tactical and locational – some of which are independent of the specific function of the site.

The most obvious independent factor is the human body. For the past 30,000 years all humans have been members of the species *Homo sapiens sapiens*. For example, they have two hands, which are fundamental to flint knapping; they can reach an area of about three square metres from a sitting position; they occupy about the same amount of space when lying down; their needs for warmth are similar; they do not like the wind and are scared of the dark! Similarly, social intercourse, a vital human trait, involves speech and eye contact, which impose their own limits on spacing. Lewis Binford has documented the operation of these factors in a fascinating series of studies of recent hunter-gatherer groups and has shown how they may be used to help us to understand archaeological sites, while at a more detailed level Newcomer and Sieveking have demonstrated how the dispersal of flint-knapping waste is partly dependent upon the posture and stance of the flint knapper.

Universal characteristics are also found on the broader scale of human social organization. Hunter-gatherers acknowledge ties between the nuclear and the extended family and the kin group, but many also have formal relationships which cut across them and may be occupationally or age dependent, as in the case of huntsmen or prepubescent girls. The organization of tasks has to take these familial and other relationships into account. For example, we can expect residential facilities at a home base to be partly contingent on the prevailing social structure (figs 3.2 and 3.3).

Other factors can be described as tactical, in that they arise from the normal human desire to make life easy. Many repetitive tasks such as fine flint knapping or bone carving are often most comfortably carried out in a seated position and, requiring little space, may take place inside. Butchery requires space so that the operative can move around the carcass and, because it is associated with unpleasant smells, it is usually considered to be an outside activity. Stationary tasks may require warmth and need to be carried out by the fire while detailed tasks may require light and, if they are undertaken inside, will need to be located near an opening. It is

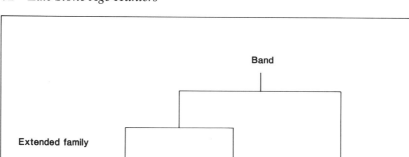

Figure 3.3 Schematic social organization of the home base featured in figure 3.2: The sector of the residential area occupied by an individual family is partly dictated by its social relations, probably based on kinship, with other families. Such relationships are unlikely to leave traces in the archaeological record.

inconvenient, and even dangerous, to walk on flint waste or fractured animal bone, and at a site occupied for a prolonged period such rubbish is likely to be cleared away.

The position and nature of the site itself can also affect the archaeological assemblage. For example, latitude determines day length and the availability of natural light as well as rain, wind and temperature – all of which have a bearing on the use, position and orientation of artifical shelters. On a smaller scale, the morphology of the site can be important. In a rock shelter activities are spatially constrained and the archaeological assemblage is partly a reflection of this. No such constraint exists on an open site and one reason why so few open sites are known may be that the dispersal of activities over a wide area makes them difficult to identify.

The extent to which archaeologists can identify the role of function in varying archaeological assemblages is an important question. How far can we infer the function of a site from the rubbish left behind there? In some cases it may be possible to establish a correlation between the finds made and the activity carried out if the tools used were discarded on site upon completion of the task. But if the tools were retained for further use no such correlation is likely to exist, except in a negative sense in that the really important items will be missing.

Some archaeologists have found it useful to employ the concept of the *tool kit*, that is a set of tools used in the execution of a particular task. But the choice of tools used by contemporary hunter-gatherers often depends on circumstances and individual tools might be used for a variety of activities; this casts some doubt on the validity of the 'tool kit' concept. In an archaeological context, the identification of tool kits is dependent on the ability of the archaeologist to recognize functionally meaningful tool types. Although 'scrapers', 'awls' and 'burins' are common, such terms are mainly used for descriptive purposes and only rarely can it be demonstrated that they were used in the ways implied.

In addition to abandoned facilities and assemblages of artefacts, the archaeological record of hunter-gatherers also includes assemblages of animal bone. The presence of animal bone at centres of human activity usually leads to the assumption that most of the bones are a further reflection of human behaviour, and faunal assemblages are generally used to make ecological and behavioural reconstructions. Many of the theoretical issues already raised in respect of artefact assemblages apply also to faunal remains, but in addition they have their own peculiar set of problems. Consideration of the faunal component of the archaeological record has a sound theoretical basis in the science of *taphonomy*, a branch of palaeontology concerned literally with the laws of burial and survival.

In practical terms the transition of animal remains from the living community (the biosphere) to the soil (the lithosphere) can be divided into two distinct stages. First, there are those events that occur between the death of the animal and the eventual burial of its remains. Second, further events affect the remains once they are buried. This second part of the taphonomic process is equivalent to the post-depositional factors which affect the accumulation of all archaeological assemblages and it is only brought to an end by the complete destruction of the animal remains or by their discovery by archaeologists. We shall consider post-depositional factors in more detail below.

Archaeological analyses of faunal remains have tended to be very simplistic and calculations attempting to equate the 'meat weight' assumed to be represented by the animal remains found at a site with population numbers via presumed calorific requirements are common. Such analyses are based on false assumptions.

The association of artefacts with faunal remains does not conclusively establish that human behaviour was responsible for the accumulation of the bones. Most faunal assemblages attributed to late Upper Palaeolithic or Mesolithic humans come from caves or rock shelters, facilities used by a wide range of animals including carnivores such as foxes, badgers, wolves, hyaenas and bears. Many of these animals die in caves, and accummulations of their remains need have nothing to do with human activity. Many also accumulate the remains of other species as their own food residues. When the prey species are not those preyed on by humans there should be no confusion, but in cases where competition has occurred with other cave-using carnivores great care is needed in assessing the status of faunal assemblages. Carnivores other than humans tend to consume the best parts of their quarry at the site of the kill and bring only those which are either difficult to process or are suitable for gnawing back to the den. Human beings usually do the opposite and bring the best bits home (plate III). In some cases such *skeletal-part analyses* can help archaeologists recognize faunal assemblages which have accumulated as a consequence of human behaviour. Similarly, carnivores break up bone in a different way from humans. Wolves and hyaenas crunch, crush and gnaw bones, leaving distinct traces, while humans carefully butcher them with tools, and cook and split them – all techniques beyond the capacity of most animals (plate IV). Such *attrition analyses* can help distinguish the human processing of carcasses from that of other animals.

In theory, attrition and skeletal-part analyses also offer the prospect of distinguishing between culturally different groups. It is well known that the butchery practices of Jews and Muslims differ from those of Christians, while cuts of meat common in Edinburgh are quite unavailable in London. The Danish archaeozoologist Nanna Noe-Nygaard has noted differences in the processing of red deer carcasses between sites in Britain and Denmark which might also be cultural, but much work remains to be done in this field.

We must also remember that animals were not killed only for food. They are the source of a whole range of products and this must be considered in evaluating the status of a faunal assemblage.

In the preceding paragraphs we have considered some of the principal factors that affect the accumulation of archaeological assemblages but we must not forget that these processes of accumulation take place through time, and time itself is an important factor. In cases where an activity is repeated many times at the same locality we might expect the remains of such an activity to be more clearly identifiable than those of single events, but in practice no two events are ever exactly the same and repetition leads to blurring of the archaeological record.

VARIABILITY BETWEEN ARTEFACTS

At the most basic level, artefacts vary in their use of raw material. Stone is good for some tasks while bone or antler may be better for others, and wood can be used for a wide range of items, examples of which survive only very rarely. The raw material used can provide important information, as for example when a particular material is found to have been used in an area where it does not occur naturally. This can provide an indication of the areas visited by a hunting band during their annual cycle of movements or the extent of their trading contacts. However, different raw materials were sometimes used to produce very similar items and most variability between artefacts arises from the functions they were designed to fulfil.

Archaeologists have always sought to ascribe functions to artefacts, both as a terminological convenience and as an attempt at behavioural recon-

struction. Archaeological *cultures*, that is recurring assemblages of artefacts thought to correspond to distinct social entities, have customarily
been identified by the presence or absence of 'diagnostic' artefacts.
Likewise, cultures having diagnostic artefacts in common have been
thought to have participated in a common technological tradition and are
grouped as *techno-complexes*. In the past the individual artefact has been
treated as the key to understanding spatial and temporal variability in the
archaeological record.

Similarly, site function has been interpreted on the basis of the presence
of particular pieces of equipment, a classic example being the 'scraper-
dominated' sites thought to be skin-working locations. In the case of stone
artefacts, which are nearly all we have, functions have usually been
ascribed on the basis of crude analogy and it is common practice to
describe assemblages of stone tools in terms of axes, arrowheads, scrapers,
points, knives, awls, burins or gravers and so on. But such 'tools' usually
comprise only a small part of an assemblage, most of which cannot be
classified in this way and is usually treated as 'waste'.

Chipped stone artefacts often exhibit signs of use regardless of whether
they have been fashioned into recognizable 'tools'. Some such traces are
clearly visible but others emerge under varying levels of magnification.
These traces consist of edge damage, abrasions, striations and glossy
polishes (plate vb). It has proved possible to replicate a number of these
features experimentally and this has led to the belief that some of the traces
observed on ancient implements can be associated with specific functions.
Microwear studies have led to some interesting insights into the use of
stone tools, but, as with many new developments, early optimism has been
tempered with realism as the limitations of the method become fully
appreciated. It has been found in most assemblages that only some items
are suitable for microwear analysis. At Star Carr for example, although 248
microliths were found, only 31 were considered suitable for microwear
study and of these only three exhibited traces of use. The extent to which
the Star Carr microliths can be interpreted on the basis of this 1.2 per cent
sample is limited. In additon to sampling problems, which are common to
much of archaeology, microwear analysis also faces a number of other
difficulties which are yet to be resolved. There has been little consideration
of how or why some forms of use produce microwear traces and whether
such traces could be produced by other processes such as manufacture or
post-depositional disturbance. While experimental replication can establish that certain traces could have been produced in a particular way it does
not prove that this is what actually happened. It is unlikely that these
problems of small sample size and equifinality (many causes leading to the
same result) will ever be completely resolved and they will continue to
place a limitation on the contribution of microwear analysis to the study of
stone tool assemblages.

Some variability between artefacts does not have a functional or utili-
tarian basis but arises from the individuality of the piece and its maker. In

days before mass production few artefacts would ever have been identical. Some of this variation would have been quite random and some due to the quirks and whims of the craftsman. In either case such individual variability has little to tell the archaeologist about past behaviour.

Non-functional variability between artefacts can, nevertheless, be systematic and variability of this kind is called *stylistic*. Style is a difficult concept to define, but it is perhaps best understood as a form of communication. In certain circumstances individuals dress in a style that expresses their affiliation to a particular group. Membership of a group, be it at the family, task group, hunting band or tribal level, has advantages for the individual and it makes sense that in most circumstances such membership should be openly expressed, both to help the cohesiveness of the group and to identify strangers. The Scotsman's kilt is an obvious contemporary example, as is the clergyman's dog-collar. The description of someone as stylish or fashionable has possible social connotations and Barbour jackets and green Wellington boots have gained a significance in England that goes some way beyond their simple utility as waterproofs. Stylistic variability in modern society is not confined to clothes but touches nearly all aspects of life from houses and cars to furniture and wrist watches. Although clothes rarely survive in the archaeological record, we may assume that stylistic variability affected a comparably wide range of material in the past. If this assumption is correct, patterns of stylistic variability may provide a means of studying, at a very elementary level, past patterns of social organization.

Although attempts have been made to identify stylistic variability in artefacts, it is difficult to be certain that the patterns observed do not have functional connotations, and clothing almost never survives. Ornaments are the one aspect of clothing that does regularly survive, and ornaments are more suitable for stylistic analysis than microliths or scrapers. We also know that ornaments are often used in modern societies as an expression of group affiliation and there is no reason to assume this was not the case in the past. Late Upper Palaeolithic and Mesolithic ornaments are varied in detail but use a limited range of raw materials. A necklace made of materials which are difficult to obtain or hard to work can tell the archaeologist quite a lot about the status of its owner and his or her social contacts and affiliations.

POST-DEPOSITIONAL PROCESSES

Material enters the archaeological record as a consequence of human actions and decisions, and it is primarily a record of these aspects of behaviour. A hunter may give up attempts to find a lost projectile point or a group may choose not to clear away domestic refuse at a temporary camp. The abandonment of facilities is also the result of a decision and it is such decisions about the discard of rubbish and the abandonment of facilities that determine much of the evidence available to the archaeologist. However, once material has been discarded, it is susceptible to modification by a number of natural processes such as burial or erosion, movement or, ultimately, destruction.

At the regional level these processes play an important role in determining the location of sites. For example, home bases are unlikely to be located in unstable environments such as flood plains, areas of wind blow or caves where roof falls are common. Such situations lead to rapid burial and preservation, but the sites preserved are more likely to be short-term scenes of activity where such dangers would have mattered less. These considerations can lead to a distortion of the settlement pattern through major sites of long-term occupation being underrepresented, because they may not have been preserved.

Natural processes also have a major influence at the level of the assemblage, though as yet there has been little research in this field except in the context of caves. Caves are mainly depositional, or burial, environments though erosion and movement do also occur, such as frost heaving in cold climates. Rates of sedimentation vary both between and within sites and have been recorded as ranging from 1.2 mm to 31 mm per decade. The more quickly material is buried, the more likely it is to be preserved, and this distorts the archaeological record towards rapidly forming deposits. On open sites it may take a long time for discarded artefacts and bones to become buried, and while they remain exposed the chances of movement or destruction must be considerable.

Natural processes also influence the archaeological record at the level of the individual artefact. For example, movement in the ground can damage working edges and remove microwear traces while scoring by wind-blown sand can produce polishes almost indistinguishable from those caused by certain forms of use.

Strictly speaking, the recovery of the archaeological record by archaeologists is also a post-depositional process. It is a form of erosion, usually involves movement of material and leads to the destruction of information.

PALYNOLOGY AND PALAEOECOLOGY

Several other categories of evidence also contribute to the archaeological record although they fall outside the province of the archaeologist. Pollen analysis, or *palynology*, is a tool of major importance in the reconstruction of past environments. As well as providing a record of natural changes in the flora, pollen spectra can preserve records of changes brought about by humans, the so-called anthropogenic factor. One of the best examples of this is forest clearance, where a sudden decrease in tree pollen may be the only record of human presence.

Palaeoecology also has an important contribution to make to the reconstruction of past behaviour, and nowhere is this better illustrated than in the realm of seasonality studies. Many animals experience an annual cycle of growth which is adjusted to the seasons. Red deer grow their antlers in the summer, wear them fully grown during the autumn and winter, and shed them in the spring (plate vɪa). Other deer experience similar cycles and it is sometimes possible to estimate the time of year an animal was killed by the growth of its antlers. The shells of many marine molluscs have an incremental pattern of growth which is most rapid during the summer and virtually non-existent during the winter (plate vɪb). By studying the last cycle of growth it is sometimes possible to estimate the season during which the animal was gathered. Most animals follow a regular cycle of reproduction, with young being born at the same time each year. Clearly, the presence of neonatal or very young animals on a site can be an indication of the time of year it was occupied. Young animals also have regular patterns of growth during their early life, and a knowledge of the season of birth can provide a further indication of the time of year they were killed. Given the cyclical and seasonal pattern of hunter-gatherer behaviour, being able to establish at which times of the year sites were occupied, or how the hunters' activities altered with the seasons, is very informative.

PALAEONUTRITION AND PALAEOPATHOLOGY

There is a popular saying that 'we are what we eat' and from the archaeologist's point of view this is fortunately more true than most people imagine. The science of *palaeonutrition* has demonstrated that our skeletons preserve a limited record of certain aspects of our diet. Stable carbon isotope ratios in human bone have been used to determine the proportions of marine and terrestrial food in the diet. The $^{13}C/^{12}C$ ratio in seawater bicarbonate is higher than that in atmospheric carbon dioxide. These differences are apparent in marine and terrestrial plants and in the bone collagen of animals that feed on them. A study of the bones of Mesolithic populations in Denmark has established that their diet was dominated by seafood. Trace elements also record aspects of diet. For example, strontium has been found to be an especially useful indicator. Herbivores have less strontium than the plants they eat and carnivores have less than the herbivores. Strontium also becomes concentrated in freshwater and marine molluscs, and marine vertebrates have higher levels than terrestrial vertebrates. Because these distinctions are passed up the food chain, trace element analyses of human skeletons can distinguish populations with different dietary habits.

The kindred discipline of *palaeopathology* is also making an increasingly important contribution through the recognition of pathological indicators of dietary stress such as enamel hypoplasia, while pathological signs of social stress are mostly traumas such as cranial contusions. It is, however, important to distinguish traces of interpersonal violence from hunting accidents.

CONCLUDING SUMMARY

In this chapter we have seen how archaeologists attempt to reconstruct human behaviour from its material remains, which constitute the archaeological record. This record is subject to many distortions, only some of which arise from human behaviour, while others may be considered more as natural processes. It is one of the tasks of the archaeologist to establish in what ways the record has been distorted so that this may be allowed for in reconstructions of the past. Inevitably, the need to make such allowances imposes limitations. However, a relatively incomplete, but soundly based, reconstruction is to be preferred to one which, although more complete, does not bear close scrutiny because it is based on insufficient evidence.

ADDITIONAL READING

The regional hierarchy of hunter-gatherer sites is adapted from that published by Foley (1981), while factors influencing the formation of archaeological assemblages have been considered in detail by Schiffer (1976, 1989), Binford (1978a and b, 1989) and Houtsma *et al.* (1996). The experimental generation and analysis of flint-knapping waste is dealt with by Newcomer and Sieveking (1980), and the existence and significance of 'tool kits' by Whallon (1978). Lewis Binford (1981) has also made a major contribution to the study of faunal assemblages, while examples of some of the processes at work are provided by Behrensmeyer and Hill (1980). In several important papers Nanna Noe-Nygaard (1977, 1987) has dealt with taphonomy within the context of mesolithic assemblages from northern Europe and Jenkinson (1984a) deals with similar issues arising in British late Upper Palaeolithic caves.

The study of use-wear traces on stone tools was initiated by Semenov (1964) and developed by Keeley (1974, 1980), while Jensen (1988) has provided a recent review of developments in this field. In Britain recent published work is by Dumont (1988, 1989). Readers especially interested in these matters will enjoy following the controversy over microwear 'polishes' argued out in the pages of the *Journal of Archaeological Science* between 1986 and 1988. A discussion of the role of style in stone tool variability will be found in Gendel (1984, 1989) while Constandse-Westermann and Newell (1988) have examined ornaments and the putative correlation between their distribution and patterns of social organization.

Palynology is too fully developed a discipline for any particular source to be recommended, but at a regional level I have drawn heavily on the work of Huntley and Birks (1983). Examples of seasonality studies are provided by Legge and Rowley-Conwy (1988) and in several papers by Deith (1983, 1986, 1989). Palaeonutrition is dealt with by Wing and Brown (1979), Hassan (1979) and Cohen (1977), while examples of what can be learned from stable isotope and trace element analyses are provided by Tauber (1981) and Price (1989a). Palaeopathology is dealt with by Zivanovic (1982) and Cohen and Armelagos (1984).

4 An interpretative framework

In the preceding chapters I have tried to delineate some of the many factors which influence the behaviour of hunter-gatherers and the ways in which that behaviour is reflected in the archaeological record. In later chapters we shall look at examples of evidence for such behaviour in order to see what may be learned about the life of Late Stone Age hunter-gatherers in the British Isles. To facilitate this we need a framework within which to marshal the evidence. This framework needs to be three dimensional in that it has to allow for consideration of the behavioural, spatial and temporal aspects of the evidence.

THE BEHAVIOURAL FRAMEWORK

In reviewing the ecology of hunting and gathering in chapter 2, I drew attention to a number of conditions which we can expect to find among all hunter-gatherer groups. These may be presented as a series of broad propositions:

First, as a consequence of the ecological relations of hunting and gathering, groups following such a way of life live at low densities.

Second, such low population densities lead to relatively simple levels of social organization, which only become more complex when densities rise above the norm.

Third, patterns of economic behaviour are closely adjusted to the nature and distribution of available resources.

Where ecological data are available it is possible to use such basic propositions to make predictions about population density, social structure, settlement pattern and behaviour. However, such data are not available in a sufficiently precise form for the British Isles during the Lateglacial and early Postglacial.

While an ecological perspective provides a context within which to review the evidence for the economic life of Late Stone Age hunters, it offers little insight into their social life. Such a perspective is both one-sided and determinist. Whilst environment may set broad limits to what can be done, the many choices that are available within those limits are just as likely to be motivated by social considerations as they are by those of ecology. The need to be conscious of such matters suggests a fourth, this time socio-ecological, proposition:

> That the social relations of production also have an important influence on economic behaviour. This will be especially the case when increasing population density leads to the development of more complex social structures, and a particular strategy might be pursued as much for its social, as for its economic, value.

Given that social organization cannot be inferred from ecological data, it is necessary to turn to the ethnohistorical record, where the social organization of hunter-gatherers can be studied in operation. This record is so diverse that much of it is irrelevant to the Late Stone Age in the British Isles and careful evaluation is necessary. In North America at the time of the European settlement, large areas were still occupied by peoples pursuing a hunting and gathering way of life in environments similar, in some respects, to those found in Britain during the Lateglacial and early Postglacial. Their tripartite social structure of family, task group and band within a higher level of tribal organization provides a useful framework within which to review hunter-gatherer social organization in Late Stone Age Britain (fig. 2.4).

Ecology and ethnohistory provide broad indications of what we might expect life to have been like for the Late Stone Age hunter-gatherers of the British Isles. Our evidence for the details of that way of life is provided by the archaeological record.

The archaeological record is created by the actions of human beings but, as we saw in chapter 3, by the time the archaeologist comes on the scene, the evidence for those actions has become distorted in a number of ways. Natural processes may have disturbed or destroyed some of the evidence and the evidence itself has usually accumulated over a period of time and is not the residue of a single event. The process of accumulation is a source of behavioural information in its own right. The fact that a group continued to use a particular location, either for the same purpose or for a variety of purposes, is not without significance. Given that most of the archaeological record consists of such accumulations, we clearly have important evidence for a conservatism which has structured most hunter-gatherer behaviour. Viewed in this light, radical disruptions in the accumulation process or its termination can be seen as significant events.

To get the clearest view of past behaviour we must seek instances where accumulation processes have been minimal, such as locations occupied over a short period of time for perhaps a limited range of activities. Such cases are uncommon and, by their very nature, provide an incomplete record of the full range of behaviour. However, the nature of the evidence precludes the attainment of a complete picture, and the explanatory value of short-period accumulations means that examples of this kind will feature prominently in the case studies examined in later chapters. In order to select the most informative case studies, I have included radiocarbon dates and biological evidence as further criteria.

When reviewing an assemblage of discarded artefacts or animal bones we have first to ask: What are these remains doing here? Were they lost or thrown away? Were they dropped where they were used? Have they accumulated in one place after being tidied away? Only when such issues have been addressed can we move on to consider in which ways the artefacts or bones were used.

We saw in chapter 3 that behaviour can be viewed as either independent of the specific function of the site or in some way determined by it. The fact that people want to sit upwind of a fireplace but be close enough to engage in conversation applies whatever the reason for their being there. Similarly, social relations also tend to structure the way tasks are undertaken and can have an important influence on spatial organization, members of one group wishing to be together and clearly separate from others (fig. 3.2). The material remains arising from such behavioural choices have little relation to the specific activities carried out. On the other hand, butchery leaves debris different from that of flint knapping and a home base witnesses a wider range of activities than is found at a field camp. In considering the case studies we shall need to take such factors into account.

At the regional level, hunter-gatherer activity usually follows an annual cycle, pursued within an area known as the annual territory (fig. 2.3). Cycles may vary from year to year depending on economic and social factors and territorial limits are flexible. Through a lifetime an individual may come to know a far larger territory than may be visited in any one annual cycle (fig. 2.5). Evidence for the existence of such a cycle is provided by indications that various locations were used on a seasonal basis and evidence for its extent may come from the distribution of raw materials such as flint beyond the area of their natural occurrence.

Activity focuses around one or more centres which may be called home bases, since most of the group spend part of their time there, and some members rarely leave it. The home base has two components: a residential area and a periphery, which is the scene of various activities including perhaps the disposal of waste (fig. 3.2). The archaeological remains should reflect these differing functions. Economic resources are likely to be distributed discontinuously and extraction will therefore focus on a number of locations. When these are more than a day's journey from the home base a field camp has to be set up. Archaeological remains which accumulate at such locations will be specific to the activity pursued there. The home bases and these secondary locations must, of course, be joined by a network of tracks, and, as people pass along them, material enters the archaeological record when items are lost, or a temporary halt is made.

Each family unit follows its own annual cycle but as families tend to operate together the co-residential group or band may comprise anything from a few tens of individuals to a hundred or more. Groups are flexible and aggregate and disperse during the course of the annual cycle according to economic and social pressures. Occasionally large aggregations occur where several co-residential groups come together, often for social and ceremonial purposes. An important reason for population aggregation is the exchange of marriage partners.

Social relations are difficult to identify in the archaeological record but in a few cases it is possible for something to be inferred. It is well known that the development of increasingly complex social structures is a mechanism by which animals, including people, deal with the stresses of population pressure, be it the pecking order in a hen house or the complex class structure of a modern state. Most hunter-gatherer groups are organized at the level of the co-resident group, or band, and social organization outside the family structure is weak and temporary. As population rises, more complex structures emerge. These may be temporary, such as during a periodic aggregation, or more permanent, as endogamous begin to replace exogamous breeding networks. In the archaeological record we may infer greater social complexity from greater population density. We may recognize it within groups by signs of differential access to material wealth, or preferential diet, and between groups by evidence for distinct styles of dress or ornamentation within specific areas and over particular periods of time.

THE SPATIAL FRAMEWORK

It is obvious from the title of this book that our spatial framework is that of the British Isles. In their present form the British Isles are a relatively recent geographical phenomenon, the familar outline having only been established when sea level reached its present height about 6,000 years ago. For most of the period covered by the book the outline was quite different and it is necessary to take this into account when we are considering the pattern of human settlement. There is uncertainty about the rate of sea-level rise and the topography of now submerged coastal areas. Accordingly, it is difficult to reconstruct the configuration of the coastline at any precise point in time and the maps which accompany chapters 5 and 9 illustrate, in a generalized and conventional manner, the extent of coastal change during rather broadly defined periods.

THE TEMPORAL FRAMEWORK

For reasons already explained in the preface, the temporal framework adopted in this book is that provided by radiocarbon dating. Archaeologists apply radiocarbon dating in two ways. First, the method

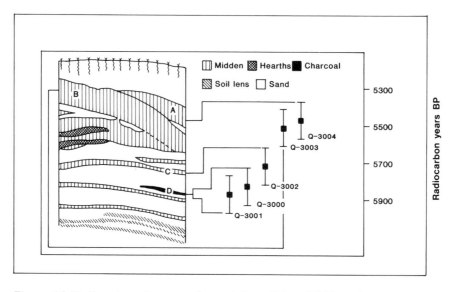

Figure 4.1 Radiocarbon dates on charcoal from Priory Midden, Oronsay: The upper layers of the midden (A and B) are dated to *c*. 5500 BP and an earlier layer (C) to *c*. 5700 BP. Layers in between accumulated during the intervening period. The charcoal lens (D) is dated to *c*. 5825 BP and earlier midden deposits and soil horizons must have accumulated before this (after Mellars 1987). (Dates: Q–3004 5470 ± 50 BP, Q–3003 5510 ± 50 BP, Q–3002 5717 ± 50 BP, Q–3000 5825 ± 50 BP, Q–3001 5870 ± 50 BP)

can provide a date for the context in which the archaeological traces of some past human activity have been found. In the example in figure 4.1, dates have been obtained on samples of charcoal from various levels in a shell midden. Other finds from the same levels would be presumed to be of broadly the same date.

Second, archaeological specimens can be dated directly if they are made from organic materials. These include artefacts made from bone and antler, animal bones with traces of human modification, usually arising from butchery practices, and remains of the humans themselves. Compared with the incidence of stone tools, all such specimens are very rare indeed, and the size of the sample required for dating, usually between about 50 and 100 grams, has until recently been prohibitive. Finds of this kind are simply too valuable to be partly destroyed in a radiocarbon laboratory. The regular, direct dating of such specimens has become possible through the application of accelerator mass spectrometry, known as AMS, to radiocarbon dating. This technique requires only a microscopic amount of material to be sacrificed for a date to be obtained and it is usually considered that the knowledge gained justifies this (fig. 4.2). This technique received wide public attention in 1988 when the dating of a few fibres from the Turin Shroud established it as a medieval forgery.

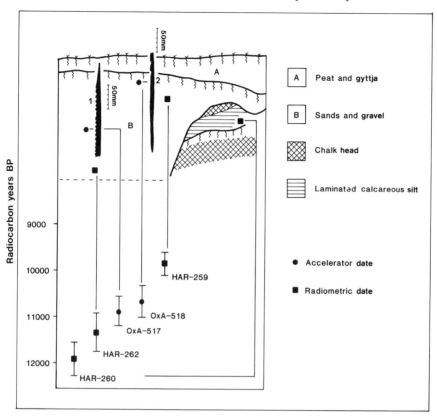

Figure 4.2 Radiometric and AMS dates from Sproughton, Suffolk: Before their direct dating by the accelerator the two barbed points were dated to between *c.* 12,300 and *c.* 9640 BP by their association with radiometric dates from the same deposits. The accelerator dates on the points themselves have narrowed this range to 11,210 to 10,380 BP (after Wymer *et al.* 1975). (Dates: HAR–259 9880 ± 120 BP, OxA–518 10,700 ± 160 BP, OxA–517 10,910 ± 150 BP, HAR–262 11,370 ± 210 BP, HAR–260 11,940 ± 180 BP)

Radiocarbon dates look deceptively precise and, by implication, convincing. For example, the bone point found at Sproughton (NGR TM 133443) in Suffolk (fig. 4.2 no. 1) provided an AMS radiocarbon date of 10,910 ± 150 BP. The second number, known as the error term, gives an indication of just how imprecise the date is and reflects the level of accuracy of the dating exercise. In our example, the way in which the date is expressed tells the specialist that there is a 66 per cent chance of the actual date lying between 11,060 and 10,760 BP. A radiocarbon date is thus a range, and is usually expressed as a mean value with a single standard deviation, the error term. It is obvious that a 66 per cent level of reliability is not very good and many archaeologists prefer to use radiocarbon dates with two standard deviations; thus the margin in the example becomes 300 years and the range 11,210 to 10,610 BP. At two standard deviations the level of reliability is 95 per cent, which is much more acceptable and genuinely significant in a statistical sense. The range has perhaps become rather wide, but in relatively remote periods this is of less importance than the confidence gained by opting to use a date at two standard deviations. In figures 4.1 and 4.2 date ranges are shown at two standard deviations.

The concepts outlined in this chapter provide a framework within which the archaeological record can be used to provide insights into the life of the Late Stone Age hunters of the British Isles. But these people lived in an environment that was at times changing rapidly and it is first necessary to say something about the ecological framework within which they lived out those lives.

ADDITIONAL READING

This chapter is mainly a synthesis of points covered in more detail in chapters 2 and 3, and reference should be made to the 'Additional reading' sections of those chapters. The technique of radiocarbon dating is widely used and well known. The most recent summaries of the principles involved can be found in Aitken (1990) and Bowman (1990), who also discuss the problems involved in interpretation, while the arguments in favour of the direct dating of artefacts are considered in Bonsall and Smith (1990).

Plate 1 (a) Hunters of the open grasslands: a Blackfoot band camped on the Canadian plains in the late nineteenth century; note the tepees are erected in several discrete clusters which perhaps reflect the social relations of their occupants (cf. figure 3.2) (Museum of Mankind).

(b) Hunters of the woods and forests: domed Ojibwa wigwams at Sault Ste Marie in 1845–8. They are covered with birch bark and hides and may be compared with the putative reconstruction of the Mesolithic hut at Mount Sandel in figure 7.12 (from a painting by Paul Kane, courtesy of the Royal Ontario Museum, Toronto, Canada).

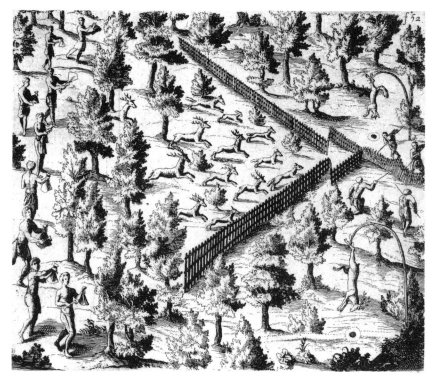

Plate II (a) In this seventeenth-century French engraving, illustrating a Huron deer hunt, we see a hunting party or task group in action (for comparison with figure 5.10); deer are driven towards a fenced enclosure where they are trapped and speared (plate V of Samuel de Champlain, *Voyages et descouvertures faites en la Nouvelle France depuis l'année 1615 à la fin de l'année 1618*, Paris, 1619, by permission of the British Library).

(b) A group of Copper Inuit in the Canadian Actic tundra spearing salmon at a fish weir (National Museums of Canada, Canadian Museum of Civilization negative no. 37080).

Plate III (a) Hyaenas dismember and consume a carcass at the scene of the kill (Hans Kruuk).

(b) A family butcher's shop in Hexham, some distance from the scene of the kill (author).

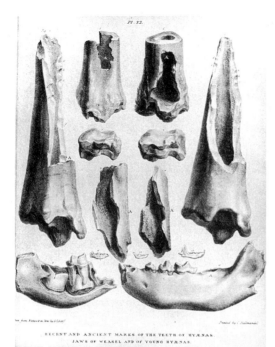

Plate IV (a) Attrition analysis: animal bones gnawed by hyaenas (plate 23 from William Buckland's *Reliquiae Diluvianae*, 1824). Nos 1, 3 and 5 were gnawed by a Cape hyaena in 'Mr Wombwell's travelling collection' at Oxford in 1822 while nos 2, 4 and 6 are from Devensian deposits at Kirkhead Cave, Lancashire (University of Newcastle upon Tyne).

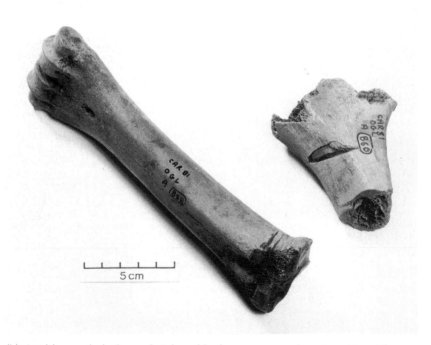

(b) Attrition analysis: bones butchered by humans; second-century AD cattle bones from Carlisle with clear butchery traces (University of Newcastle upon Tyne).

Plate V (a) It is very rare for such ephemeral traces as footprints on a beach to be preserved, but erosion caused by storms in 1986 exposed these tracks left by a Mesolithic hunter in the mud of the Severn Estuary (Derek Upton).
(b) The use to which stone tools have been put can sometimes be determined by the examination of microscopic traces left on their cutting edges. These two flint blades from the late Mesolithic site of Deby 29, Poland (examined at × 300), both show traces of bright polish, probably caused by cutting plant material (Richard Willis).

(c) Mesolithic shell midden dated to the sixth millennium BP at Ferriter's Cove, Dingle Peninsula. This small accumulation may represent the rubbish from just a few hours' collecting along the foreshore (Peter Woodman).

Plate VI (a) Red deer stags shed their antlers in the spring and grow a new set in time for the autumn rut. The stage of antler growth can be used to provide an indication of the time of year the animal was killed and shed antlers can usually only be collected in the spring. The skull is from a young red or sika stag which died of natural causes late in the winter of 1987/8; the antlers are still firmly attached to the skull. The shed antler, probably from the same species, was collected in April 1988 (University of Newcastle upon Tyne).

(b) An acetate peel of a section through the edge of a cockle (*Cerastoderma edule*) shell showing tidally deposited growth increments. During the winter growth is very slight or non-existent: a study of the incremental patterning can indicate the season during which the mollusc was collected (Margaret Deith).

Plate VII Beyond the margins of the ice sheet much of Britain was affected by permafrost and periglacial phenomena. These two aerial photographs show crop marks formed over patterned ground features in Essex (a) and Suffolk (b) (Cambridge University Committee for Aerial Photography).

Plate VIII (a) Birch scrub in Argyll. During the Lateglacial Interstadial and early Postglacial birch was a major component of the British flora (author).

(b) Light deciduous woodland in Argyll. By 9000 BP mixed deciduous woodland covered much of the British Isles (author).

Plate IX (a) Stumps of Scots pine, exposed at low tide on Borth Beach, Cardigan Bay, are an eloquent testimony to the fact that sea levels in the past have been much lower than at present (author).

(b) Raised beaches and former sea cliffs at Tiretigan in Argyll, set many metres back from high-water mark, indicate that at times present sea levels have been considerably exceeded (author).

Plate X Hunting lesions retaining embedded flints noted in a reindeer cranium and vertebrum from Lateglacial Ahrensburgian levels at the Stellmoor site near Hamburg (general views and details) (Archäologisches Landesmuseum Schleswig).

Plate XI (a) Mother Grundy's Parlour at Creswell Crags: the fireplace excavated by Armstrong lay to the left of the iron grille, under the overhang (author).

(b) Robin Hood's Cave at Creswell Crags: the fireplace excavated by Campbell lay just outside the entrance (author).

(c) Ulva Cave: the Mesolithic shell midden lies to the left of the cave entrance (Clive Bonsall).

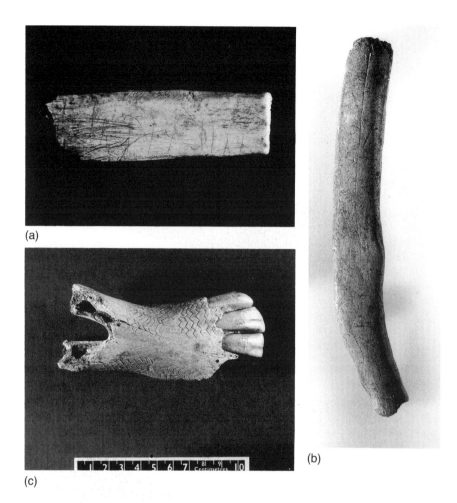

(a)

(b)

(c)

Plate XII Examples of British late Upper Palaeolithic art: (a) horse head engraving from Robin Hood's Cave, (b) anthropomorphic engraving from Pin Hole and (c) an engraved mandible of *Equus* from Kendrick's Cave (British Museum).

Plate XIII (a) Skin boat of umiak type (Museum of Mankind).

(b) The putative Mesolithic dugout canoe from Pesse in the Netherlands (Fotoarchief, Drents Museum, Assen).

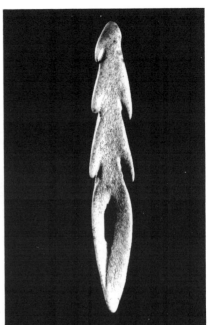
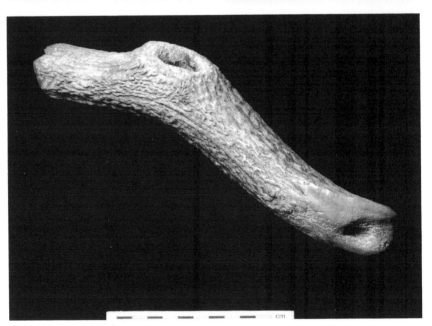

Plate XIV Late Mesolithic bone and antler artefacts: (a) the Whiburn harpoon (Museum of Antiquities, University of Newcastle upon Tyne) and (b) the Meiklewood mattock (Royal Museum of Scotland).

Plate XV (a) Cnoc Coig midden, Oronsay, during the recent excavations (Paul Mellars).

(b) A detailed view of a section through the Caisteal nan Gillean II midden, Oronsay, during recent excavations (Paul Mellars).

5 The Lateglacial and early Postglacial environment

Evidence for environmental change is widespread and commonplace. At the level of the individual we can all remember sequences of good or poor summers, and harsh or mild winters, while the view that over the span of several generations such variations have been considerable amounts to more than mere nostalgia for long hot summers and white Christmases. At a broader scale still, landscapes in many parts of the British Isles exhibit evidence for glacial erosion of a kind found today only in polar or alpine regions, while the exposure of submerged forests at low tide testifies to formerly much lower sea levels (plate ixa). More subtly, the present and past distribution of plants and animals can monitor climatic changes in quite a precise way. For example, the present distribution of the dwarf birch (*Betula nana*) is confined to the area where maximum summer temperatures do not exceed 22°C, namely the highlands of central and northern Scotland. However, fossilized grains of pollen found in lake sediments have shown that 11,000 years ago dwarf birch had a more widespread distribution which extended into southern England (fig. 5.1). Bones of reindeer (*Rangifer tarandus*), the quintessential animal of the tundra, have been found in cave deposits in Staffordshire dated to 10,000 years ago.

Eighteen thousand years ago large areas of the British Isles were uninhabited and uninhabitable. Over half of the area was covered by an ice sheet, and not even the highest summits broke its surface. But by 13,000 BP most of this ice had melted and temperatures, at least in the summer, had reached or even slightly exceeded those of the present day. It may have taken rather longer for winters to ameliorate by a comparable amount and continuing low sea levels ensured that mainland Britain remained part of the continental land mass until about 8,500 years ago. During this period the environment of the British Isles changed radically in its physical appearance, its climate, and the plants and animals that came to live here as the ice sheets melted.

The Late Stone Age hunters of the British Isles had continually to adapt to a changing environment, at times a rapidly changing one. It has been estimated, for example, that at about 13,000 BP summer temperatures may

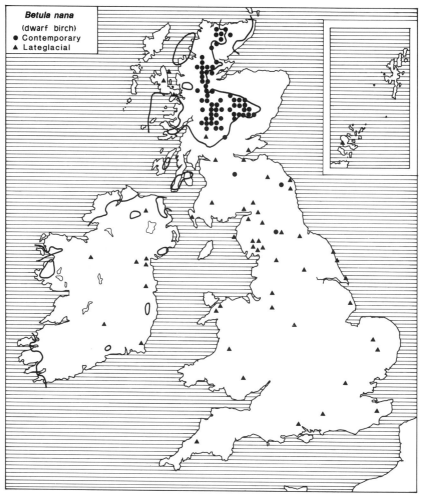

Figure 5.1 The contemporary and Lateglacial distribution of dwarf birch (*Betula nana*), with the present 22°C maximum temperature isotherm (after Conolly and Dahl 1970).

have been increasing by as much as 1°C per decade. Many changes were sufficiently marked to be perceived over a few generations and we should not make the mistake of thinking that the early inhabitants of Britain viewed their world as unchanging.

Situated in middle latitudes, the British Isles lie directly in the path of the major weather systems which, in the northern hemisphere, track from west to east. This westerly exposure is further enhanced by a location at the western extremity of the Eurasian landmass and fronting on to one of the world's largest oceans. Few other areas experience the same combination of circumstances.

A general cooling of the climate on a global scale has been detected in the palaeontological record from the time of the transition between the Miocene and Pliocene epochs, about 5 million years ago, by the appearance of increasing numbers of species adapted to cool conditions. Fluctuations between cool and temperate conditions have been a feature of the past 3.2 million years of the Pliocene and Pleistocene epochs.

The beginning of the Pleistocene is conventionally placed at 1.6 million years ago. Studies of marine sediments, in which a detailed and world-wide record of climatic change is preserved, suggest that during this period there have been at least ten periods during which the climate became sufficiently cold for glacial conditions to have become extensive in the northern hemisphere. The last of these episodes began about 118,000 years ago and is often referred to in Britain as the *Devensian* period. In the northern hemisphere, the growth of the Arctic ice cap modified patterns of oceanic and atmospheric circulation. In particular precipitation increased. Against the background of a global lowering of temperature, this led to the formation of ice sheets and glaciers in middle-latitude regions such as Scandinavia and the British Isles, while on a world-wide scale the accumulation of ice lowered sea levels by over 100 metres. When temperatures began to ameliorate after about 16,000 years ago, the contraction of the Arctic ice cap reversed this process. Precipitation decreased, and with warmer temperatures the British and Scandinavian ice sheets wasted away. Sea levels rose rapidly and many low-lying areas such as the North Sea Lowlands were inundated. These changes in climate and terrain were mirrored by changes in the plants and animals in north-western Europe at the time.

OCEANIC CIRCULATION AND WEATHER SYSTEMS

It is well known that the British Isles benefit from lying directly in the path of the North Atlantic Drift. This oceanic current, which is an extension of the Gulf Stream, begins in equatorial latitudes and flows up the eastern seaboard of the United States. Off Newfoundland it meets the cold Labrador Current and the warmer waters are deflected eastwards. The boundary between these cool, Arctic, and rather warmer, temperate, waters is called the *Polar Front* and its latitudinal position is a major controlling influence on the weather systems of the North Atlantic and north-west Europe (fig. 5.2). Studies of microfaunas in marine sediments document variations in the latitudinal position of the Polar Front. At the present time the Polar Front lies to the north of Shetland but at the time of the glacial maximum it lay well south of Britain, between latitudes 40°N and 45°N. With rising temperatures after the glacial maximum the Polar Front retreated northwards and reached the latitude of Iceland by about 11,000 years ago. However, a return to lower temperatures brought it south again and the final, major northward retreat was not completed until about 9300 BP.

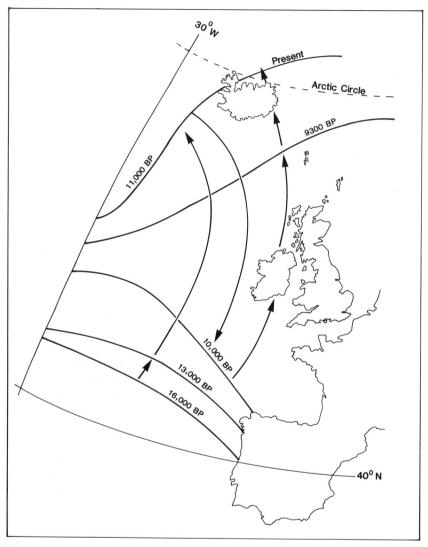

Figure 5.2 Movements of the Polar Front since 13,000 BP (after Gamble 1986 and Lowe and Walker 1987).

PRECIPITATION AND TEMPERATURE

The position of the British Isles, in the middle latitudes of the northern hemisphere, at the western extremity of a continental landmass and in the path of the major weather systems, has led to the region being subject to both maritime and continental influences. The north and west tend to be under maritime influence, with high humidity and limited temperature range, while the opposite applies to the south and east. During periods of low sea level, when eastern England was joined to the Continent, this distinction was more marked. Even today, with Britain an island, precipitation and temperature still vary considerably between the west and east coasts.

Throughout the Devensian period Britain remained joined to the Continent and precipitation was generally low, at about 300 mm per year, or roughly half that of the present day. However, for extensive glaciation to have occurred towards the end of the period an increase in precipitation, at least in western Britain, is implied. This can be associated with increased cyclonic activity arising from the southward movement of the Polar Front. Values for upland Britain of between 550 mm and 740 mm per year have been suggested for the period from 30,000 BP to 18,000 BP. Reconstructions of patterns of atmospheric circulation indicate that most of this precipitation fell during the summer months, but nevertheless must have fallen as snow. As the Polar Front moved up and down the Atlantic seaboard during the three millennia after 13,000 BP, further, short-term, increases in precipitation occurred. But this period of instability was relatively short lived, and by 9000 BP the present pattern of atmospheric circulation had been established and it took only the flooding of the North Sea Lowlands to give the British Isles a fully maritime precipitation regime.

Past temperatures cannot be studied directly and must be inferred from a variety of sources of evidence. Most such evidence has been derived from studies of fossil pollen and insect faunas. Different types of plant require different temperature regimes to maintain growth and reproduce. Their presence at various times enables such temperature conditions to be inferred. We have already seen how the distribution of the dwarf birch is limited by the 22°C isotherm (fig. 5.1). Similarly, various species of insects are also adjusted to particular climatic conditions and their remains can provide an indication of the climate prevailing at the time of their death.

Studies of pollen and insect remains clearly document the rise in temperature that followed the glacial maximum and led to the melting of the ice sheets. However, the insect remains suggest that the rise in temperature was rather more rapid than might by judged from a study of pollen alone. This contradiction is more apparent than real in that insects, being generally more mobile than plants, are able to respond to changes far more quickly.

The pattern of temperature fluctuations over the period between 18,000 BP and 5000 BP, inferred from a variety of sources, is illustrated in figure 5.3. From this it can be seen that summer temperatures comparable to, or even slightly higher than, those of today had been reached by 13,000 BP. This mild interval is known as the *Lateglacial Interstadial*. However, temperatures had begun to decline again by 12,000 BP and reached a low point around 10,800 BP, only to rise rapidly again until a maximum was reached, slightly higher than today, at about 8500 BP. This event is known as the *Postglacial climatic optimum*.

The general pattern of changes in temperature and precipitation have so far been considered in their effect on the British Isles as a whole. There

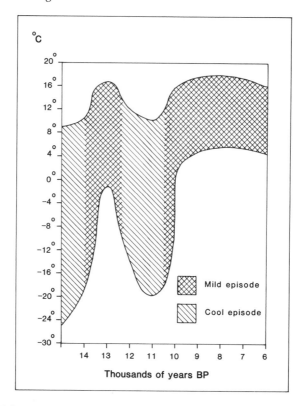

Figure 5.3 Mean temperatures for the warmest month (top) and coolest month (bottom) from 14,000 to 5000 BP (after Lamb 1985 and Atkinson, pers. comm.).

must have been local variation within these patterns and reference has been made to the present longitudinal differences between the mild and damp maritime west and the cold but dry continental east. The latitudinal extent of the British Isles, over 10° in all, is a further source of variation. Worthing and Wick experience quite different ranges of temperature and patterns of rainfall and 10,000 years ago these extremes are likely to have been greater. Altitude provides another source of variation. Air temperature falls by about 0.6°C for every 100 m gained above sea level and, as fellwalkers know, both precipitation and wind force increase with altitude. The warmest and most sheltered areas are those less than 100 m above sea level and one effect of lower sea levels would have been to make upland areas even more hostile and inimical to settlement than they are today.

GLACIATION AND DEGLACIATION

The effects of glaciation are some of the most conspicuous features in the landscape, especially in the mountainous areas of the west and north. The angular peaks, jagged ridges, high cols and broad U-shaped valleys were sculpted by ice sheets and glaciers during the last 100,000 years while, in the lowlands to the south and east, much of the material eroded from the uplands was deposited as boulder clay or till.

Although the Devensian period was generally cold, glaciation was widespread only towards the end. The British ice sheets and glaciers reached their maximum extent about 18,000 BP when over half the country was covered by ice. The southern limits of the Devensian ice sheet are well established (fig. 5.4a). To the west there is some uncertainty and it is not clear whether ice reached quite as far as the edge of the continental shelf. Northwards, it has often been assumed that the British ice sheet met, and coalesced with, the larger Scandinavian sheet. Recent evidence from the sea bed suggests that this may not have been the case and that an ice-free corridor extended the full length of the North Sea Lowlands as far as the latitude of Shetland.

At its maximum the British ice sheet was over 1,800 m thick over central Scotland, covering even the highest of the Cairngorms and Ben Nevis. Towards its margins the thickness was greatly reduced and some of the uplands of northern England such as the northern Pennines and Teesdale may have remained as unglaciated *nunataks* while the surrounding lower ground was engulfed by ice. Beyond the margins of the ice sheets and glaciers stretched a broad zone of permafrost and periglacial activity, traces of which can still be detected as crop marks (plate vII).

Compared with the tens of thousands of years during which the climate had been deteriorating, the amelioration was rapid and the British Isles were ice free within less than 8,000 years. Deglaciation was not constant and was interrupted on several occasions by increases in precipitation associated with the movements of the Polar Front which led to renewed ice accumulation. These episodes are marked by glacial moraines where the stationary or readvancing ice sheets left accumulations of eroded debris. The best known is the *Loch Lomond Readvance*, dated mainly to the period between 11,400 and 10,800, though ice accumulation may have been under way by 12,000 BP (fig. 5.4c).

During these episodes of readvance, ice also accumulated in other mountainous areas such as the Isles of Skye and Mull, where small ice sheets formed. In the Lake District and in the mountains of Wales corrie glaciers developed, and Britain as a whole experienced a return to harsh conditions, with snow lying in upland areas for many months each winter. By 10,000 BP the ice sheets and glaciers had all wasted away and this date is conventionally taken as marking the end of the Devensian, and with it the end of the Pleistocene. Like all conventional boundaries this is quite arbitrary and its relevance to human behaviour should not be stressed.

CHANGING SEA LEVEL

One day in September 1931 the sailing trawler *Colinda* was fishing off the coast of Norfolk over the Leman and Ower Banks, submarine features

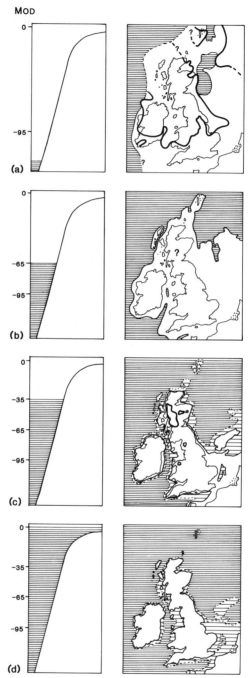

MOD

Figure 5.4 Ice sheets, coastlines and sea level during the Lateglacial and early Postglacial: (a) *c.* 18,000 BP, (b) *c.* 13,000 BP (the extent of ice cover at this time is unknown; it may have been non-existent), (c) *c.* 10,000 BP, (d) *c.* 8000 BP (after Long *et al.* 1986, Louwe Kooijmans 1985, Lowe and Walker 1987).

similar to the larger Dogger Bank. When the net was raised, in addition to a few fish, it was found to contain a large block of peat. Such finds were not uncommon and lumps of peat provide tangible scientific support for the view, long held traditionally, that much of the North Sea had formerly been dry land. What made the *Colinda*'s find special was the fact that embedded in the peat was a barbed point made from red deer antler (fig. 5.5). This has recently been dated to 11,740 ± 150 BP and the idea of humans hunting 11,500 years ago across what was to become the sea bed captures the imagination even today.

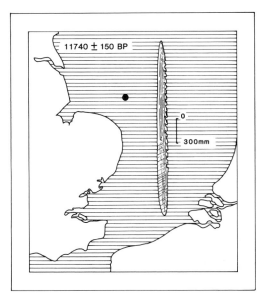

Figure 5.5 Barbed point of antler trawled from the Leman and Ower Banks by the *Colinda* in 1931 and recently dated by accelerator (after Clark and Godwin 1956 and Louwe Kooijmans 1971).

Evidence for formerly lower sea levels can be observed at many places around the British coasts in the form of tree stumps and fallen branches exposed at low tide (plate ixa). In other areas, especially in the north of Britain, extensive spreads of beach pebbles can be found many metres above the high-tide mark at the foot of cliffs now well away from the present action of the waves (plate ixb). Such submerged forests and raised beaches are eloquent testimony to the inconstancy of the British coastline.

Changing sea levels are a concomitant of the processes of glaciation and deglaciation in that the water in the ice sheets ultimately comes from the sea. At times of extensive glaciation sea levels are low and as the ice melts they rise. Because of the interlinked nature of the oceans this is a world-wide phenomenon and is known as *eustasy*, or eustatic sea-level change. Just as the melting of the ice sheets did not proceed at a constant rate, the eustatic rise in sea level proceeded in an irregular fashion with periods during which rising sea levels, or *transgressions*, were separated by episodes when levels were simply maintained or actually fell, the latter being known as *regressions*.

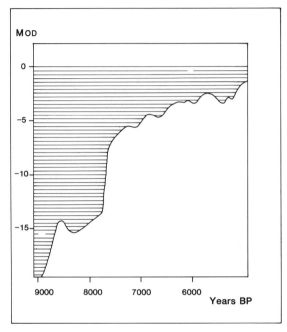

Figure 5.6 Eustatic fluctuations in mean sea level for north-west England from 9000 to 5000 BP; to estimate mean mean high water of spring tides add 4 m (after Tooley 1974).

The sequence of transgressions and regressions which has affected the coasts of the British Isles since the Lateglacial is complex (fig. 5.6), but for northern coasts a further complexity is added by movement of the land relative to the sea known as *isostasy*, or isostatic recovery. When the British ice sheet was at its maximum extent and thickness, its enormous weight was sufficient to depress the underlying portions of the earth's crust by an appreciable amount. As the ice melted this pressure was removed and so the surface began to recover. However, the processes of melting and recovery were not simultaneous and recovery of the land surface continued long after the final melting of the ice sheets. Indeed, parts of Scotland are still rising at a rate of a few millimetres per century. In northern Britain, while global sea level was rising at varying rates, isostatic recovery was sometimes proceeding faster, leading to a very complex sequence of events (fig. 5.7). In the following paragraphs we will look at the effects of eustatic sea-level change which affected the whole region and then consider some of the extra complexities in the zone of isostatic recovery.

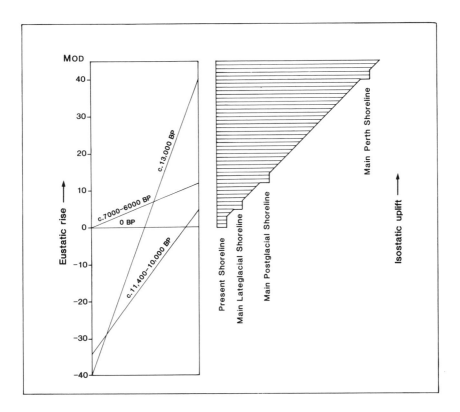

Figure 5.7 Sea-level fluctuations and raised shorelines in the zone of isostatic uplift at the north end of the Sound of Jura (after Lowe and Walker 1987).

A careful study of coastal deposits both above and below the present high-water mark has made it possible to establish the broad outlines of eustatic sea-level change around the British Isles. When the British ice sheet was at its maximum, sea level was at least 130 m lower than at present. The British Isles, as such, did not exist and the coastline of the unglaciated portion of north-west Europe lay along the edge of the continental shelf. The southern North Sea was dry land consisting mainly of sandy ridges of loess and moraine, while to the north, if the British and Scandinavian ice sheets did not actually join, the intervening area was probably occupied by melt-water lakes. The English Channel consisted of a broad valley occupied by the 'Greater Seine', the waters of which may have been augmented by those of the 'Thames–Rhine' system if the course of the latter across the the North Sea Lowlands was blocked by moraines or grounded ice (fig. 5.4a).

With the onset of the climatic amelioration and the melting of the ice sheets eustatic rise was well under way by 16,000 BP and it is estimated that sea level stood at 100 m below the present level by 15,000 BP. Over the next two millennia the sea rose further, so that by about 13,000 BP, shortly before human groups are thought to have begun to return, it stood at about −65 m (fig. 5.4b). Continued eustatic rise led to the Straits of Dover being penetrated by 9600 BP and the breaching of the land bridge between north-east Ireland and south-west Scotland (fig. 5.4c). The full insulation of Britain was effected by the inundation of the North Sea land bridge a thousand years later. Sea levels had reached those of the present day, and even slightly exceeded them, by about 7000 BP and this event is known as the *Main Postglacial Transgression* (fig. 5.4d).

This general pattern applies to the whole of the British Isles but in the north it is also necessary to allow for the effects of isostatic recovery (fig. 5.7). In this area at 18,000 BP the coastline lay at the edge of the continental shelf and there is some doubt as to whether the ice sheet ever extended quite this far. With significant deglaciation by 13,000 BP, the effects of eustatic sea-level rise, combined with the fact that isostatic recovery was yet to begin, led to an episode of relatively high sea level in northern Britain. Evidence for this event, in the form of raised beaches and other shoreline features at about 40 m above present sea level, has been recorded in both western and eastern Scotland and in the latter area these features are referred to as the *Main Perth Shoreline*.

Once isostatic recovery began, the effect was to produce a lowering of sea levels relative to those of the land because the rate of recovery exceeded that of sea-level rise. From the point of view of any human occupants of this part of Britain, this was a time of falling sea level. With the return to conditions of ice accumulation during the Loch Lomond Readvance isostatic recovery was slowed down, though eustatic rise, operating on a world-wide scale, continued. This led to sea levels standing at between 5 m to 10 m above those of the present day and the formation of raised beach features at the *Main Lateglacial Shoreline*.

The two processes of eustatic sea-level change and isostatic recovery have continued to affect the coastline of northern Britain down to the present day, the effect of isostasy being most marked in western Scotland and around the shores of the Inner Hebrides. In these areas beaches formed at the time of the Main Postglacial Transgression 7,000 years ago have been elevated 10 m to 14 m above the present shore by continuing isostatic recovery.

THE TERRESTRIAL FLORA

While deglaciation and sea-level change determined the extent of the terrain, and temperature and precipitation the plants and animals that came to occupy it, it was the abundance and utility of the latter which led bands of hunters to return to the British Isles after an absence of many millennia. Our main source of evidence for the Lateglacial and Postglacial flora consists of fossil pollen grains from cave and former lake sediments. The interpretation of such evidence on a regional scale can be difficult. Analogies with other areas are sometimes used but the trouble with this approach is that such analogies are always flawed.

Extending from approximately 50°N to 60°N, the British Isles are a mid-latitude region with a mainly maritime aspect; no other area in the world experiences a climate exactly similar to that which prevailed here during the Lateglacial and early Postglacial. The Antarctic and the Greenland ice sheets are high-latitude features, extending no further than 65°S and 60°N respectively, while the Arctic sheet is entirely polar. The great tundras and boreal forests of Eurasia and North America are continental phenomena. Latitude determines both day length and the angle at which solar radiation strikes the earth's surface, both considerations which influence the length of the growing season, the period during which mean daily temperatures reach 6°C. The length of the growing season determines what plants can grow. Thus the tundra may be defined as the zone with temperatures rising to 6°C for three to four months a year, permitting limited plant growth during a short, but prolific, growing season, while in deciduous woodlands the average temperature for the coldest month does not fall below −3°C and there are less than six months when temperatures lie below 6°C.

Notwithstanding the difficulties in finding analogous environments, it is possible to identify a number of vegetational types which extend in concentric zones away from the North Polar ice sheet. Similar zones can be recognized on a smaller scale in mountainous areas regardless of latitude but adjusted to altitude. This suggests that the general pattern of zonation may have more to do with temperature and precipitation than latitude, which probably has more bearing on the composition of the zones. The study of fossil pollen has shown that a similar pattern of latitudinal and altitudinal zones prevailed throughout the Lateglacial and early Postglacial. Three broadly defined zones can be recognized: tundra, boreal forest and deciduous woodland (plates IIb, IIIa and VIIIb), and these zones provide a convenient ecological framework within which to review the archaeological evidence.

The tree line marks the boundary between the tundra and the boreal forest and during the maximum extent of the ice sheets this lay at approximately the same latitude as Rome and Madrid (i.e. 42°N). At this time the unglaciated parts of the British Isles were to a large extent treeless, apart from some scrubby clumps in sheltered valleys near the contemporary coastline. The Lateglacial and early Postglacial are characterized by shifts in the boundaries between vegetational zones as each type moved northwards and upwards with the ameliorating climate.

Pollen assemblages are usually illustrated in the form of diagrams which show the varying contribution made to the pollen rain by different plants

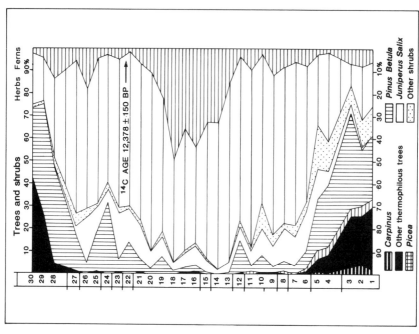

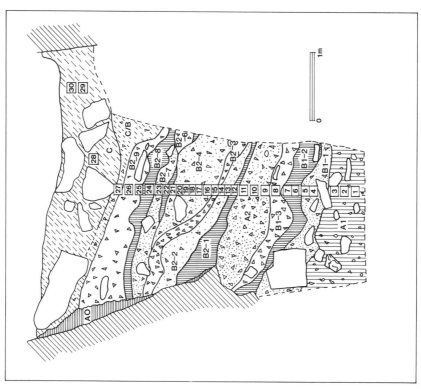

Figure 5.8 Section and summary pollen diagram from the Sun Hole (after Campbell 1977).

during the history of the site (fig. 5.8). Comparison of a large number of pollen diagrams has led palynologists, notably Sir Harry Godwin, to suggest that the development of the Lateglacial and Postglacial vegetation of the British Isles can be divided into a sequence of distinct stages, or zones, numbered from i to viii. Being sequential, these zones have come to be regarded as synonymous with distinct chronological stages in the Lateglacial and early Postglacial. The fact that peat deposits, from which most pollen data have been obtained, are especially suitable for radiocarbon dating has enabled a chronometric dimension to be added to this sequence, although problems arise if it is used indiscriminately.

Today it is possible, within the confines of the British Isles, to visit examples of most of the vegetation types characteristic of Godwin's various zones, and this is likely to have been the case throughout most of the period with which we are concerned (plates viiia and viiib). Plant communities consist of a mosaic of different species varying according to latitude, temperature, precipitation, soil type, exposure and a whole host of factors. As these factors change, changes in the plant community are also to be expected. But such changes are rarely abrupt and almost never simultaneous. Thus while southern Britain began to develop boreal forests typical of Godwin's Zones iv and v, in the north tundra, more typical of Zones i or iii, prevailed. The time-transgressive, or diachronic, nature of the boundaries between the Godwin pollen zones makes them difficult to use as a framework within which to view the prehistory of human settlement, except on a local scale.

The development of the Lateglacial and Postglacial vegetation of Europe as a whole is clearly illustrated in the atlas of pollen maps published by Huntley and Birks. This fascinating collection of maps spans the period back to 13,000 BP and illustrates the fluctuating extent of tundra, boreal forests and deciduous woodland in the British Isles. Each of these vegetation types is made up of a combination of plants, many of which are characteristic of more than one of them. The differences between vegetation types reside in the varying proportions of the components, as illustrated by table 5.1.

TERRESTRIAL FAUNA

Although we can assume that Late Stone Age hunters and gatherers made frequent use of plant resources when these were available, for most of the period covered by this book existence in Britain would not have been possible without the exploitation of animals. The relative importance of plant and animal resources has often been debated, and in the deciduous woods plant products may have been major subsistence items. However, this could not have been the case in the boreal forests or on the tundra, and at no time could plants alone have supplied all subsistence needs.

All animals, either directly or indirectly, meet their energy requirements

Table 5.1   Lateglacial and Postglacial vegetation units

Unit	% tree and shrub pollen (TSP)							
	1	*2*	*3*	*4*	*5*	*6*	*7*	*8*
Tundra	<50		<5			<50	>10	
Boreal forests:								
Birch forest	>50	<5	<5			>50	<10	
Birch-conifer	> 50	<5	<5			<50		
Conifer-deciduous	>50		>5					>50
Deciduous-woodland	>50		>5	<5	<10			

(1 Total TSP; 2 total TSP excluding birch and pine; 3 mixed deciduous; 4 Mediterranean; 5 birch; 6 willow; 7 pine)

(after Huntley and Birks 1983, p. 614, table 6.11)

by extracting what they need from the plant community. Some do this by eating the plants while others eat the plant eaters. The fauna is thus, to a large extent, determined by the flora, though other factors such as sea-level change also play a part. The limited range of the Irish fauna may be attributed to rising sea levels early in the Postglacial, which prevented the migration of a number of species found in mainland Britain.

Animals were important not only as sources of food and raw materials but also as competitors. A number, such as wolves, bears and foxes, hunted many of the same species as humans and there was competition for accommodation in that wolves and bears also use natural shelters. In assessing the life of Britain's Late Stone Age hunters, we need to take into account the role of both useful animals and competitors. The following paragraphs provide details of the main relevant species, concentrating on those aspects of physiology and behaviour of interest to a hunter.

Mammoth (*Mammuthus primigenius*)

Until recently it was believed that these immense animals (fig. 5.9a) were not part of the Lateglacial fauna of the British Isles, having become locally extinct during the maximum of the last glaciation. That this was not the case has been shown by the spectacular discovery of the remains of four mammoths, dated to *c.* 12,700 BP, in a Shropshire gravel pit in 1986. It is no longer necessary to doubt the authenticity of occasional finds of mammoth bone and ivory associated with artefacts. However, it is unlikely that mammoths were ever regularly preyed upon by humans. Moving across the mainly open landscape in herds of hundreds, with each animal weighing several thousand kg and standing up to 4 m high, mammoths would have been formidable prey for hunters armed only with spears and arrows.

However, natural deaths did occur, as was the case in Shropshire, and these animals could have been scavenged. When death occurred in winter the human hunters' ability to employ fire to thaw a frozen carcass gave them an advantage over other scavengers. We do not know when mammoths finally became extinct in Britain, but as yet there is no evidence that they survived the Lateglacial Interstadial.

Woolly rhino (*Coelodonta antiquitatis*)

In no case is there an unequivocal association between woolly rhino remains and human artefacts, and no specimens have been directly dated to the Lateglacial. But if conditions, at least during the early part of the Lateglacial Interstadial, were suitable for mammoths they would have also been suitable for woolly rhino.

Bison (*Bison priscus*) and wild cattle (*Bos primigenius*)

These two closely related genera of bovids are difficult to separate skeletally and there has been a tendency to regard Lateglacial specimens as bison and Postglacial specimens as wild cattle, mainly on the basis of assumed habitat preferences. Recently, several Lateglacial specimens have been identified as wild cattle and this animal appears to have been present in Britain from at least the mid-thirteenth millennium BP until it became extinct, probably in the second. On the basis of horn-core evidence, bison were also present, at least early in the Lateglacial, and some remains identified as *bovine* will probably always remain ambiguous. Adult bison and wild cattle were of roughly equivalent weight at about 1,400 kg (fig. 5.9c and d). Both animals were grazers which also browsed on bushes and shrubs as well as the new growth of trees such as willow, and occasionally ate bark and mast, according to the season. Shelter was an important consideration in winter, especially for wild cattle, and a predominantly open landscape with some tree cover was preferred. Although there is no evidence that the European bison ever formed huge herds or entered on large-scale migrations, they could probably be encountered in larger groups than wild cattle, which are virtually solitary. It was, however, the latter animal that was the more important of the two, and bison may not have long survived the mammoth and woolly rhino. Hunting wild cattle is likely to have involved stalking and shooting at close quarters with bow and arrow. Carcasses exhibiting wounds and retaining flint projectiles have been found at Vig and Prejlerup in Denmark, while animals could be speared if caught in dead-fall traps or mired in boggy ground.

Horse (*Equus ferus*)

Remains of wild horse are some of the most common in Lateglacial

Figure 5.9 Terrestrial prey species: (a) mammoth, (b) woolly rhino, (c) bison, (d) wild cattle, (e) horse, (f) giant deer, (g) elk, (h) red deer, (i), reindeer, (j) roe deer, (k) saiga antelope and (l) wild pig (after Stuart 1982).

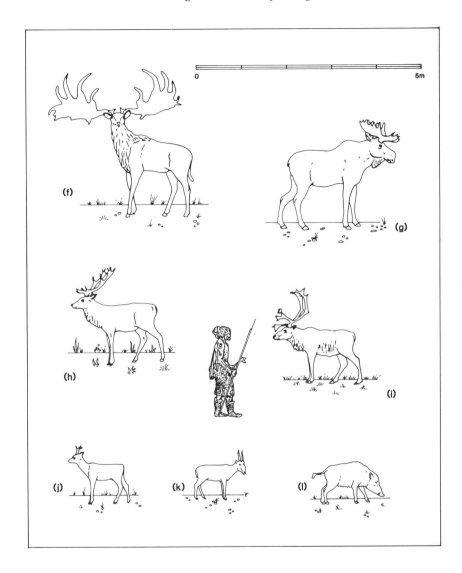

assemblages and this animal was clearly one of the most important prey species in Britain (fig. 5.9e). Horses were present in Britain by the middle of the thirteenth millennium BP and survived into the Postglacial. Little is known of their behaviour as they have few surviving relatives, and none in environments analogous to Lateglacial Britain. They were open-country grazers eating grasses with a high fibre content and varieties of *Artemisia* such as mugwort or wormwood, perhaps also grubbing for acorns and tubers when they were available. Large herds would have been a rare sight and most would have been encountered in small bands led by a stallion. A fully grown adult weighed about 350 kg. There are accounts of European wild horses being caught in dead-fall traps and they could have been shot by hunters lying in ambush. At Flixton in Yorkshire a shouldered point and a flint blade were found with the remains of at least three horses, in a deposit dated to the closing stages of the Loch Lomond Readvance.

Giant deer (*Megaloceros giganteus*)

This animal, the largest of the British deer, weighing almost as much as a wild bull (fig. 5.9f), does not appear to have survived the Lateglacial Interstadial. Little is known of the habits of this extinct animal, but its extraordinary 3 m span of antlers must imply that it spent most of its time in the open. Like most other deer, it is unlikely to have lived in large social groups or indulged in extensive migrations.

Elk (North American moose) (*Alces alces*)

Elk were the largest deer to be regularly taken by the Late Stone Age hunters of the British Isles (fig. 5.9g). Animals of boreal forests and lakes, elk were nevertheless present as far north as Morecambe Bay by the mid-thirteenth millennium, where a band of hunters successfully brought an animal to bay. It remained an important prey species into the Postglacial but died off with the spread of deciduous woodlands. Elk, which weigh between 300 kg and 400 kg, feed on herbaceous aquatic and waterside plants and the foliage of trees. They are generally solitary and within their present range are sparsely scattered, rarely exceeding one animal per km^2. Stalking was probably the main method of hunting.

Red deer (*Cervus elaphus*)

The herds of red deer seen wild in the Highlands of Scotland give a false impression of this animal's preferred habitat, which consists of a mixture of grassland and open woodland, similar to that inhabited by wild cattle. Similarly, modern red deer are rather small compared to their Lateglacial and early Postglacial ancestors which, being better nourished, weighed between 250 kg and 350 kg (fig. 5.9h). It was once thought that this species undertook large-scale seasonal migrations, but this was based on analogies with contemporary deer living in less than optimum conditions. In the rich Lateglacial and early Postglacial environment such migrations were unlikely, and small-scale altitudinal movements were probably all that were necessary. The largest groups could be found in the winter when deer gathered in valleys for shelter, but the need for stags to drive off competing males provides a natural mechanism operating against the formation of large herds. In spite of their preference for partially wooded conditions, radiocarbon-dated specimens show that red deer were present in Britain from an early stage in the Lateglacial Interstadial. They could be caught by ambush or stalking, and dead-fall traps may have been used. They have remained a popular prey species to the present day.

Reindeer (*Rangifer tarandus*)

It is generally accepted that modern reindeer populations can be divided into woodland and barren-ground ecotypes, but it is difficult to apply this distinction to fossil material. Behaviourally, the two types are quite different. Woodland reindeer remain in small groups throughout the year and undertake only limited migrations, usually of an altitudinal nature, whereas barren-ground animals form immense herds of tens of thousands and migrate over distances of several hundred kilometres between their calving and summer feeding grounds, and the forest margins where they spend the winter. But these are extremes of what is really a behavioural continuum, and Lateglacial and early Postglacial reindeer in Britain need not have conformed to either type.

Their remains are found in most faunal assemblages attributed to the Lateglacial Interstadial but they are generally much less numerous than those of horse. In assemblages dating from the Loch Lomond Readvance, especially in central and northern Britain, this relationship is reversed and reindeer may be virtually the only food animal represented. It seems that conditions during the thirteenth millennium BP did not really suit reindeer, but that it came into its own during the subsequent climatic deterioration. It remained important into the early Postglacial, but traditions that it survived much later in Scotland seem to be unfounded.

Adult reindeer weigh between about 80 kg and 150 kg depending on their sex and the time of year (fig. 5.9i). They have a natural tendency to form herds that can be driven, and there are numerous examples of the use of drive fences and hides in the hunting of large herds (fig. 5.10a). Such herds do appear to have been present on the North European Plain during the Lateglacial and their remains are numerous at a number of Hamburgian and Ahrensburgian sites. At one of the latter, Stellmoor, the reindeer seem to have been slaughtered in great numbers while trying to swim across a lake. A number of the bones still bear embedded flint points and from these it is possible to demonstrate that the animals were shot mainly from behind, once they were in the water (plate x). No examples of this kind are known from Lateglacial Britain, and if our native reindeer only ever formed small aggregations and were relatively non-migratory, stalking, trapping and snaring were probably the preferred techniques.

Wild pig (*Sus scrofa*)

The wild pig, a rather solitary denizen of broad-leafed forests, was an exclusively Postglacial species (fig. 5.9l). Quoted weight estimates vary between 35 kg and 200 kg, and a large adult boar could weigh rather more than a reindeer. Trapping and stalking are the most likely hunting methods.

Roe deer (*Capreolus capreolus*)

Also a mainly solitary, woodland animal, roe deer are not known in Britain before the early Postglacial, during which period they were hunted regularly (fig. 5.9j). Adults, which weigh about 35 kg, would require careful stalking, though snares and traps may also have been employed. The tendency for juveniles, especially inexperienced males, to congregate in small groups in the open would make them more vulnerable.

Ibex (*Capra ibex*) and saiga antelope (*Saiga tartarica*)

There are a few records from Lateglacial contexts in Britain of ibex and saiga antelope (fig. 5.9k). The former are tentative, and await confirmation. Ibex are animals of the high mountains and the British Isles seem hardly suitable, even in the Lateglacial. There are, however, authentic records of saiga antelope, and butchery marks on a specimen from Gough's Cave show that they were hunted. These small animals, about the size of a sheep, now live on the steppes of central Asia, which indicates a preference for a dry, cold climate. They may have spread to Britain during a short-lived episode of more continental conditions within the Lateglacial Interstadial, and equated with Godwin's Pollen Zone ic.

Small mammals

Carefully excavated and recorded faunal assemblages often include a range of small mammals, many of which were probably victims of the hunt. The most common species are the beaver (*Castor fiber*), brown hare (*Lepus europaeus*) and mountain or arctic hare (*Lepus timidus*), otter (*Lutra lutra*), marten (*Martes martes*), badger (*Meles meles*), red fox (*Vulpes vulpes*) and arctic fox (*Alopex lagopus*). All of these animals were probably caught with traps and snares and are likely to have been valued for their pelts as much as their meat. There are also records of small artefacts such as needles made from hare bones.

Game birds and bees

Game birds, especially grouse (*Lagopus lagopus*) and ptarmigan (*Lagopus mutus*), are not uncommon, and a range of waterfowl including ducks, geese and swans were also taken. Birds of prey are represented, and were probably valued for their plumage, which would be required to fletch arrows, and perhaps also for personal adornment. The only insects to be

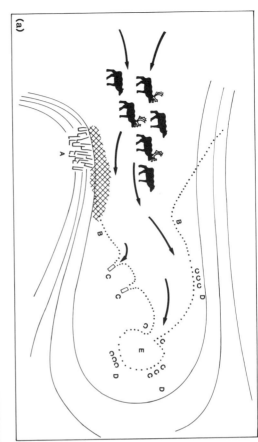

(a)

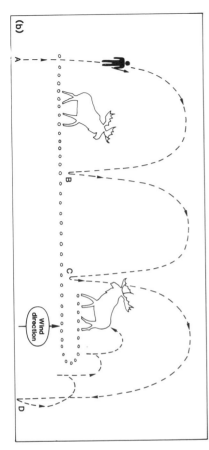

(b)

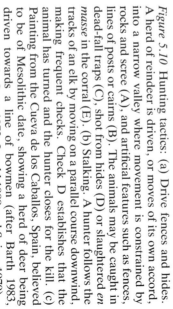

(c)

Figure 5.10 Hunting tactics: (a) Drive fences and hides. A herd of reindeer is driven, or moves of its own accord, into a narrow valley where movement is constrained by rocks and scree (A), and artificial features such as fences, lines of posts or cairns (B). The animals may be caught in dead-fall traps (C), shot from hides (D) or slaughtered *en masse* in the corral (E). (b) Stalking. A hunter follows the tracks of an elk by moving on a parallel course downwind, making frequent checks. Check D establishes that the animal has turned and the hunter closes for the kill. (c) Painting from the Cueva de los Caballos, Spain, believed to be of Mesolithic date, showing a herd of deer being driven towards a line of bowmen (after Barth 1983, Beltran 1982, Coon 1972, Ingold 1988 and Spiess 1979).

Figure 5.11 Painting from La Arana Rock Shelter, Spain, dated to *c*. 8000 BP, showing a figure collecting honey and surrounded by bees (after Crane 1983).

regularly exploited were bees, whose combs were robbed for honey (fig. 5.11), though grubs, caterpillars and slugs are known to be viewed as delicacies in some societies.

Carnivores

It remains to consider those animals with which humans were in competition. Bones and coprolites of spotted hyaena (*Crocuta crocuta*) are common in cave deposits dating from the Lateglacial. These animals make their dens in caves and they were probably the most important non-human bone accumulators. There is, however, no evidence that they survived as late at the Lateglacial Interstadial. The brown bear (*Ursus arctos*) did compete with humans for the use of caves and preyed on some of the same species. Bears are also the only carnivores to be regularly eaten by humans and the status of bear bones in an archaeological deposit can often be ambiguous. The main competitor in the hunt was undoubtedly the wolf (*Canis lupus*), but by the early Postglacial the emergence of the domestic dog is evidence of a spirit of co-operation between *Homo* and *Canis* that has lasted to the present day. There are also a number of Lateglacial and Postglacial records of the northern lynx (*Lynx lynx*). It was never numerous, but it did manage to spread to Ireland, which it must have accomplished before rising sea level flooded the land bridge with south-west Scotland around 9500 BP.

THE MARINE BIOMASS

Although humans occasionally eat and do a variety of things with seaweed, it is unlikely to have been a major resource for hunter-gatherers. The archaeological evidence from shell middens indicates that exploitation concentrated on marine animals, chiefly mammals such as whales and seals, anadromous and pelagic fish, such as salmon and saithe respectively, and shellfish. All are relatively high up the food chain and depend upon lesser organisms such as the phytoplankton. Productivity varies with temperature, and whereas the plankton biomass of the North Atlantic Drift exceeds $300 \, mg/m^3$, in the cooler waters to the north it can be less than half this. Since 18,000 BP there have been considerable changes in the temperature of the seas around the British Isles due to the various movements of the Polar Front. This variability in productivity has a bearing on the extent to which the early inhabitants of the British Isles looked to the sea for sustenance.

The cetaceans regularly found in British waters belong to two main groups, the baleen whales and the toothed whales. The former group includes the rorquals (*Balaenoptera* sp.) (fig. 5.12a) and the latter the dolphins (*Delphinus* sp.) and porpoises (*Phocaena*) (fig. 5.12b and c), all of which were at one time common. While there is no evidence that any of these animals was actively hunted in British waters during the Stone Age some of the smaller ones, such as the killer (*Orca gladiater*) and pilot (*Globiecephalus melas*) whales, dolphins and porpoises could have been driven ashore, or into narrow bays and inlets by hunters in open boats. They could then have been dispatched with spears or harpoons. A Stone Age carving from Sweden appears to show a pilot whale caught in a net (fig. 5.13). Natural strandings were certainly taken advantage of. Such events are not as rare as they may seem: 407 instances of strandings were recorded between 1913 and 1926, and at the time of writing the severe gales of January 1990 have left at least one baleen whale stranded on the south coast. But humans are unlikely to have included such adventitious events in their economic planning, and whale remains in archaeological assemblages must arise from opportunism.

Remains of both grey (*Halichoerus grypus*) and common seals (*Phoca vitulina*) (fig. 5.12d and e) are regularly encountered in archaeological deposits and it is clear that they were systematically hunted. Both spend much of their time close inshore but are unlikely to have been hunted in the open water owing to the difficulty of recovering the carcasses. The common seal, also known as the harbour seal, can penetrate quite far inland following tidal rivers. Both usually spend part of their day ashore basking, and grey seals have to come ashore to breed in the autumn, when they form large colonies. At such times they are very vulnerable, as are their pups, which have to remain ashore for several weeks until after their first moult. Animals caught on shore can be harpooned or clubbed, and examples are known from Scandinavia of harpoons found with seal carcasses.

The only fish remains encountered in large numbers on Stone Age sites are those of salmonids (*Salmo* sp.), eel (*Anguilla anguilla*), saithe (*Pollachius virens*) and cod (*Gadus morhua*) (fig. 5.14a, b, c, and d). The salmonids are anadromous and can be caught, by net or spear, in large numbers in British rivers in the summer and autumn when they return to their spawning grounds. A mature salmon can weigh 35 kg, as much as a roe deer, but this must be an exception. Eels are catadromous: they live in lakes and rivers but in the autumn return to the Sargasso Sea to spawn. The average weight for an eel is 4.5 kg. The pelagic saithe spawn between January and April and young fish can be abundant in inshore waters, usually forming schools of the same year-group. Today saithe are caught in trawl or seine nets or by anglers with rod and line. Fish hooks and nets are very rare archaeological finds and it is not known how the large numbers of saithe found at some sites were caught. Adult saithe can grow to 14 kg, but if mainly young fish were caught they would be smaller. Cod weigh about 45 kg and are not usually found close inshore. Most cod found on archaeological sites must have been caught at sea. Remains of freshwater fish are very rare in archaeological assemblages, pike (*Esox lucius*) (fig. 5.14e) being the only species regularly mentioned.

The shells of marine molluscs, often heaped up by the thousand in middens, can be very conspicuous archaeological finds but we should not exaggerate the role played by shellfish in Stone Age economies. Of low nutrient value and labour intensive to gather, shellfish can only ever have been a dietary supplement, or an emergency food in times of shortage. Many were probably collected for bait. The range of types found in middens is broad but a few tend to predominate. These include gastropods such as limpets (*Patella* sp.) and periwinkles (*Littorina littorea*), and bivalves such as the cockle (*Cerastoderma edule*). Crustaceans are also reported from middens, but being less robust appear less common.

In this chapter I have described, in some detail, the environment with which the Late Stone Age hunters of the British Isles were confronted and some of the natural resources it had to offer. Both were changing, and at times rapidly. The following three chapters provide examples, in the form of case studies, of the ways in which people coped with these changes.

ADDITIONAL READING

Environmental change is a complex phenomenon involving many often interlinking factors. The first part of this chapter is largely based on the summary of the main developments published by Lowe and Walker (1987). A more recently published authoritative account is that of Jones and Keen

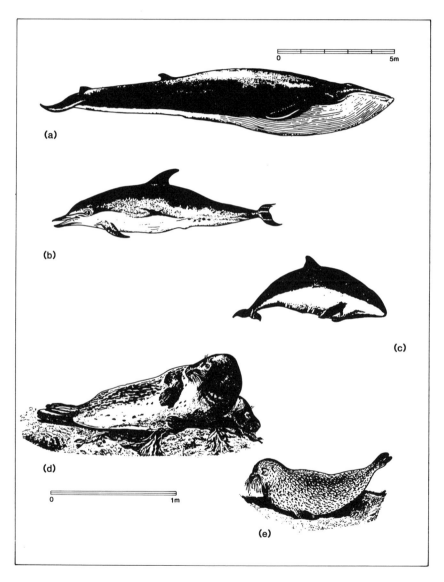

Figure 5.12 Marine prey species: (a) rorqual, (b) dolphin, (c) porpoise, (d) grey seal and (e) common seal (after Thorburn 1984).

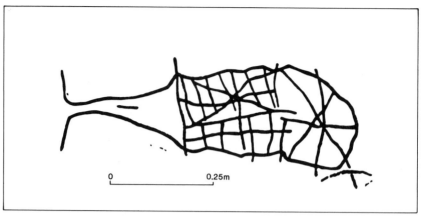

Figure 5.13 Stone Age engraving from Sweden of a whale, apparently caught in a net (after Clark 1952).

(1993). Additional information on climatic change has been obtained from Lamb (1985), Morner and Wallin (1977), Price (1982) and papers presented by Coope and Atkinson at the 'Late Glacial of North-West Europe' conference held at Oxford in the autumn of 1989 and published in 1991 (Barton *et al.* 1991). The complexities of sea-level change are dealt with by Kidson and Tooley (1977), Oele *et al.* (1979), Simmons and Tooley (1981), Tooley (1978) and van Andel (1989, 1990). Details of plant distributions are from Conolly and Dahl (1970) and Huntley and Birks (1983), while the potential importance of plant foods to humans is discussed by Bonsall (1981), Clarke (1976) and Zvelebil (1994).

Details of terrestrial mammals are mainly taken from Stuart (1982), supplemented by further information from Chaplin (1975), Currant (1986, 1987), Forsberg (1985), Grigson (1978), Jenkinson (1984b), Jochim (1976), Legge and Rowley-Conwy (1988), Mellars (1975) and Spiess (1979). Lateglacial mammoths in the British Isles were discussed by Lister at the 'Late Glacial North-West Europe' conference. Hunting methods are dealt with by Barth (1983), Burch (1972), Fischer (1989), Ingold (1988), Noe-Nygaard (1974), Spiess (1979) and the evidence from Stellmoor was dealt with by Bratlund at the 'Late Glacial North-West Europe' conference. Birds are discussed in several publications by Bramwell (1960), Grigson (1989), Harrison (1986, 1987, 1988 and 1989) and Jenkinson *et al.* (1984), while Crane (1983) deals with the exploitation of bees.

I have taken details of marine mammals from the 1984 American edition of Archibald Thorburn's *Mammals*, while Clark (1946, 1947, 1952) has discussed their role as prey species in prehistoric times. The data on fish have mainly been taken from Wheeler (1978b).

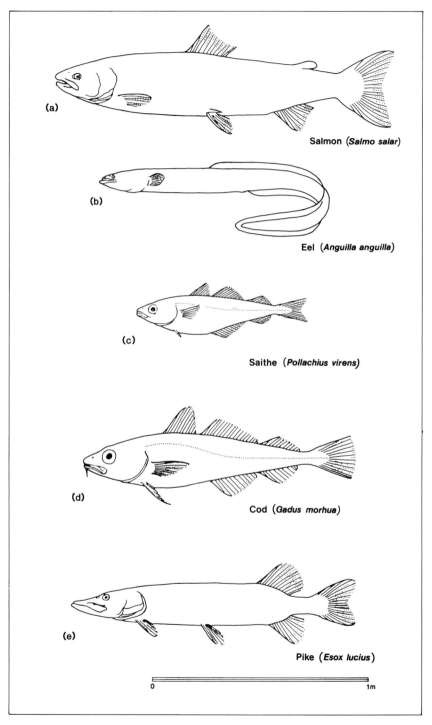

Salmon (*Salmo salar*)

Eel (*Anguilla anguilla*)

Saithe (*Pollachius virens*)

Cod (*Gadus morhua*)

Pike (*Esox lucius*)

0   1m

Figure 5.14 Marine prey species (after Wheeler 1978b).

6 Case studies I: Hunters of the Lateglacial tundra

The archaeological record for the period between *c*. 13,000 BP and *c*. 10,000 BP is limited in extent when compared with many other parts of Europe because at the time the British Isles lay on the margin of human settlement in the Old World. It is also intractable, most of our data having been acquired during the pioneer days of archaeology when standards of recovery and recording fell far short of what can be expected now. It constitutes a most inadequate basis for reconstructing human behaviour over a period of three millennia. However, it is all we have, and careful analysis does lead to a number of interesting insights. The framework of analysis proposed in chapter 4 suggested that the archaeological record could be subdivided according to whether it represented refuse discarded at a home base or within its periphery, material left at a field camp or other location where specific activities were carried out, or finds casually lost or discarded.

THE KENT'S CAVERN VESTIBULE

Situated a kilometre to the north of Torbay, on the west side of a small valley, Kent's Cavern (NGR SX 934641) (fig. 9.4a no. 3) has produced a rich series of archaeological finds including material of Lower and Middle Palaeolithic age, in addition to the Lateglacial finds with which we are concerned. It is a large cave (fig. 6.1b), and evidently at one time had a deep stratigraphy which would have had considerable archaeological potential had it not been completely removed over a century ago. These early excavations are poorly published, but John Campbell's careful analysis of notebooks kept by William Pengelly, who excavated in the cave between 1865 and 1880, enables some limited reconstruction of the evidence to be made.

While finds were widespread throughout Kent's Cavern the greatest concentration was in the Vestibule (fig. 6.1b). The Lateglacial material was found over an area of about 67 m² from within a deposit referred to by Pengelly as a 'cave earth'. This was sealed by a layer of stalagmite and Campbell's analysis suggests that the finds came from a number of narrow

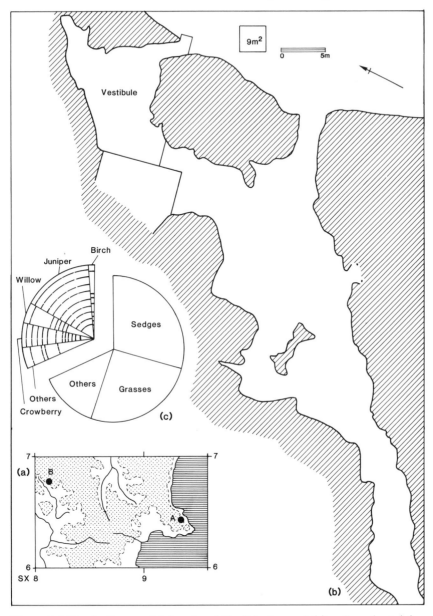

Figure 6.1 Kent's Cavern: (a) location (A), (b) plan and (c) pollen chart (after Campbell 1977).

lenses within the cave earth. One, an 8 cm thick lens of charcoal-rich soil assumed to mark the position of a series of hearths, has become known as the 'black band' (fig. 6.2).

Three radiocarbon dates for material from the cave earth are very

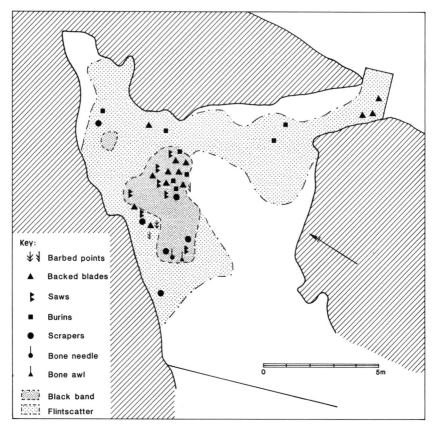

Key:

⇓⇓ Barbed points

▲ Backed blades

⦌ Saws

■ Burins

● Scrapers

⦙ Bone needle

⅄ Bone awl

▦ Black band

▦ Flintscatter

0   5m

Figure 6.2 Kent's Cavern Vestibule (after Campbell 1977).

similar: *c.* 12,320 BP, *c.* 12,180 BP and *c.* 11,880 BP. The first is on a humanly modified piece of bone and is the best evidence for the date of the human occupation. It also came from the black band, as was the case with the third specimen. However, as both the second and third specimens are not humanly modified their presence does not necessarily arise from human activity, and they could have become incorporated in the deposit naturally. This is almost certainly the case with a fourth date of *c.* 14,275 BP, on a metatarsal of giant deer, a species which may have been extinct in southern Britain by the thirteenth millennium BP, while a very wide standard deviation (11,570 ± 410 BP (BM–2168)) makes a fifth date too imprecise to use. The finds did not all come from the same lens of deposit and may have accumulated as a result of a succession of visits rather than a single occupation. The date from the humanly modified piece of bone suggests this occurred in the latter part of the thirteenth millennium BP.

Campbell managed to identify 64 pollen grains from a small sample of cave earth adhering to the north wall. This is insufficient for a statistically acceptable analysis but may provide an indication of conditions around the cave at the time of the human occupation (fig. 6.1c). Trees and shrubs accounted for about 33 per cent, with juniper being the most in evidence, and willow and crowberry also important. But open country plants, at 61 per cent, were dominant and the picture is of open grass and sedge tundra with clumps of crowberry, while stands of juniper and willow were to be found in selected locations. Fragments of charcoal from the black band have been identified as oak, elm and buckthorn, none of which occurs in the pollen assemblage. But with a total count of only 64 grains this is not significant. All three could have been present in southern Britain in small numbers during the thirteenth millennium, and they probably made better firewood than the other shrubs which were more widely available.

Published faunal evidence from the Vestibule is limited to Campbell's identification of mammal teeth and post-cranial fragments identified during the course of radiocarbon dating. Horse is the most common, with seventeen teeth identified. There are seven bear teeth and a tibia of this species was sampled for dating (GrN–6203). To the dated giant deer metatarsal should be added four teeth, while Campbell also identified two of reindeer or red deer, two of hyaena, two of woolly rhino and one of bison or wild cattle. None of these is burnt or modified and may have accumulated through natural, rather than human, agency. Indeed hyaenas, which are represented, are known to return to their dens with bones for gnawing. However, the hyaena seems to have been extinct in Britain by the thirteenth millennium BP and the remains, along with those of giant deer, probably do not relate to the human occupation. Horse, reindeer, red deer and wild cattle are all known to have been part of the thirteenth-millennium BP fauna. This is also true of the cave bear, but these animals hibernate in caves and the bear remains may originate from natural deaths. If these data mean anything, horse appears to have been the most favoured species.

The archaeological assemblage from the cave earth includes 161 late Upper Palaeolithic items, but Campbell mentions a further 378 recorded by Pengelly which are now missing. It is also likely that many small items were not spotted at the time of the excavation. Of the 155 extant stone artefacts 50, or 32 per cent, have been retouched. In more recently conducted excavations at other sites, the proportion of retouched pieces is usually found to be far lower than this, around 3 per cent being a commonly recorded value, and the original assemblage was probably much larger than the 539 of which we have some record.

A home base can be expected to be the scene of a range of activities where, in addition to the daily tasks of preparing and consuming food, equipment and clothing were manufactured and repaired. The assemblage includes eight burins, items usually associated with bone or antler working (fig. 6.3a), eight scrapers, two flint awls, two bone awls and a bone needle, all of which suggest hide preparation and perhaps clothing manufacture (fig. 6.3b), eight flint 'saws', perhaps used for dismembering portions of carcass, cutting tendons and stripping flesh from bone, and fifteen backed flint blades. This latter class is assumed to have been the tips of arrows or spears, and several are broken (fig. 6.3c), suggesting that they may have been brought back to the cave embedded in carcasses. However, when they were complete they would have functioned very well as knives, perhaps used for defleshing joints during meals. The only certain pieces of hunting equipment are fragments of three antler points, one of which was found in the black band (fig. 6.4). They were probably brought back to the cave in carcasses and, being broken, were thrown away. The variety of items found is good evidence that we are dealing with a home base.

Although the material in the Vestibule may have accumulated as the result of several visits, the spatial distribution suggests that the process of accumulation has not caused much distortion (fig. 6.2). Butchery, and perhaps the actual consumption of meat, appears to have taken place on either side of the group of hearths represented by the black band, the extent of which argues for more than a single visit. The fact that burins tended to be found towards the east side of the area and scrapers towards the west may be a hint that bone and skin working were spatially segregated. Waste from stone tool manufacture and repair was scattered throughout, though a clear zone about 2.5 m wide immediately to the east of the black band may be significant. The concepts of 'residential area' and 'periphery' apply less in the confined space of a cave than on an open site, but the area to either side of the entrance, which has not been investigated, may have been important for discarding refuse. Alternatively, this may have been the scene of a range of activities best undertaken out-of-doors.

The hearths were situated so as to allow all-round access to heat and light for a fairly small group. We can do no more than guess population size but the 67 m^2 of space available in the Vestibule could not have accommodated more than about ten people without overcrowding. However, we should not forget that the Vestibule is just a small part of a much larger cave, though there are few Lateglacial finds from its other chambers.

In the absence of seasonality data, we have no way of knowing the duration of the occupation, and whether this amounted to successive seasonal visits or a single prolonged stay, though the former is more likely, given our understanding of hunter-gatherer behaviour. The Kent's Cavern band probably foraged widely over the terrain between the south-east slopes of Dartmoor and the coast, which then lay about 50 km away (fig. 5.4b).

Evidence for Lateglacial settlement is reported from five other caves in the area, but in each case the number of finds is small. Faunal remains recovered during the 1957 excavations at Three Holes Cave (NGR SX 814675) (fig. 6.1a Site B) have recently provided radiocarbon dates contemporary with the Kent's Cavern series. The occupation of the Vestibule was probably not an isolated event, but part of a regular pattern of settlement in south-western Britain during the Lateglacial Interstadial.

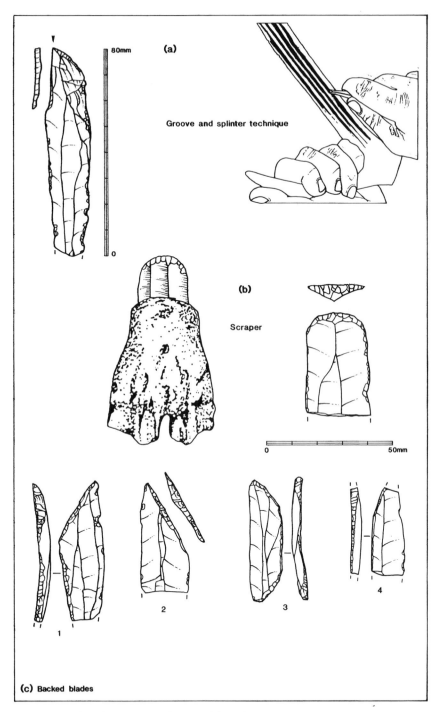

80mm

(a)

Groove and splinter technique

(b)

Scraper

0   50mm

1

2

3

4

(c) Backed blades

Figure 6.3 Finds from Kent's Cavern: (a) burin and 'groove and splinter' technique of bone and antler working, (b) scraper with suggested mode of hafting in a section metapodial, (c) backed blades, possibly used to tip spears or arrows, or as knives; nos 1 and 3 respectively are examples of 'Creswell' and 'Cheddar' points (after Campbell 1977).

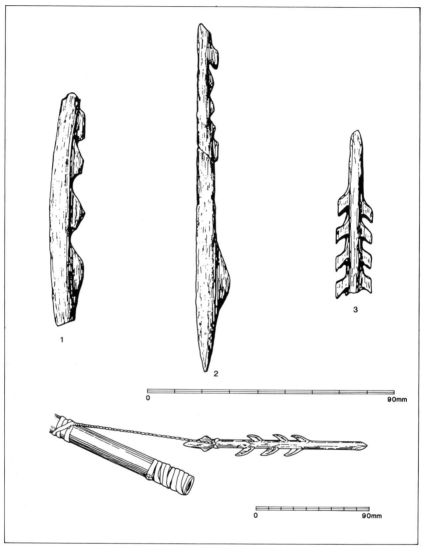

Figure 6.4 Antler points from Kent's Cavern: no. 2 is almost certainly a harpoon and was probably mounted in the manner shown (after Garrod 1926).

I have dwelt on the evidence from the Kent's Cavern Vestibule at some length because, for all its shortcomings, it remains one of the most informative Lateglacial assemblages.

CRESWELL CRAGS

Records survive of Lateglacial occupation in four of the well-known caves at Creswell Crags, a gorge cut through Magnesian Limestone on the border between Derbyshire and Nottinghamshire (fig. 9.4 no. 1). Although three of the caves, Mother Grundy's Parlour, Robin Hood's Cave and Church Hole, were devastated by the activities of nineteenth-century diggers, work at the first two in the 1920s and since 1959 has produced evidence under more controlled conditions. A fourth cave, Pin Hole, while receiving some attention in the nineteenth century, was mostly excavated during the 1920s and 1930s and the evidence is of a higher standard than most of that from the other caves.

From the records available it is clear that Mother Grundy's Parlour, Robin Hood's Cave and Pin Hole all at one time preserved long stratigraphical sequences, and these caves have been the focus of much interest by specialists concerned with the development of stone tool typology. Our interest lies in a few isolated cases where we can recognize detailed behavioural evidence, that is episodes of cave use of relatively short duration which are well dated and accompanied by biological material.

Mother Grundy's Parlour (NGR SK 536743) is situated on the north side of the gorge towards its east end (fig. 6.5a; plate XIa). It consists of a broad chamber 6.7 m wide and 10.7 m deep with a narrow fissure leading off the back. A platform extends about 5 m in front of the cave before the ground slopes gently down to the lake about 14 m away. This lake is a recent feature, and during the Lateglacial the valley floor would have been occupied by a small stream. The interior of the cave and the fissure were entirely emptied in the nineteenth century and virtually all our evidence comes from the platform. In this area, Armstrong, digging in the 1920s, and McBurney and Campbell working in the period between 1959 and 1969, found evidence for a succession of occupations of which the most interesting was an assemblage of stone tools and animal bones around a hearth in the upper part of Armstrong's 'Base Zone' (fig. 6.5b and c).

Two radiocarbon dates of *c.* 12,190 BP and *c.* 12,060 BP have been obtained on individual bones from within the hearth and imply that the occupation occurred towards the end of the thirteenth millennium BP or early in the twelfth, that is during the Lateglacial Interstadial. The hearth was an insubstantial feature consisting of an oval hollow 0.75 m across and 0.25 m deep lined with tabular fragments of limestone. Although the cave may have been visited on many occasions, the hearth is likely to date from a single occupation.

Campbell's excavation abutted the east side of Armstrong's trench and his 'Layer LB' appears to correspond to Armstrong's 'Upper Base Zone' and 'Lower Middle Zone'. As part of his work, Campbell undertook a pollen analysis but the count from Layer LB was very low, 129 grains between two samples. However, it clearly records an open landscape of grass and sedge tundra with stands of birch and willow (fig. 6.5d), while birch charcoal has been identified from Armstrong's excavation.

Identified faunal remains from Armstrong's 'Base' and 'Lower Middle' Zones, and Campbell's 'Layer LB' are listed in table 6. l:

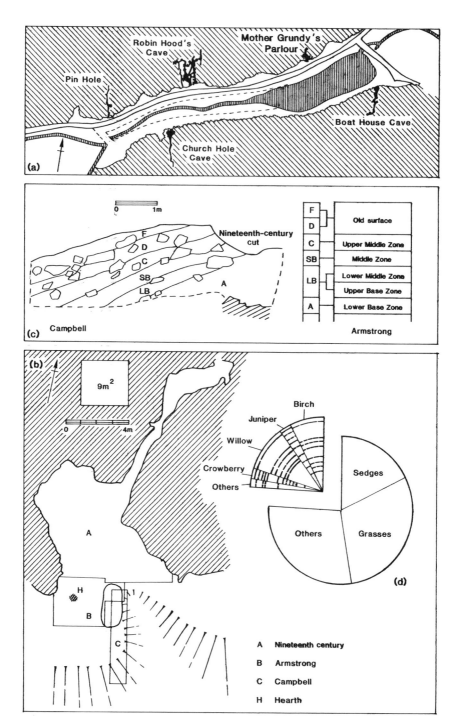

Figure 6.5 Mother Grundy's Parlour: (a) location, (b) plan, (c) section from Campbell's excavation as correlated with the stratigraphy of Armstrong by Jenkinson, (d) pollen chart for Campbell's Layer LB (after Campbell 1977 and Jenkinson 1984a).

Table 6.1   Large mammal bones and teeth from Mother Grundy's Parlour

	Base Zone	*Lower Middle Zone*	*Layer LB*
Hyaena	2	2	
Cave bear			1
Cave lion	1		
Woolly rhino	1	1	
Mammoth	2		
Horse	8	3	6
Reindeer	1	1	
Giant deer			3
Bovid	?	?	

(after Jenkinson 1984a: 185–7)

Bovid remains are known to have been recovered by Armstrong. Indeed, several have been used for radiocarbon dating, but no such specimens were in the collections studied by Jenkinson. Armstrong identified most of these as bison but it is more likely that they were wild cattle, the bones of which can be difficult to distinguish from those of bison. In his original publication, Armstrong also reported red deer remains in all the deposits he examined, but these have not been recognized in more recent analyses.

The hyaena and giant deer are thought to have become extinct in Britain before the thirteenth millennium BP and the cave lion is unknown in contexts post-dating the last glaciation. The faunal assemblage is clearly a mixture of specimens of various ages and the only items that can be certainly associated with human activity are some burnt bovid fragments from the hearth, used for dating, two fragments of mammoth ivory and several crude bone and antler tools, two of which Armstrong identified as from reindeer. He also commented on the large number of highly fragmented and burnt bone fragments in the vicinity of the hearth, believing that horse was the most common prey, and remains of at least six horses seem to be represented.

Armstrong found 1,557 stone artefacts, but only 847 can be attributed to one or other of his 'Zones'. This stratified sequence has provided one of the key assemblages for the period, but only those items from the 'Base Zone' were associated with *in situ* traces of occupation. Of the artefacts from the 'Base Zone', 33 were retouched pieces. Most were found in two concentrations, one within 1 m of the hearth, the other in front of a recess in the rock. From within this second area Armstrong recovered 284 items from 'a cubic foot' (0.0283 m³) of deposit. Twelve, or 4 per cent, were implements.

The occupation of the platform was confined to the western side, a large slab of rock providing a natural limit towards the east (fig. 6.5b). McBurney's and Campbell's trenches were on the other side of this and

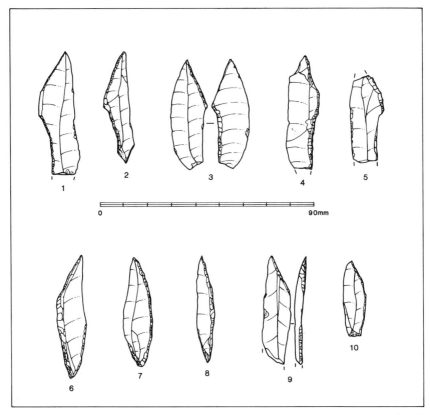

Figure 6.6 Backed blades from Mother Grundy's Parlour: Nos 1–5 are examples of 'shouldered' points. All may have been used to tip projectiles but would have been suitable for use as knives also, and no. 10 is an example of a 'penknife' point (after Armstrong 1924).

they found little. The occupation area amounts to 14 m^2 and the surviving assemblage has a density of 16 items per m^2, although the original total may have been several times this.

Armstrong did not publish the distribution of his finds, but in any case activity on the platform was probably continuous with that in the cave itself, and about this we have no details whatsoever. Although the number of retouched pieces is small, their range is typical of a home base assemblage. Over half are variously described by Armstrong as points or blades, including several shouldered points and backed blades (fig. 6.6), normally regarded as the tips of spears or arrows, but possibly knives. In addition there are seven burins, four scrapers and two piercers, implements conventionally associated with bone, antler and hide working. The assemblage also includes several items of worked or utilized bone. Two of these Armstrong interpreted as fragments of a bone or antler point. The others are fractured pieces of bone, the sharp ends of which may have been worn through use, perhaps as piercers or awls. Armstrong also believed that he found a number of bone engravings of animals, but most other workers who have seen the specimens seem to regard this as wishful thinking.

Robin Hood's Cave (NGR SK 534742) lies about 180 m west of Mother Grundy's Parlour. It is the largest of the Creswell group, with several large chambers and many passages (fig. 6.7b; plate xib). Like Mother Grundy's Parlour, it was almost entirely emptied in the nineteenth century and reliable information is limited to Campbell's small excavation in front of the west entrance in 1969. Even here the uppermost levels had been disturbed and *in situ* occupation deposits only survived at a low level.

Below the nineteenth-century tips Campbell found what he took to be *in situ* deposits, his Layers USB, OB and LSB (fig. 6.7d). More recently, Jenkinson has suggested that these layers consist of lenses of material washed out of the cave mouth, a view which resolves a number of anomalies in Campbell's dating and interpretation. Campbell's Layer B/A does appear to be an *in situ* occupation deposit for it has, set in its upper surface, a stone-lined hearth, similar to that in the 'Base Zone' at Mother Grundy's Parlour (fig. 6.7c).

A series of radiocarbon dates has been obtained on animal bones, some of them modified, from Layers LSB and OB. They range from the early thirteenth millennium to the late eleventh, and if these layers have been washed out of the cave the dates tell us nothing about the age of the hearth in Layer B/A. It could have been in use at any time during this period, though it must have been a short-lived feature.

Campbell analysed 87 pollen grains from Layer B/A and, although not statistically significant, the picture obtained is consistent with expectations, with open country plants accounting for 86 per cent (fig. 6.7e). Willow is the most important of the trees and shrubs, and probably grew in the gorge. Juniper and birch were present in small numbers. Faunal remains from Layer B/A are set out in table 6.2.

The only one of these animals that can be definitely associated with the human occupation is the mountain hare, several bones of which have been modified. Hares were probably caught by trapping, and were perhaps valued as much for their pelts as their meat. The main prey animals are likely to have been horse and reindeer, and the ibex, if correctly identified, must have been something of a novelty. The most famous single find from Robin Hood's Cave is a fragment of bone bearing an engraving of a horse's head. Although a controversial find at the time of its discovery in the 1870s, there seems little reason to doubt its authenticity and it offers a powerful insight into Late Stone Age visual perceptions (plate xiia). The reindeer remains include antlers, which may have been collected as raw material, while some of the other bones may have been accumulated by the hyaenas who also used the cave, probably somewhat before the humans moved in.

The Layer B/A assemblage also includes remains of arctic lemming

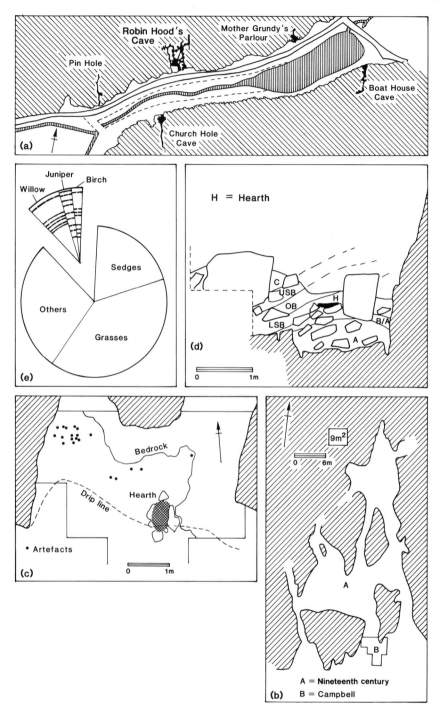

Figure 6.7 Robin Hood's Cave: (a) location, (b) general plan, (c) plan of Campbell's Layer B/A, (d) section from Campbell's excavation, (e) pollen chart for Layer B/A (after Campbell 1977).

Table 6.2 Large mammal bones and teeth from Layer B/A Robin Hood's Cave

	Number of bones and fragments	*Individuals*
Hyaena	3	1
Red fox	6	2
Woolly rhino	4	1
Horse	1	1
Reindeer	7	2
Ibex	2	1
Mountain hare	7	2

(after Jenkinson 1984a: 197)

(*Dicrostonyx torquatus*), kestrel (*Falco tinnunculus*), magpie (*Pica pica*), grouse and ptarmigan, of which the latter two can be considered prey species. Particularly interesting is the presence of grey plover (*Pluvialis squatarola*). Today these small birds are mostly seen on the coast during winter, moving north in summer to breed on the tundra of northern Siberia. The British Isles are at the northern edge of their present winter range and during the Lateglacial this would have been much further south. The Robin Hood's Cave bird was probably in its summer breeding territory.

Campbell found only 36 artefacts in Layer B/A, all but five of which came from a square metre immediately outside the cave entrance (fig. 6.7c). It appears that he excavated on the edge of an area of occupation, the centre of which lay within the cave. Experiments have shown that any fire lit within Robin Hood's Cave creates severe smoke problems, while the use of embers carried into the cave from fires lit outside reduces this considerably. The hearth uncovered outside the entrance may have been used to provide such embers.

Pin Hole (NGR SK 533742) is the last of the sites at Creswell from which substantial archaeological information is available. It lies at the west end of the gorge, on its northern side (fig. 6.8a). A fissure, which varies in width from about 1 to 3 m, Pin Hole is known to extend into the hillside for over 40 m, though only about the first 25 m have been excavated (fig. 6.8b). The layout of the cave makes it most unsuitable for occupation, but its deep, stratified deposits, which were excavated by Armstrong in the 1920s, have produced evidence of human use extending back to before the maximum stage of the last glaciation.

The narrowness of the cave encouraged Armstrong to record his finds in two dimensions only, a horizontal distance from the cave entrance and a vertical depth below a layer of travertine, or flowstone, which formed the floor at the time he began work. Using this information Jenkinson has made a convincing attempt at analysing the stratigraphy of the cave. However, although the cave is very narrow, natural processes at work within it have led to lateral variation within the deposits. Finds made at

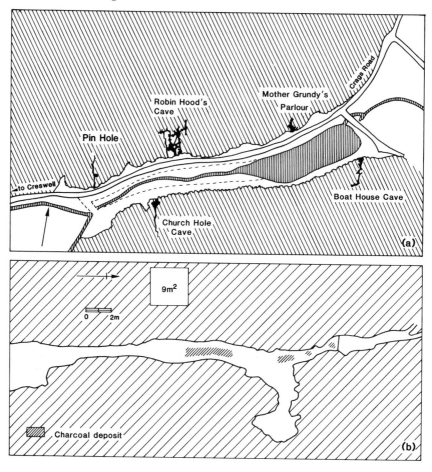

Figure 6.8 Pin Hole: (a) location, (b) plan (after Jenkinson 1984a).

both the same distance from the entrance and the same depth from the travertine floor, could nonetheless have originated from quite different deposits depending on whether they came from the western or eastern side of the passage. This leads to some inevitable blurring between the deposits that can be identified from Armstrong's records, and makes it difficult to reconcile the recently obtained series of radiocarbon dates with Jenkinson's analysis of the stratigraphy.

Of these recently obtained dates, five lie within the span of the Lateglacial Interstadial. Although the range is broad, four have mean values within a century of 12,400 BP. Only one of these specimens, a cut proximal radius of mountain hare dated to *c.* 12,350 BP, can be definitely associated with human activity, and is very similar in date to modified hare bones from Robin Hood's Cave.

The stratigraphical problems at Pin Hole mean that it is not possible to isolate evidence for the kind of small-scale, short-term activity that we were able to examine at Kent's Cavern and Mother Grundy's Parlour. However, some observations on what appear to be aspects of Lateglacial behaviour within Pin Hole are worth making, particularly in the light of the recent discoveries at Gough's Cave, to be discussed below.

Jenkinson has noted two concentrations of charcoal, which appear to have been the remains of hearths. The larger, some 2.5 m in extent, was situated in the centre of the cave, while the other was smaller and lay towards the rear. Human bones were found with both hearths and, although not burnt, they are very fragmentary. They represent at least four individuals. As well as tools and waste, artefacts include a bone pendant found a few metres south of the central hearth, and a fragment of a bovid rib with a highly stylized engraving of a human figure from near the inner hearth (plate xiib).

Its shape means that Pin Hole is unlikely to have been used for occupation in the normal domestic sense, and the presence of human remains suggests that it may have been the focus for some rather special activity. Formal burial seems unlikely, as more human remains should have survived, but some form of post-mortem ritual must be a distinct possibility.

Creswell Crags is one of the richest complexes of Late Stone Age hunter-gatherer sites in Britain and several of the caves have produced large assemblages of animal bones and artefacts. The inadequate recording methods of most of the excavators has meant that these collections are less informative than they might be. However, a number of useful observations can be made.

To begin with, the fact that such rich deposits accumulated testifies to the conservatism of patterns of landuse and settlement. For generation after generation bands of hunters returned to Creswell during the course of their annual cycle. All three of the sites considered have a series of radiocarbon dates extending through the Lateglacial. We have no idea of the size of the bands but, from the space available, Mother Grundy's Parlour could have accommodated a group of about twelve, while the various chambers at Robin Hood's Cave could have been used by several such groups. They are only a few hundred metres apart and it is probably a mistake to treat the individual caves separately. Rather, the whole complex should be regarded as a single settlement, with each cave being repeatedly used by members of the same group, a practice common among cave users into recorded times. Perhaps the gorge was the focus for one of the larger social gatherings which are known to be a regular feature of hunter-gatherer life. Such an event would offer a context for the kind of ritual we may be able dimly to perceive taking place in Pin Hole. We have little idea of what time of year such gatherings may have occurred, though difficulties over maintaining supplies of food and firewood make the winter unlikely. If hares were trapped mainly for their pelts, these would have been in prime condition in the autumn. This is also the best season for game birds such as grouse and ptarmigan, while grey plovers can remain in their summer nesting areas until October or November. Perhaps Creswell Crags was occupied by a group of extended families, held loosely together by ties of kinship and dialect, who met each autumn before dispersing to winter quarters.

GOUGH'S CAVE, CHEDDAR GORGE

The largest assemblage of archaeological material dating from the Lateglacial has been found in Gough's Cave (NGR ST 467539) at the southern end of Cheddar Gorge (figs 6.9a and 9.4a no. 2). Over 7,000 artefacts are reported from this cave, and there is a large faunal assemblage. However, virtually all of this material was recovered during poorly recorded excavations in the years between the First and Second World Wars, and what records were made have since been lost. A little more is known about work in the 1940s and 1950s and a small-scale excavation of a surviving fragment of deposit, begun in 1986, is proving very fruitful. This has led to a thorough reappraisal of the earlier finds.

The poor state of the archaeological record at this site means that we cannot isolate, from the mass of data, a well-dated occupation deposit accompanied by biological evidence. Nevertheless, Gough's Cave is of such importance that we must try to gain at least a general impression of the human activity that took place there.

Parry, who conducted the main excavations, recorded his finds in twenty-five 6-inch (0.15 m) spits and, although his records have been mislaid, many artefacts and bones have spit numbers written on them. Apart from these details of 'depth', we have little idea of where within the cave the finds were made, though most of Parry's work was done within 30 m of the entrance. Artefacts of Lateglacial date were recovered from Spits 9 down to 25 but later finds also occurred down to Spit 12 and Parry believed that material below Spit 16 had been subject to post-depositional displacement. Spits 13 to 16, a depth of about 0.6 m, are the nearest we can get to an *in situ* occupation deposit. Although part of this vertical spread may be due to the unevenness of the original surface, it is highly unlikely that all this material could have originated from a single episode of occupation.

Direct dates have been obtained on five animal bones from Spits 13 to 16 and, although their total span is broad, three have mean values within a century of 12,450 BP. We may tentatively conclude that Gough's Cave was occupied during the latter half of the thirteenth millennium BP.

Blocks of sediment from Parry's excavation have been preserved and various attempts have been made to use them for pollen analysis. Counts of 206 and 115 grains were obtained by Leroi-Gourhan from samples from Spits 15 and 13 respectively, and the results are presented in figure 6.9c. In

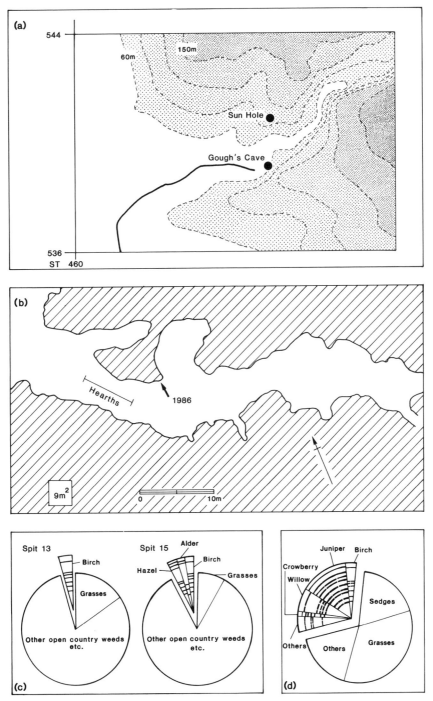

Figure 6.9 Gough's Cave: (a) location, (b) plan, (c) pollen charts for Spits 13 and 15, (d) pollen chart for Layer B2–7 at Sun Hole Cave (after Campbell 1977, Jacobi 1985 and Leroi-Gourhan 1985).

both, although open-country plants predominate, grasses and sedges amount to less than 20 per cent and others such as dandelions (Cichorieae), chamomile (Anthemideae) and meadow rue (*Thalictrum* sp.) seem over-represented. This may be an anthropogenic effect. The plants in question would have been growing in the damp ground at the bottom of the gorge, and pollen could have been brought back to the cave on clothing, muddy feet or bunches of flowers. Trees account for less than 10 per cent and, in addition to the ubiquitous birch, it is interesting to note the presence of alder and hazel, both trees of deciduous woodland. They probably grew in the sheltered gorge and serve to emphasize the diversity of the landscape of the Lateglacial Interstadial.

Pollen analyses have been undertaken for other caves in the gorge and Campbell's work at Sun Hole provides an interesting comparison (fig. 5.8). Sun Hole lies opposite Gough's Cave, at a higher level, with an exposed south-facing aspect (fig. 6.9a). Its pollen assemblage may therefore be more representative of the area as a whole. Campbell believed Layer B to be of Lateglacial age and this has been confirmed by dates of *c.* 12,378 BP on a humerus of brown bear, and *c.* 12,210 BP on a fragment of a human ulna, both of which came from Layer B2.

Campbell found pollen throughout B2, and I have selected the data from B2/7 for comparison with Gough's Cave (fig. 6.9d). A total of 245 grains was identified and of these 30 per cent came from trees or shrubs, with juniper, willow and birch being the most common. The picture is of a generally open landscape, especially on the higher ground, but with a good deal of tree cover at lower levels.

Mammal bones were abundant in Gough's Cave and the principal species identified in Spits 13 to 16 are listed in table 6.3:

Table 6.3 Mammal bones from Spits 13–16, Gough's Cave

	13	*14*	*15*	*16*
Mountain hare	3	9	2	
Beaver		1		
Wolf	1	3	2	1
Brown fox			1	
Brown bear		3		
Horse	27	63	21	15
Red deer	8	8	3	1
Wild cattle			1	
Saiga		1	1	

(after Currant 1986: 290)

The great predominance of horse is clear, and bones of this species, along with examples of red deer, wild cattle, saiga and mountain hare, bear cut marks which testify that these animals were hunted. A detailed study of cut marks on bones of horse and red deer indicates that, in addition to the normal processes of butchery and filleting, sinews were being systematically removed. The use to which such a raw material was put is a matter for speculation, but backing for composite bows, bow strings, harpoon lines and nooses for snares are all uses which spring readily to mind.

Bird bones from Spits 13 to 16 include open-country species such as ptarmigan and grouse, and others favouring a more wooded habitat such as stock dove (*Columba oenas*) and blackbird or ring ouzel (*Turdus merula* or *T. torquatus*). A notable identification from Spit 14 is whooper swan (*Cygnus cygnus*). Today this bird breeds in the Arctic and spends winter in the British Isles, but in the Lateglacial its breeding range may have included Britain. Remains of a peregrine falcon (*Falco peregrinus*) were scattered between several spits and this bird may have been deliberately caught, perhaps for its talons or plumage.

The several thousand artefacts found during the various excavations at Gough's Cave include the largest group of Lateglacial finds from any site in Britain. Precise totals cannot now be established, owing to the incomplete nature of the surviving assemblage, but in a recent study Jacobi has identified 388 late Upper Palaeolithic stone tools among those available for study. The assemblage is of key importance to studies of stone tool typology and is currently being subjected to reappraisal. It includes backed points of the so-called *Creswell* and *Cheddar* types as well as shouldered points (fig. 6.10). Burins, scrapers and awls were also present and these indicate bone, antler and skin working, as do several bone needles, piercers and awls. This is a typical assemblage from a home base, where various maintenance and industrial tasks were carried out and the evidence for sinew removal is part of the same picture.

Gough's Cave has long been well known among archaeologists for the number of 'decorated' pieces of bone and antler that have been found there, and these have been added to by the excavations which began in 1986. These items include three *bâtons de commandement*, consisting of sections of antler or bone with a neat perforation towards one end. Their function is unknown, but a plausible suggestion is that they were used for straightening arrow shafts. Extra interest attaches to one because of a series of roughly parallel scratches which can be seen on one face (fig. 6.11a). These scratches are in regularly arranged groups, and similar markings have been noted on two other items, a segment of rib, and a tibia of mountain hare (fig. 6.11b and c). To this group can be added six similarly marked small fragments of ivory found during the recent excavations. The purpose of these marks is unknown. They appear to be some form of notation, but whether for use as a tally, as a system of measurement or a record of the passage of time can only be guessed at. They suggest a hitherto unsuspected level of numeracy, and provide a fascinating insight into the mental life of hunters living at Cheddar over 12,000 years ago.

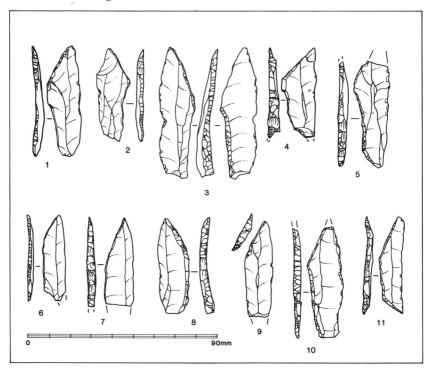

Figure 6.10 Backed blades from Gough's Cave: nos 1–5 are examples of 'shoul-dered' points, no. 10 is a 'Creswell' point and no. 11 a 'Cheddar' point (after Campbell 1977).

Gough's Cave is also well known for the fragmentary finds of human remains recovered during the earlier excavations and a virtually complete skeleton of early Postglacial age, the so-called 'Cheddar Man'. More recently, it has become notorious through the discovery of more human remains, which bear clear traces of butchery. They are all very fragmen-tary, and butchery marks are not in themselves evidence for cannibalism. They might just as easily arise through the defleshing of corpses as part of a funerary ritual. What is certain is that remains of both adults and children underwent some post-mortem processing, and then seem to have been discarded along with the other animal remains.

We have little indication of the spatial distribution of these finds but Parry found traces of hearths just inside the entrance, and we can expect these to have been the focus of a range of activities, while other tasks were carried out on the platform outside. The daylit portion of the cave amounts to about 150 m^2 and provided sufficient space to accommodate a group of about twenty, that is twice the number estimated for the Kent's Cavern Vestibule or Mother Grundy's Parlour. There is also some evidence that occupation was seasonal.

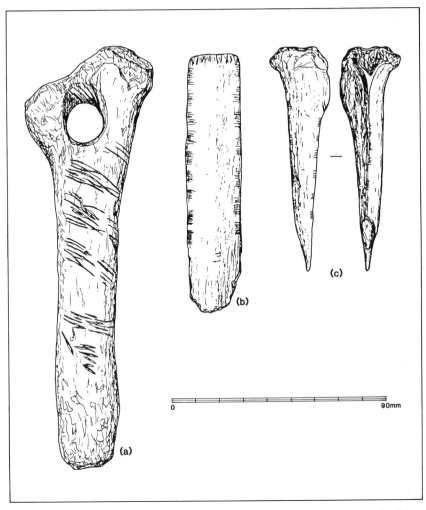

Figure 6.11 Incised bone and antler from Gough's Cave: (a) reindeer antler *bâton de commandement*, (b) rib segment, (c) tibia of a mountain hare. All three pieces are marked with regularly spaced groups of carefully incised lines (after Campbell 1977).

Red deer and horses give birth to their fawns and foals over a fairly short span of time and after birth growth is generally rapid and regular. This is especially marked in the development of the dentition, in both tooth eruption and the formation of cementum. Studies of tooth eruption in five red deer jaws suggest that the animals were killed in the winter, while cementum development in three horse and one red deer give summer as the time of death. A further hint of activity during the summer is provided by a record of whooper swan from Spit 14. These results are not as contradictory as they first seem. The season of occupation at Gough's Cave may have changed over a period of time, or the cave may have been used intermittently throughout the year. That use was intermittent is implied by evidence for carnivore activity at broadly the same time as the humans were present. As they are unlikely to have shared the cave we can assume that the wolves moved in while the humans were absent, perhaps to scavenge the rubbish heaps.

Given the, putatively, intermittent nature of the occupation, we can also speculate a little about where the Gough's Cave people spent the rest of the year. A clue is provided by the raw material used in stone tool manufacture. Over 95 per cent was Upper Cretaceous flint which had probably been collected in the Wiltshire area, while the assemblage also includes small amounts of Greensand and Portland chert, suggesting that their annual cycle took them as far as the English Channel Plain.

Cheddar Gorge is a far larger feature than the gorge at Creswell Crags and the various caves which have produced evidence for human activity during the Lateglacial need to be treated as distinct sites as well as components in a larger complex. The evidence from Gough's Cave offers the best picture of that activity, but remains very incomplete. What we can glimpse is a rich and diverse environment that could sustain several bands of hunters at any time of the year. We can also gain some impression of life at their home base, where much time was devoted to making and repairing equipment. Certain grisly tasks were also undertaken from time to time, the nature of which we can only guess at. At Creswell Crags such activities seem to have been confined to Pin Hole and segregated from daily life. We can only hope that such segregation also occurred at Gough's Cave, and that, while the band elders were dismembering corpses in the rear of the cave, children were not playing in the entrance!

HENGISTBURY HEAD

It would be easy to gain the false impression that during the Lateglacial humans lived only in caves. That this is unlikely is indicated by evidence for open encampments from areas as far apart as south-western France and the Ukraine. We also know from ethnography that recent hunting and gathering peoples have been reluctant to use caves except in emergencies. Even in Britain, nineteenth-century cave dwellers in Scotland preferred to move into tents for winter, which were presumably easier to heat and draught-proof. Although caves may have been more popular in the relatively harsh conditions of the Lateglacial, our home base case studies would be incomplete without consideration of at least one open encampment. The only such location for which sufficient information is available is Hengistbury Head (NGR SZ 178904) on the Dorset coast (figs 6.12a and 9.4a no. 5).

This site has been excavated on several occasions: in 1957 by Mace, from 1968 to 1969 by Campbell and from 1981 to 1985 by Bergman and Barton. The Lateglacial occupation at Hengistbury Head is poorly dated and there

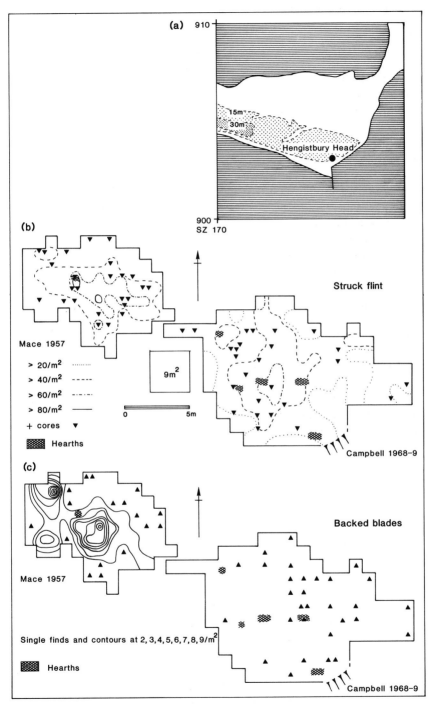

Figure 6.12 Hengistbury Head: (a) location, (b) struck flint, (c) backed blades (adapted from Mace 1959 and Campbell 1977).

are no reliable biological data. The best indication of its age is provided by a series of thermoluminescence (TL) dates obtained on burnt artefacts recovered during the recent excavations. These dates range from 14,800 BP to 10,020 BP and have immense standard deviations. However, the mean value has been calculated as 12,500 ± 1150 BP, which is in broad agreement with the radiocarbon dates obtained for the other case studies considered in this chapter.

In caves, deposits accumulate rapidly through natural agencies and this leads to the preservation of much archaeological material. On open sites the opposite is often the case. Burial is a slow process, and archaeological traces of human activity are only rarely preserved. When they are, it is not usually in a neat stratigraphical sequence. Evidence simply accumulates through time and the traces of activity become blurred and distorted. Allowing for this distortion is the chief problem we face in trying to consider the meaning of the Lateglacial assemblage from Hengistbury Head.

Although Campbell believed that two distinct assemblages of different age were present, this is now thought unlikely and I shall treat the finds as part of a single group. Spatial details from the recent excavations are yet to be published and this case study will concentrate on the findings of Mace and Campbell. The total finds from the two excavations are summarized in table 6.4:

Table 6.4   Finds from Hengistbury Head

	Area	Finds	Density	Implements	%
Mace	73m²	3,057	41.7/m²	177	5.8
Campbell	125m²	3,518	28.4/m²	110	3.1
Total	198m²	6,575	33.2/m²	287	4.4

(after Mace 1959 and Campbell 1977)

Campbell's finds were the more numerous, but they were distributed across a larger area and more artefacts were discarded on the part of the site examined by Mace. It also seems clear that neither excavator uncovered the full extent of the assemblage, although both exposed clearly defined concentrations (fig. 6.12b). If we assume that the distribution of distinct categories of artefact corresponds to areas where particular activities were carried out, a number of interesting patterns can be identified.

Although they could be used to work bone or wood, scrapers are usually associated with skin and hide working; microwear studies of scrapers from various sites have tended to support this view. Campbell found traces of red ochre, and this may also have been associated with the preparation of hides, into which it may have been rubbed as a preservative. Scrapers are distributed evenly across the two areas at Hengistbury Head except for a slight concentration in Mace's area (fig. 6.13a). It is unlikely that at any one time this activity would be so widespread, and we may infer that the distribution of scrapers is the residue of several occupations.

The distribution of burins, to be identified with the processing of bone or antler, suggests that this activity was confined to the area excavated by Mace (fig. 6.13b). Mace, but not Campbell, also recorded blade segments as a distinct category (fig. 6.13c) and these were found concentrated in the same area as the burins. This is especially interesting as Mace regarded the blade segments as an early stage in burin manufacture. We may conclude that, unlike hide processing, bone or antler was worked on only this part of the site.

A clear discrimination between the two areas also emerges in the distribution of backed blades (fig. 6.12c). Although they were widely scattered, two concentrations of these implements were found by Mace. This assemblage includes a range of items such as tanged, shouldered and backed blades or points, usually taken to be projectile tips (fig. 6.14). It looks as if the preparation and repair of hunting gear was mainly carried out to either side of the hearth identified by Mace.

Areas of stone working are indicated by the distribution of cores (fig. 6.12b). No clear pattern is evident, except that little was done in the eastern part of Campbell's area.

It seems that the Hengistbury Head site was occupied on a number of occasions and that patterns of use varied, with a range of artefacts being discarded across the areas examined. However, there was a marked concentration of industrial activity on the western part of the site. This suggests two things: first, that visits were sufficiently frequent for this pattern to be maintained, and second, that on most visits the eastern area was reserved for another function.

Campbell, under the influence of discoveries made in northern Europe (fig. 6.15), thought he found traces of a shelter. The evidence for this consisted of a line of three hearths, and on either side of them, to the north and south and set back about 3 m, two curving lines of discarded cores defining an area about 6 m by 5 m. He suggested that the cores were weights used to hold down the sides of a tent-like structure. As some of these cores weighed only 200–300 grams (hardly more than a half-pound bag of toffees!) this seems a bit far-fetched. Campbell also drew attention to the concentration of late Upper Palaeolithic artefacts within his putative tent as part of his argument. In my view, the contrary argument is stronger. People were very unlikely to want a lot of stone tool debris in their living area and, if a structure was ever erected on the eastern part of the site, this would have been when it was not being used for flint knapping.

For part of the time the site was occupied there was a clear distinction in the way the two areas were used and at Hengistbury Head we may, for the first time, be seeing the juxtaposition of a residential area with a peripheral zone devoted to industrial activity (fig. 3.2).

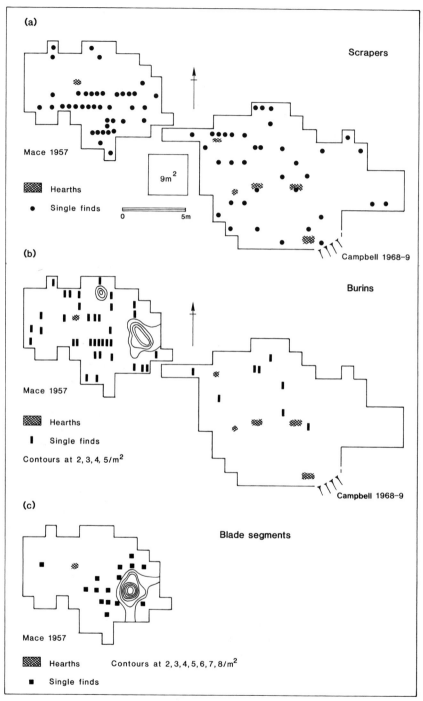

Figure 6.13 Hengistbury Head: (a) scrapers, (b) burins, (c) blade segments
(adapted from Mace 1959 and Campbell 1977).

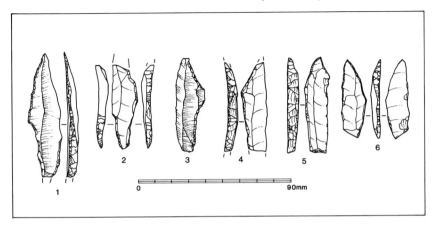

Figure 6.14 Backed blades from Hengistbury Head: nos 1 and 2 are 'tanged' points, no. 3 a 'shouldered' point and nos 4–6 'Creswell' points (after Campbell 1977 and Bergman and Barton 1986).

In the earlier case studies I used the available floor area as a rough basis for estimating group size. In each case the area was defined by the walls of the cave. With an open site no such unambiguous definition exists, and without clear structural traces such estimates are impossible. Campbell's 'tent' would have had a floor area of 30 m^2, and would be unlikely to have offered shelter to more than a family.

The different categories of material found by Mace occurred in distinct concentrations within the general background scatter. These vary in size between about 1 m^2 and 4 m^2, and may provide just a hint of the scale of individual activity areas.

We can say nothing about the season of occupation and very little about the economic activities of the groups who camped at Hengistbury Head. The site lay within an area of predominantly grass and sedge tundra with some birch scrub (figs 9.2 and 9.3) which was probably cut for firewood. At *c.* 12,500 BP it was a long way from the coast (fig. 9.4a no. 5) and we can assume that the hunters of Hengistbury were primarily engaged in hunting open-country herbivores, of which the most common would have been the horse.

The case studies examined so far have all been examples of home bases. We have noted evidence for a range of activities of the kind we would expect, such as the manufacture and maintenance of equipment, the processing and consumption of food and, presumably, residence. But the main preoccupation of most Lateglacial hunters would have been the need to acquire food and raw materials. They would hope to supply these needs from the territory around the home base, or at least the territories around several such centres visited during the course of an annual cycle (fig. 3.1).

Figure 6.15 Campbell believed the three hearths found in his excavation at Hengistbury Head marked the position of a tent-like structure, but the evidence is very slight. These reconstruction drawings are based on rather better evidence from the site of Pincevent, near Paris (after Leroi-Gourhan 1984).

Some of these activities are undetectable archaeologically. For example, the demand for firewood must have been considerable but deforestation is hard to identify in pollen spectra from what was basically an open environment. The gathering of vegetable foods is also very difficult to detect unless pips or stones happen to get preserved in archaeological deposits, and Lateglacial sites are not blessed with the almost ubiquitous hazel-nut of later periods.

Other activities we can recognize, either directly or indirectly. In areas with rich flint deposits we should be able to identify locations where the main activity was the extraction of raw material, though there are no clear examples of this until the Postglacial. However, the hunters who sheltered in Gough's Cave acquired most of their flint some distance from Cheddar, in Wiltshire. We may infer that their annual round took them to a flint-bearing area and that part of the group must have devoted time to acquiring sufficient raw material to last until the next visit.

The one category of raw material about which we have clear evidence is animal products, for as well as being the major source of food, animals provided a useful range of raw materials such as bone, antler, sinew, oil and hide. Some examples of kill sites known from the Continent were referred to in chapter 5 and these may be compared with two examples from Britain.

The Poulton elk (NGR SD331387) (fig. 9.4a no. 4), whose bones have been dated to 12,400 ± 300 BP, bore on its carcass traces of wounds inflicted by flint implements, while two bone points were found amongst its bones (fig. 6.16). Some of the wounds had begun to heal and the animal appears to have been encountered on at least two occasions. Hunters in the North American sub-arctic will track a wounded moose (i.e. European elk) for more than a week and the hunting of the Poulton animal may have been a similarly extended event (fig. 5.10b). Weighing over 300 kg, an elk would be worth a considerable investment of time.

Our second example of a kill site is provided by the fragmentary remains of three horses found at Flixton Site 2 in Yorkshire (NGR TA 028807) (fig. 9.4c no. 3). The deposit containing the remains has been dated to *c.* 10,413 BP. The particular interest of this find is that two flint artefacts, an unretouched blade and what appears to be a broken shouldered point, were associated with the bones. No wounds or butchery traces are reported on the skeletons, but they were very incomplete, suggesting that a number of joints had been removed from the site by the hunters.

As the Poulton example may imply, tracking big game could have been a protracted business and a hunting party might have to travel a considerable distance from the home base in order to secure a quarry (fig. 3.1). Many of the records of Lateglacial settlement in Britain consist of just a handful of finds and such small assemblages may be the debris discarded by hunting parties making overnight stops. When a kill was made far from base the hunters had to face the problem of how to get it home. The difficulty could be alleviated partly if some of the kill was stored, or cached, for collection or use at a later date, and during the cold Lateglacial winters joints of meat could be stored frozen.

Human behaviour did not revolve exclusively around the acquisition of food and raw materials. In the Pin Hole and Gough's Cave case studies we glimpsed evidence, in the form of the post-mortem processing of human remains, for what could have been ritual activity. A fissure like Pin Hole may have been reserved for such activities. A further, possible example comes from Kendrick's Cave on the Great Orme in North Wales (NGR SH 780828) (fig. 9.4c no. 4). During the nineteenth century, in very poorly recorded circumstances, a number of finds were made in this cave which

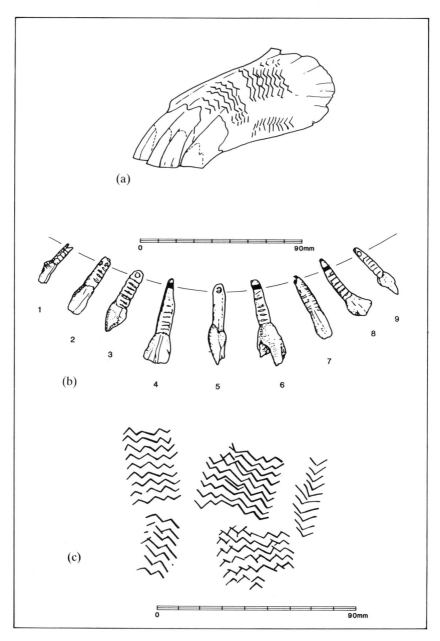

Figure 6.17 Finds from Kendrick's Cave: (a) the decorated horse mandible, (b) perforated ungulate incisors believed to have been found with the mandible and human burials (nos 1, 8, 9 red deer; 3, 4, 6 bovid; 2, 7 giant deer or elk, 5 unidentified), (c) design on the mandible (after Sieveking 1971).

may be the remains of a Lateglacial funeral. They comprised parts of four human skeletons, portions of two horse mandibles, and two perforated canine teeth of brown bear. Nine other perforated teeth of various species are also thought to have come from the cave. All the teeth and one of the mandible fragments are decorated; the latter with a complex pattern of incised zigzags in groups of seven and nine (fig. 6.17), a further example of Stone Age numeracy (plate xiic). This has provided a date of *c*. 10,000 BP and is the first piece of Upper Palaeolithic art from Britain to be directly dated.

The archaeological record for the Lateglacial can be seen to consist of a series of home bases, and various other locations which were the scene of particular activities, such as hunting and ritual. A third component consists of items lost or casually discarded as people moved between their various centres of activity. Good examples of such finds are provided by a series of barbed projectile points of bone or antler (figs 4.2 and 5.5). These are usually single finds and were presumably lost during the hunt. They are often our only evidence for the presence of Lateglacial hunters in the area.

ADDITIONAL READING

Several of the sites considered in this chapter have provided important evidence for the study of stone tool typology. I have not attempted to treat this subject, but interested readers are referred to Campbell (1977), Jacobi (1980), Jenkinson (1984a) and Barton and Roberts (1996). An alternative approach, based on the direct dating of artefacts made from bone and antler is discussed in papers by Bonsall and Smith (1990) and Smith and Bonsall (1991).

The account of Kent's Cavern is based on Campbell (1977), while Rosenfeld reported on Three Holes Cave (1964), though work at that site was resumed in the 1990s. Most of the information on Creswell Crags comes from Campbell (1977) and Jenkinson (1984a), though Armstrong (1924) and McBurney (1959) provide additional information in the case of Mother Grundy's Parlour. Gentles and Smithson (1986) describe their experiments with fires in Robin Hood's Cave and Charles and Jacobi (1994) have recently discussed the dating of the faunal assemblage from that site. Gough's Cave has recently been the focus of much attention and an important series of papers dealing with various aspects of the site has been published in the *Proceedings of the University of Bristol Spelaeological Society* since 1985. Of particular note are papers dealing with the exploration of the cave (Jacobi 1985), sedimentology (Collcutt 1985), pollen analysis (Leroi-Gourhan 1985), hominid remains (Stringer 1985 and Cook 1986), mammals (Currant 1986 and 1987), birds (Harrison 1986), and seasonality and taphonomy (Parkin *et al.* 1986 and Beasley 1987). Other general accounts have been published by

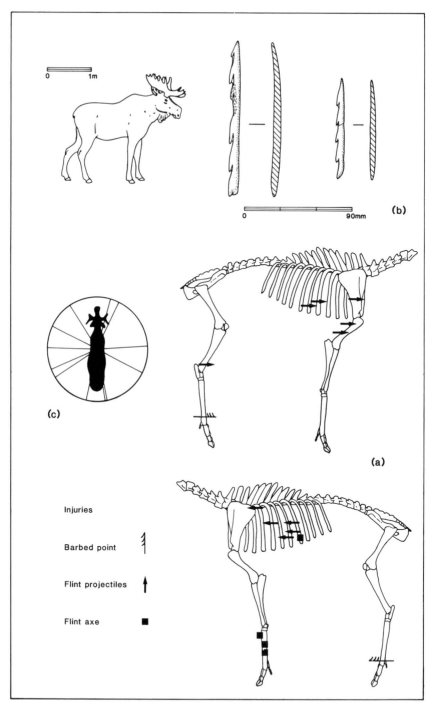

Figure 6.16 The Poulton elk: (a) injuries noted on the skeleton, (b) the two bone points (after Hallam *et al.* 1973), (c) injuries on the carcass. The directions of fire are conjectural.

Currant *et al.* (1989) and Jacobi (1986a and b). Details of Sun Hole are from Campbell (1977). The excavations at Hengistbury Head during the 1950s and 1960s, which form the basis for the study presented in this chapter, are described by Mace (1959) and Campbell (1977) while Campbell's results have also been reviewed by Houtsma *et al.* (1996). The excavations undertaken at the site in the 1980s have now also been published (Barton 1992) and readers are referred to that report for the most complete account. The discovery of the Poulton elk is dealt with by Hallam *et al.* (1973), though note should be taken of subsequent comments by Noe-Nygaard (1975) and Stuart (1976). The Flixton horses are described by Moore (1954), and Sieveking (1971) discussed the finds from Kendrick's Cave.

For estimations of population size based on artefact densities and floor area see Price (1978), and references quoted by him. For information on tents and shelters in northern Europe see Binford (1983), Leroi-Gourhan (1984), Leroi-Gourhan and Brezillon (1966). Burleigh (1986) has discussed radiocarbon dates from the Cheddar sites, and accelerator dates for these sites, Creswell Crags, Kent's Cavern, Three Holes Cave, Poulton and Kendrick's Cave are published in the *Archaeometry* Datelists nos 2, 3, 4, 6, 7, 9 and 10.

7 Case studies II: Hunters of the boreal forest and deciduous woodlands

With the amelioration of the climate which followed the Loch Lomond Readvance and finally released the British Isles from the grip of ice sheets and glaciers, the landscape rapidly changed from a mainly open tundra to one in which trees became increasingly predominant. To begin with, this closing of the landscape was accomplished by boreal forests in which birch was the most common tree, and indeed birch had been a locally important component of the Lateglacial vegetation. However, the period of the birch forests was relatively short lived. By 10,000 BP deciduous woodland was well established in southern Britain and within a thousand years had reached the west coast of Scotland and southern and eastern Ireland. Birch remained important in these areas, but as part of a mixed woodland community in which pine, hazel, oak and elm were also important, and to which lime had been added by 7000 BP (figs 9.5, 9.6, 9.9 and 9.10). As a legacy of the melting of the ice sheets the early Postglacial landscape was at first dotted with numerous lakes, but as time passed they began to dry out and became progressively overgrown with reed swamp, peat and fen. A final stage in this process was the development of alder carr, a type of deciduous woodland typical of damp ground, and by 7000 BP alder had become the dominant tree in many parts of lowland Britain (fig. 9.10a). These changes, and accompanying changes in the fauna, presented the human population with new challenges and opportunities.

STAR CARR AND THE VALE OF PICKERING

Star Carr (NGR TA 027809)(fig. 9.4d no. 3) is the best known early Postglacial site in Britain, and since its excavation by Grahame Clark between 1949 and 1951 it has hardly been out of the archaeological headlines. Exceptional conditions of preservation and meticulous excavation led to the recovery of large amounts of organic material in addition to stone tools, and Clark was able to draw an unusually detailed picture of life for a band of hunters living in East Yorkshire 9,500 years ago. The quality of the original data and the high standard of its publication have encouraged a succession of re-evaluations of the site, the first of which was by Clark himself in 1972. In 1977 further archaeological and palaeo-environmental research was begun in the area.

During the Lateglacial a lake formed at the eastern end of the Vale of Pickering and drained westward into the River Derwent. Star Carr was situated near its outlet. The full extent of the lake is known only in outline, but recent research has provided a very detailed picture of its western end (fig. 7.1b). The area was a focus of activity in the Lateglacial and the horse kill site at Flixton 2, described in chapter 6, lay on an island in the lake, while the recent excavations at Site K in Seamer Carr have identified an occupation site of Lateglacial age on the northern shore.

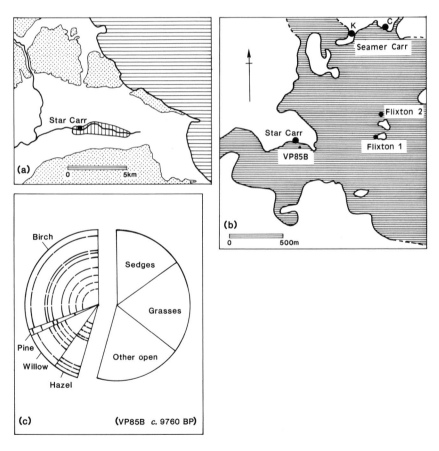

Figure 7.1 Star Carr: (a) location map showing the putative extent of Lake Pickering in the tenth millennium BP (redrawn from Legge and Rowley-Conwy 1988); (b) Lateglacial and early Postglacial sites at the west end of Lake Pickering (redrawn from Cloutman 1988); (c) pollen chart for *c.* 9760 BP from core VP85B (data from Cloutman and Smith 1988).

A series of radiocarbon dates obtained for Star Carr indicates that occupation occurred during the middle of the tenth millennium BP. The range is wide and the site may have been used intermittently over a long period. Further along the north shore, early Postglacial occupation has been dated to *c.* 9400 BP at Site K and to *c.* 9200 BP at Site C, and it is clear that Lake Pickering remained a focus of interest throughout the tenth millennium BP (fig. 7.1b).

Star Carr and Site K at Seamer Carr were by the northern shore of the lake and both were to some extent protected by spits of slightly higher ground to the east and south respectively. They could also be reached over dry land from the north, as was probably the case at Site C, whereas Flixton 1, an early Postglacial site investigated in the 1940s, appears to have been on an island.

There are numerous pollen analyses of deposits from the lake and these have been used to produce a very detailed picture of the environment at the time the sites were occupied; figure 7.1c is based on data from Sample VP85B published by Cloutman and Smith in 1988. It must be emphasized that this is a general indication only, and is offered for comparison with similar diagrams in this and the previous chapter. Birch dominated the tree and shrub species and probably grew on dry ground away from the lake margin. Willows were more in evidence on the damper ground, while fen was developing at the water's edge with sedge and reed swamp beyond, though the Star Carr site had access to open water. There is an indication that pine was beginning to appear in the area, on drier ground away from the lake, and hazel was becoming locally important. The 20 per cent contribution of grass pollen implies that the birch forest was either discontinuous or comparatively open.

The aspect of the finds from Star Carr that has been most fully studied is undoubtedly the faunal assemblage. Animal remains were dominated by those of red deer, of which a high proportion was antler. In the original report these were treated along with bones as a basis for establishing the minimum number of animals represented on the site. One of the main activities at Star Carr was antler working. This being the case, antlers may have been brought to the site as raw material and should not be used in estimating the meat consumed or processed there. Excluding antlers has a dramatic effect on the minimum numbers calculation, reducing red deer from 80 to 26 and roe deer from 33 to 17. The other main food animals identified were elk, wild cattle and wild pig. A recent re-examination of the faunal assemblage has led to a number of bones being re-identified. Taking this into account, and disregarding antlers, we find that, although red deer remain the most numerous, they are no longer the main food animal.

Over half the animals killed by the Star Carr hunters were deer, and a study of dentitions has shown that they tended to concentrate on three-year-old red deer and one-year-old roe. This is probably because the behaviour of these animals made them more easily taken than their older

Table 7.1   Principal food animals at Star Carr

Species	Number	Individual weight in kg	Total meat[1] in kg
Wild cattle	16	700	6,720
Elk	12	350	2,520
Red deer	26	150	2,340
Roe deer	17	23	235
Wild pig	4	89	214

[1] Meat weight = 60% live weight

(after Legge and Rowley-Conwy 1988:67)

and more experienced relatives. All of the large animals were probably hunted by stealth and in three instances, two elk and one red deer, lesions have been noticed which were probably caused by flint-tipped hunting weapons. In each case the wounds are in shoulder blades, suggesting that the hunters were aiming for the heart or lungs, and one of the elk appears to have been shot from behind. It is particularly interesting that all three wounds healed; this would indicate that the animals escaped, though the presence of their shoulder blades at Star Carr shows that they were eventually caught a second time. The chances of the same animals being encountered more than once must have been quite small, and may suggest that red deer and elk populations around Lake Pickering were relatively sedentary.

Other animals represented in small numbers include two pine martens, a red fox and six or seven beavers. In each case the range of bones is wide and suggests the presence of whole carcasses rather than fortuitous fragments. These animals were probably taken in traps for their pelts, though the fact that most of the beavers are said to be immature suggests that a whole family was caught in its lodge. This would be most likely to have happened in the winter. The Star Carr hunters also had domestic dogs.

Birds are poorly represented. There are single records of a number of waterfowl and, in spite of its lakeside position, no fish remains were recovered. Wheeler has explained this anomaly by suggesting that the Postglacial river system had yet to become fully stocked, but several of the birds found, such as red-breasted merganser (*Mergus serrator*), red-throated diver (*Colymbus stellatus*) and great crested grebe (*Podiceps cristatus*), feed on fish. Clark referred to the Star Carr people as hunter-fishers and interpreted their barbed points as fishing spears. The absence of fish remains may be due to recovery bias, in that they survive only in exceptional circumstances and require exceptional recovery procedures.

Full details of the faunal remains from the two sites in Seamer Carr are yet to be published, but horse, wild pig, wild cattle and red and roe deer are reported from Site C. The record of horse is intriguing, given its total absence from Star Carr, though horses were hunted in the area during the Lateglacial, as we saw at Flixton Site 2 (chapter 6).

The excavators at Star Carr found nearly 17,000 flint artefacts, of which about 14 per cent were either retouched or utilized in some way. This is a high proportion, but Clark acknowledged that the total does not include small spalls, and the original proportion of worked and utilized pieces must have been smaller. The 446 scrapers form the most common type of implement, but a third of these had first been used as cores and such recycling hints at economy in the use of flint, which was nevertheless available locally. Fifty-four were broken, indicating heavy use. There were 114 awls, some of which, along with the scrapers, have been shown by microwear studies to have been used for processing hides, while the 336 burins may be associated with bone and antler working, for which there is abundant independent evidence. Hunting gear was represented by 248 microliths. These almost certainly served as the tips and barbs of arrows and one retained traces of the resin which had held it in the shaft. The microliths are typical of a so-called early Mesolithic broad-blade assemblage, 126 being obliquely blunted points (fig. 7.2). The assemblage also included seven heavy duty tools referred to as axes or adzes, which must have been used in the creation of the clearing by the lakeside in which the hunters set up camp.

Although there is abundant evidence for flint working, one of the main activities at Star Carr was the manufacture of barbed points of antler, nearly 200 of which were found. The first stage in this process was the removal of splinters from red deer antler beams with a burin, by means of the groove-and-splinter technique (fig. 6.3a). A number of unworked splinters was found, but study of the discarded beams shows that at least 360 splinters were removed. Some were over 300 mm long and it must often have been possible to fashion two points from a single splinter. The finished points were very varied but Clark defined a number of types distinguished by the number and spacing of the barbs, and the size of the tang (fig. 7.3). Many were found broken and had been discarded. Some of the smaller ones may have been mounted at the ends of arrow shafts and there is evidence that such points were used in hunting terrestrial game (cf. the Poulton elk, chapter 6). The larger specimens are more likely to have been used as fish spears, either singly or mounted in pairs as leisters. One example with a perforation near the base was presumably a harpoon.

Objects which have attracted a good deal of comment are a series of red deer antler frontlets, each consisting of part of the skull with the antlers still attached. In each case the antlers have been greatly reduced in such a fashion as to lessen their weight but maintain their profile. The portions of skull have also been thinned and the better preserved examples exhibit pairs of artificially created holes (fig. 7.4). It is assumed that these antler frontlets were intended to be worn, and debate revolves around whether this was as part of a ritual activity or, more mundanely, a disguise used in

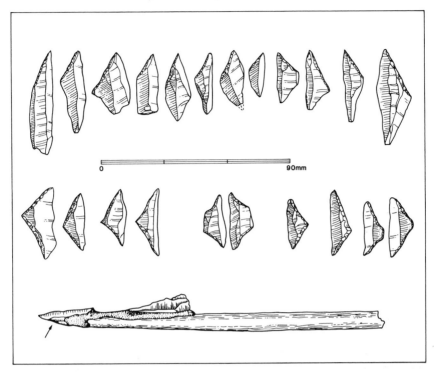

Figure 7.2 Broad-blade microliths from Star Carr: The top row displays typical examples of obliquely blunted points while the remainder are geometric forms (after Clark 1971). The arrow shaft is from Loshult, Sweden, and has an obliquely blunted point at the tip.

stalking deer. The Star Carr hunters may not have made the same distinction between ritual and secular activity that we do, but the fact that twenty-one frontlets were found argues for a practical use.

Other pieces of equipment made from organic materials include several elk antler mattocks, perhaps used for digging traps, scraping tools made from the split metapodials of wild cattle and bodkins made from elk metapodials (fig. 7.5). The only wooden item was a paddle, and, as the trees of the birch forest would have made poor dugout canoes, skin boats were probably used. Non-utilitarian items include several groups of beads and lumps of haematite. This latter material may have been used for body painting.

Seamer Carr C and K, and Flixton 1 each produced about 8,000 stone tools, but overall densities vary from 8 per m^2 to 20 per m^2 at Seamer Carr C and K and 64 per m^2 at Flixton 1. At Site C most of the finds came from three small concentrations, each of about 40 m^2 while the main concentration at Flixton was 35 m^2 across. Flixton is a classic broad-blade early Mesolithic assemblage with retouched and utilized pieces making up 6.8

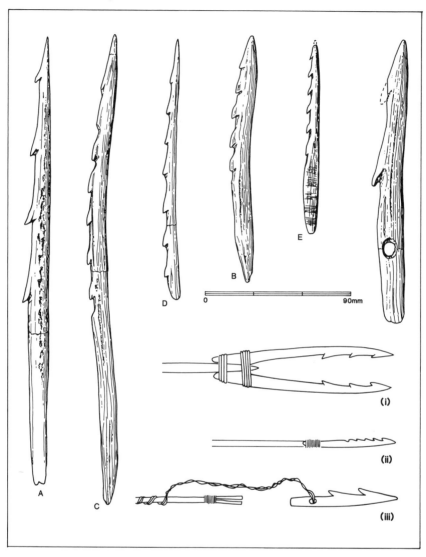

Figure 7.3 Examples of Clark's five types of antler barbed point from Star Carr and the harpoon (after Clark (1971). The reconstructions show similar barbed points used as prongs for a fish spear or leister (i), as an arrowhead (ii), and as a harpoon (iii).

per cent. Scrapers are the most common implement but, unlike Star Carr, burins are virtually absent and there is no worked bone or antler. All three sites contain little in the way of organic material.

Star Carr consisted of a spread of brushwood and birch trees about 16.5 m by 14.5 m which had been dumped at the watery margin of the lake, whereas the other sites were mainly concentrations of stone tools around

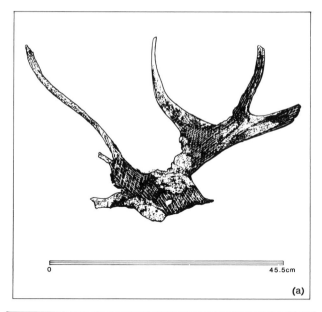

0   45.5cm

(a)

(b)

Figure 7.4 Modified red deer antler frontlet from Star Carr (a) and Sandra Hooper's imaginative reconstruction of a similar frontlet in use (b).

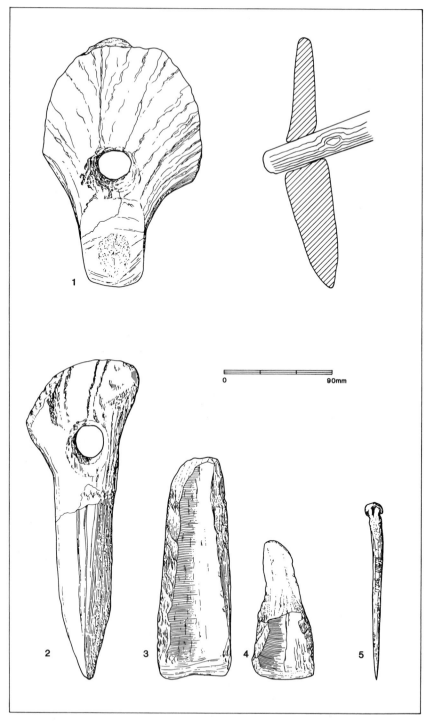

Figure 7.5 Antler and bone artefacts from Star Carr: elk antler mattocks (1, 2); scrapers made from metapodials of wild cattle (3, 4) and a bodkin made from an elk metapodial (after Clark 1971).

hearths. These differences may be more apparent than real. Clark believed he had found a deliberately constructed platform on which the hunters encamped, but apart from two putative hearths there was little sign of such activity. It seems more likely that the brushwood and birch trees were debris from making a clearing which had been thrown into the reed swamp and subsequently became an area where industrial tasks were undertaken and rubbish dumped. It is likely that the main residential area lay on drier ground and that Clark excavated part of its peripheral zone. The stone-working debris at Star Carr is known to extend upslope and, had the area away from the lake margin been excavated, remains similar to those at Seamer Carr and Flixton would probably have been exposed. Similarly, the hunters at these other sites may also have thrown their rubbish into the lake, but these discard zones have not been located.

The wealth and range of finds from Star Carr led to its being regarded as a classic example of a home base where a variety of maintenance activities was undertaken, while hunting took place in the surrounding area. In their recent study of the animal bones Legge and Rowley-Conwy point out that the butchery debris left at Star Carr consisted mainly of low-utility parts such as mandibles, shoulder blades and lower limb bones. Notably lacking, or present in small numbers only, are the main meat-yielding bones such as femora. Comparison of the Star Carr assemblage with the bones from a number of sites of known function led Legge and Rowley-Conwy to suggest that it was a temporary hunting camp rather than a home base (fig. 7.6). The trouble with these comparisons is that the sites used lay in the Arctic, the hunters in question were preying exclusively on a single species, namely caribou, and were part of a system in which hunting often occurred at a considerable distance from the home base. None of these factors applied at Star Carr. The environment was becoming increasingly temperate, a wide variety of animals was preyed upon and there seems little evidence for the kind of marked seasonal fluctuation in resources that would lead hunters to travel far from home in order to encounter prey. However, the faunal assemblage at Star Carr does lack the best bits and these were presumably removed for consumption elsewhere, though the distance involved may not have been great. Within the framework used here the area excavated at Star Carr would appear to be the peripheral zone of a home base.

Mainly on the evidence of antlers, which follow a very regular annual cycle of growth and shedding, Clark believed that Star Carr was occupied in the winter. But, as we have seen, antlers were brought to the site as a valued raw material and could be stored from season to season. If antlers are disregarded, other seasonality evidence, mainly tooth eruption in deer mandibles, points to occupation during the spring and summer. However, there are slight hints of activity at the site later in the year as well. The dentition of an elk mandible implies a late summer or autumn kill, the beaver family may have been trapped in the winter and it is perhaps

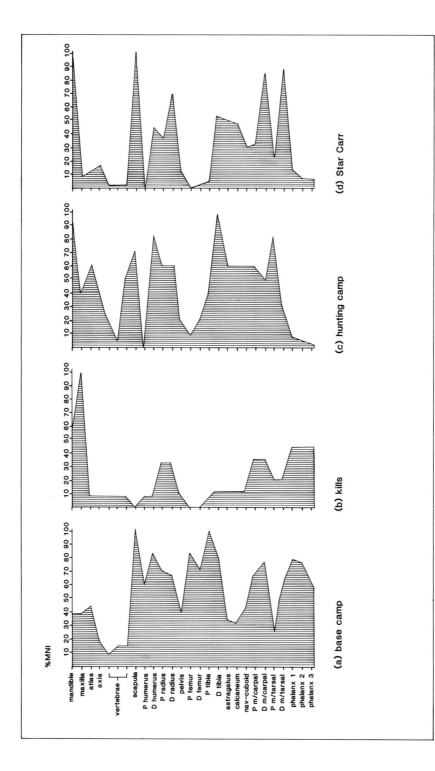

Figure 7.6 Skeletal-part analysis of red deer bones from Star Carr compared with analyses of caribou (reindeer) bones from recently occupied Nunamiut sites of differing status (redrawn with modifications from Legge and Rowley-Conwy 1988).

unreasonable totally to disregard all the antler evidence. It seems certain that Star Carr was mainly used in the summer, but occasional visits throughout the year are also likely.

THATCHAM

The site at Thatcham was an open encampment on the edge of a gravel terrace overlooking a tributary of the River Kennet, in Berkshire (NGR SU 502668) (fig. 9.4d no. 2). At the time the site was occupied the valley floor held a shallow lake and archaeological material has been recovered from both the terrace edge and the former margin of the lake (fig. 7.7a). The main excavations at the site were those of John Wymer between 1958 and 1961.

Radiocarbon dates have been obtained for material from the terrace edge and the lake margin. The former range from the mid-eleventh to mid-tenth millennium BP and thus span the conventional Lateglacial/Postglacial transition, and the transition between the late Upper Palaeolithic and the Mesolithic. Finds from the lake margin are on average several centuries later. They appear to be rubbish discarded from the adjacent encampment and suggest that occupation in the vicinity continued until towards the end of the tenth millennium BP.

Pollen analyses of the lake sediments have been carried out by Churchill, and I have selected two of his samples for comparison. Sample 5 came from towards the bottom of the sediments excavated and gives an indication of conditions early in the history of the site (fig. 7.7b). Tree and shrub species account for over 60 per cent of the pollen, with birch, pine and willow the most important, but hazel, elm and oak also present. The open-country plants were mainly grasses and sedges, and there was a range of weeds of broken-ground and lakeside species. Sample 2 (fig. 7.7c) came from a later context. The value for trees and shrubs has risen to nearly 70 per cent, mainly through an increase in pine, which becomes the most common species. Birch remains important and hazel has a similar value to willow. Open-country plants are similar to those in the lower sample, though there are fewer varieties. It seems clear that during the period the Thatcham site was used, the surrounding landscape changed from birch to birch/pine forest, with occasional other trees. Willow grew in abundance by the lake margin while hazel was the main understorey shrub and may have been prolific in openings in the canopy.

The most numerous mammal remains from the excavation of the lake margin were red and roe deer and wild pig, with remains of six, six and five individuals respectively. Horse, elk and wild cattle were also present, along with badger, marten, fox, cat, wolf and domestic dog. A skeletal-part analysis of red deer bones reveals a preponderance of limbs (fig. 7.8), suggesting that carcasses were butchered elsewhere and only useful joints brought back to the site. Of the six antlers found four were unshed.

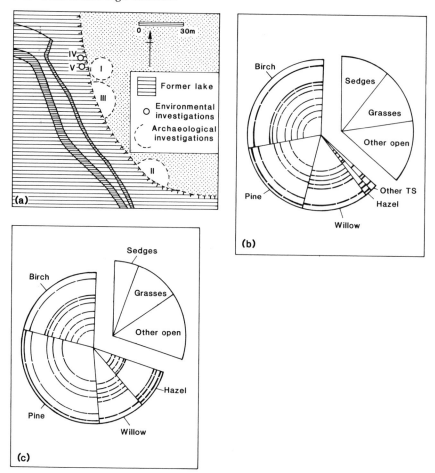

Figure 7.7 Early Postglacial sites at Thatcham: (a) location (redrawn with modifications from Wymer 1962); (b) and (c) pollen charts for Samples 5 and 2 respectively from Thatcham Site V (based on data from Churchill 1962).

Bird remains, some of which were food waste from the occupation area, were mostly of waterfowl, including mallard (*Anas platyrhynchos*), teal (*A. crecca*) or garganey (*A. querquedula*), goldeneye (*Bucephala clagula*) and possibly smew (*Mergus albellus*). Both goldeneye and smew winter in Britain but breed in northern Scandinavia and Russia. However, crane (*Grus grus*) was also identified. This bird breeds in Scandinavia, north-east Europe and Russia but flies to the Mediterranean for winter. In the tenth millennium southern Britain may have been within the breeding range of all three species. Fish remains are mentioned but not identified.

Wymer found 18,402 stone artefacts, of which 3.5 per cent were finished tools, including 285 microliths, the most common single item. Most, as at

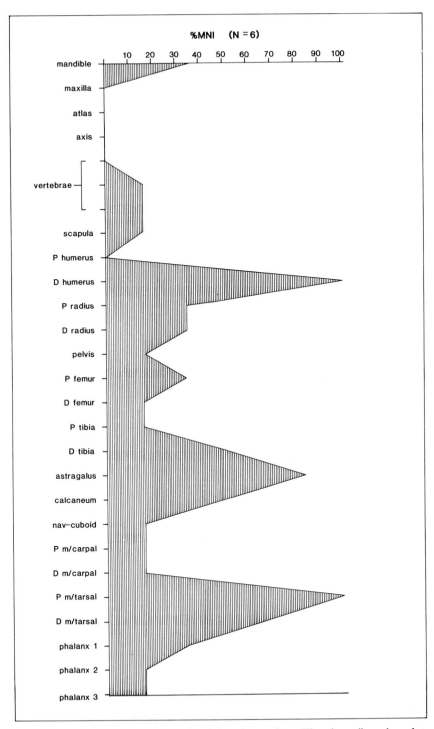

Figure 7.8 Skeletal-part analysis of red deer bones from Thatcham (based on data from King 1962), for comparison with figure 7.6 (p.120).

Star Carr, are obliquely blunted points (fig. 7.9a(i)). The assemblage also includes 61 burins, 132 scrapers and 15 awls, suggesting the familiar range of bone, antler and hide-working activities associated with a home base. Heavy-duty items include 17 axe/adzes (fig. 7.9b) used for clearing trees around the encampment, and perhaps also the making and use of dugout canoes if sufficiently large trees were available. A series of slender bone or antler points may have been fish spears or bodkins.

Wymer has published details of the density of finds made in the areas excavated on the terrace. The range is considerable – from 1 per m^2 to over 900 – and suggests that part of the site was devoted to flint knapping. The finds in Area III (fig. 7.10) formed two major clusters about 15 m apart, within which were numerous smaller clusters a metre across. Many of the clusters are alongside small hearths, and we may be able to glimpse the individual knappers at work.

The hearths included food debris in the form of burnt bone and hazel-nut shells. If these were not flint knappers' snacks, this may imply that domestic occupation also took place on the terrace. There is no clear evidence of shelters but if we assume that flint working was mainly an outside activity, a zone of low discard in Area III could mark the position of a light structure. This putative shelter would have been about 6.4 m by 5.3 m, with a floor area of 35 m^2. As such it would compare well with a number of buildings of the same age excavated at various early Postglacial sites in northern Europe. For example, a building at Duvensee in Germany was 5 m square with a floor of birch and pine bark and a similar building at Ulkestrup in Denmark was 6.7 m by 4.5 m. In each case a superstructure could have been provided by bent and tied birch saplings. Buildings of this size could accommodate no more than a single family. Occupation at Thatcham extended over a considerable area and at any one time several small shelters might have been erected on the terrace. The Scandinavian buildings are interpreted as summer residences, and this may have been the case at Thatcham also, where migratory bird evidence points to the same season.

In summary, at Thatcham we seem to have the remains of a home base used by one or more families during the summer. It occupied a clearing in birch and pine forest overlooking a lake. A wide range of animals was hunted, though red deer, roe deer and wild pig were particularly import-ant. The extent of the occupation and the range of dates suggests that this was a pattern that was maintained over a long period.

MOUNT SANDEL

Hitherto, Ireland has not featured in our case studies. Having been cut off from mainland Britain by rising sea level during the mid-tenth millennium BP, the settlement of Ireland had to be a maritime adventure. The site of Mount Sandel (INGR C 8631), on a gravel ridge overlooking the River

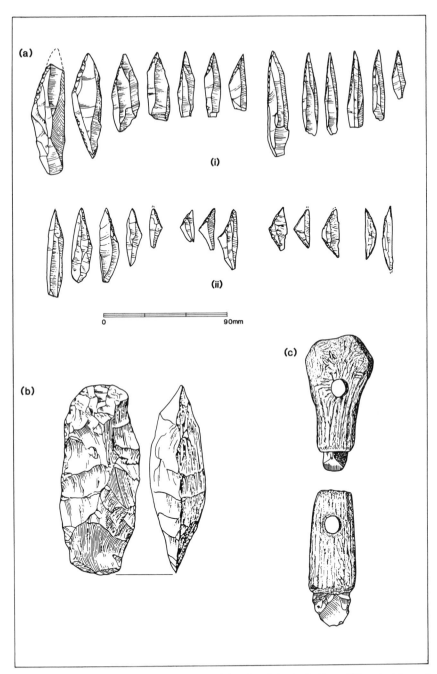

Figure 7.9 Stone tools from Thatcham: (a) microliths including obliquely blunted points (i), and geometric forms (ii); (b) an axe or adze with a suggested hafting (c) ((a) and (b) after Wymer 1962).

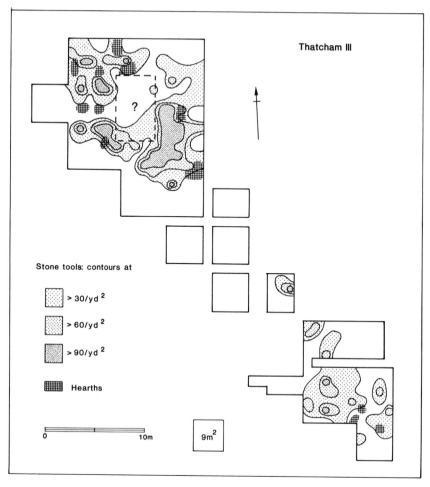

Thatcham III

Stone tools: contours at

> 30/yd²

> 60/yd²

> 90/yd²

Hearths

0   10m

9m²

Figure 7.10 Density distribution of stone tools at Thatcham Site III with the outline of a putative structure superimposed (redrawn with modifications from Wymer 1962).

Bann, lies about 9 km from the Antrim coast (figs 7.11a and 9.7a no. 2). It has been extensively excavated by Peter Woodman and is the earliest site so far recorded from Ireland, with radiocarbon dates suggesting two phases of occupation, from *c.* 9100 BP to *c.* 8500 BP, and from *c.* 8100 BP to *c.* 7650 BP.

By 9000 BP north-east Ireland was dominated by birch forest with hazel understorey (figs 9.5 and 9.6). Changes in the vegetation of the area are documented in studies of pollen from Garry Bog 7 km to the east of Mount Sandel. During the early period of occupation hazel became increasingly important but by *c.* 8500 BP elm had begun to expand into the area, followed by oak at *c.* 8000 BP (cf. fig. 9.9a and c). Plant remains from the

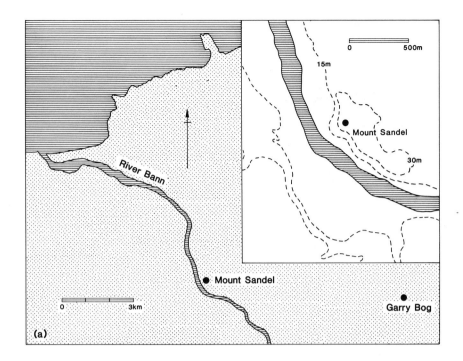

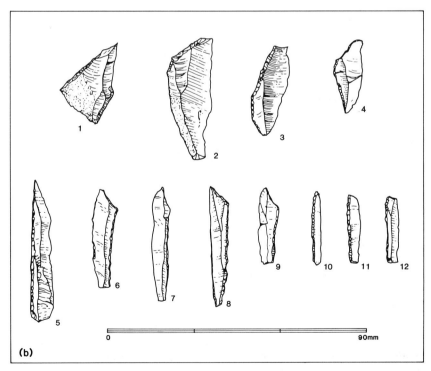

Figure 7.11 Mount Sandel: (a) location and (b) microliths including obliquely blunted points (1–4), geometric (6–9) and rod-like (10–12) forms (after Woodman 1985).

excavation include abundant hazel-nut shells, pear or apple pips, and seeds of white water-lily, all from plants which probably contributed to the diet.

Soil acidity inhibited the preservation of animal bones and only burnt fragments greater than 20 mm were studied in detail, of which 2,192 could be identified. Mammals constitute 15 per cent of the assemblage and of this 98 per cent of the fragments were from wild pig, with mountain hare, and wolf or dog making up the remainder. The number of wild pigs represented is unclear, but there were evidently several and 50 per cent were juveniles hunted during their first winter. All elements of the skeleton are present but foot and lower limb bones are overrepresented and this may have arisen from the way the Mount Sandel hunters disposed of their refuse: that is, these parts were thrown on the fires and got preserved while more useful bits of the skeleton were recycled for tool manufacture and have not survived. In addition, complete carcasses were not necessarily brought back to the encampment.

An interesting series of bird remains was found, and these can be subdivided according to whether whole birds appear to be represented or just bits. In the former case we may be dealing with prey, whereas the latter may arise from natural deaths, parts of which were preserved fortuitously. Remains of whole birds make up 75 per cent and consist of various ducks such as mallard, teal or garganey and widgeon (*Anas penelope*), and the game birds grouse, capercaillie (*Tetrao urogallus*), snipe (*Gallinago gallinago*) or woodcock (*Scolopax rusticola*), rock-dove (*Columba livia*) and wood-pigeon (*C. palumbus*). They represent a wide range of habitats including woodland, open moor and lakes, and may have been an important part of the diet. We have no idea how they were hunted, but some of the game birds and waterfowl could have been caught with nets. The more fragmentary bird remains include divers, song birds, and birds of prey including a golden (*Aquila chrysaetos*) or white-tailed (*Haliaeetus albicula*) eagle, which may have been taken for its plumage.

Eighty per cent of the bones found at Mount Sandel were of fish, and of these 48 per cent and 32 per cent came from salmon (*Salmo salar*) and sea trout (*Salmo trutta*) respectively. Eel made up 7 per cent and bass (*Dicentrarchus labrax*), an inshore fish found also in estuaries, accounted for a further 8 per cent. Weights of salmon and eel were provided in chapter 5, and sea trout and bass have average weights of 13 kg and 9 kg respectively. Salmon and sea trout are migratory and highly seasonal, entering rivers in the summer and autumn to spawn, while eels move downstream in autumn as they begin their migration to the Sargasso Sea. These species could have been caught close to the site in traps or by spearing as they moved through the rapids on the River Bann.

The animal remains suggest that the site was mainly occupied during the second half of the year and it is interesting to make the comparison with the faunal assemblage from Lough Boora, a ninth-millennium BP lakeside camp in the Irish Midlands (INGR N 1518) (fig. 9.7a no. 3). Here, wild pig were also the most important species but dentition evidence indicates that the animals were killed in the summer. Eels were the most common fish and these would only have been available in the lake in large numbers in the summer, as was also the case with another common species, the brown trout (*Salmo trutta fario*).

A total of 44,386 stone artefacts were found at Mount Sandel, and of these 1,451 or 3.3 per cent have been retouched. Microliths are the most common type, with 1,179 in the assemblage. These are mostly of the narrow-blade variety typical of later Mesolithic assemblages (fig. 7.11b nos 5–12), though some early broad-blade forms are also present (fig. 7.11b nos 1–4). Other types, such as scrapers and burins, are present in small numbers only, though a group of nearly 50 ochre-stained blades and 40 awls may indicate hide working. John Dumont studied utilization traces on 84 items and identified wood, hide and bone working in addition to the processing of meat, but it is impossible to generalize from data based on less than 0.2 per cent of the assemblage.

Although the overall pattern is distorted by the incomplete survival of occupation deposits, interesting comparisons can be made between different areas:

Table 7.2 Artefact distribution at Mount Sandel

Type	Industrial zone	Occupation area
Cores	107	23
Blades	1,579	1,270
Flakes	1,379	255
Microliths	83	210
Other 'tools'	13	36

(after Woodman 1985)

While all categories were present in both areas, the proportions vary. Cores and flakes were concentrated in the industrial zone while microliths and 'tools' were found mainly in the occupation area. Blades were common in both. From this we may infer that while maintenance activities such as the repair of equipment took place in the occupation area, flint knapping was segregated on another part of the site. This is a classic example of the relationship between the residential area and periphery expected at a home base.

Perhaps the most important aspect of the fascinating discoveries made at Mount Sandel is the unequivocal evidence for buildings, the earliest from anywhere in the British Isles. Structures of two kinds were identified, of which the most substantial were a series of oval shelters about 5.5 m across with a central pit containing a hearth (fig. 7.12). Walls were of stakes which, from the traces left in the ground, appeared to be inclined inwards, suggesting an arrangement of bent and tied saplings, while the lower parts may have been supported with turves. Six such structures were identified, but four were rebuildings on the same site. These shelters had about 30 m² of floor space and could not have accommodated more than a single family. The second kind of structure was smaller and had an external hearth. Surviving traces consisted of four lengths of curving gully enclosing an area 2.5 m across (fig. 7.13). These look like the drainage trenches campers dig, and this second structure at Mount Sandel, of which only a single example was identified, may have been a tent stance. It could have accommodated only two or three people, and is more likely to have been used by a hunting party than a larger group. This tent stance dates from the second phase of occupation and it is possible that the use of the site changed from being initially a home base to a hunting camp.

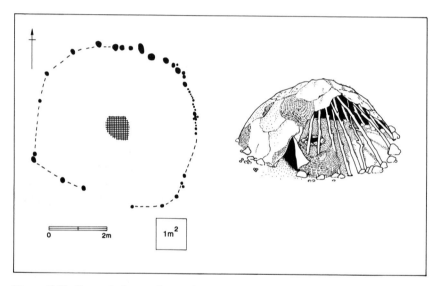

Figure 7.12 Ground plan and putative reconstruction of Hut W at Mount Sandel (plan redrawn with modifications from Woodman 1985).

A range of other features was also identified, of which the most numerous were pits. Some may have been used for storage – hazel-nuts can be stored underground – but many of the pits contained domestic refuse and we can infer that, at least while the site was used as a home base, efforts were made to keep it clean. There were numerous external hearths and, if groups of postholes can be interpreted as drying racks, we can probably infer that some of the salmon and sea trout were artificially dried, in order to preserve them for the winter.

Mount Sandel provides one of the most complete pictures we have of a hunters' home base, occupied during the late summer and autumn when supplies were abundant but when it was necessary to lay by stores for the coming winter. The diet consisted mainly of pork and smoked salmon,

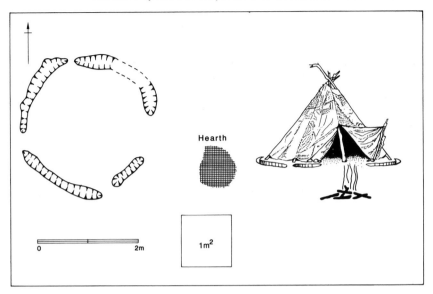

Figure 7.13 Putative tent stance at Mount Sandel (plan redrawn with modifications from Woodman 1985).

garnished with hazel-nuts! Game birds and waterfowl provided variety. The Mount Sandel hunters seem to have lived as a family-sized group, though others may have camped further along the ridge. Where they spent the rest of the year is unclear. Ireland has many coastal sites dating from early Postglacial and a move to the coast would have been a viable proposition, given the year-round availability of shellfish. Some of the flint used at Mount Sandel may have come from the north Antrim coast.

Star Carr and Thatcham were situated beside lakes and Mount Sandel overlooked a major river. The wide range of animal and plant resources available may have led to the preferential selection of such locations by early Postglacial hunters, but the fact remains that there are many thousands of sites where Mesolithic stone tools have been found which were not by lakes or rivers. Those on the coast are the subject of the next chapter, while those in the uplands will be considered below. But in order to get a balanced view we should look at one further case study from the lowlands: a home base situated in deciduous woodland and not beside a lake or river.

BROOM HILL

The site at Broom Hill in Hampshire (NGR SU 38425)(fig. 9.7a no. 5) is one of the most prolific early Postglacial settlements to be excavated in the British Isles, over 89,000 stone artefacts having been recovered. However, this is due in part to the meticulous standards of excavation and recovery employed by the excavator Michael O'Malley, though the site does seem to have been occupied over a long enough period for a substantial quantity of material to accumulate.

The remains consist of a series of hollows, one of which was almost certainly the site of a shelter. Hollow number 3 was about 0.35 m deep and virtually full of occupation debris in the form of burnt soil, charcoal, burnt hazel-nut shells and worked flint. This material has provided a series of radiocarbon dates which indicate that the hollow began to fill up around *c.* 8500 BP.

The hollow is irregular in outline and about 4 m x 3 m across (fig. 7.14). Around its outside was found a series of postholes defining an area about 5 m × 4.5 m overall. Several of the postholes were inclined inwards and, as at Mount Sandel, it appears that the hollow may have been roofed with a structure of bent and tied saplings. There was a hearth inside the shelter and the hollow is probably no more than the result of wear and tear in the central area. An extension of the hollow to the south-east might mark the position of an entrance – an area which would also receive a lot of wear.

Details of plant remains have not been published, but from regional studies we know that Broom Hill was situated in deciduous woodland in which hazel was an important component while the main canopy was made

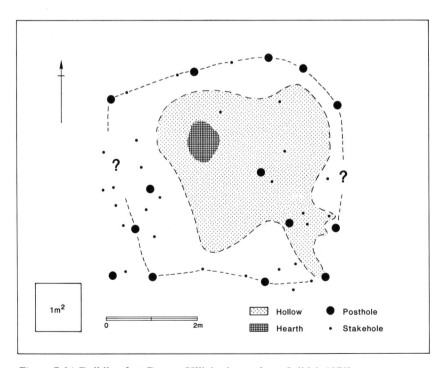

Figure 7.14 Building 3 at Broom Hill (redrawn from Selkirk 1978).

up of oak, elm and birch (figs 9.5 and 9.6). Activity at the site continued intermittently until the middle of the seventh millennium BP and during this period the composition of surrounding woodland changed significantly, with birch virtually disappearing and lime and alder becoming important (figs 9.9 and 9.10).

Several other hollows at Broom Hill, all smaller than number 3, are very irregular in outline and may mark disruption of the soil profile where trees have blown over. Such tree-fall pits are not uncommon on early Postglacial sites in deciduous woodland. The fact that such natural features often incorporate archaeological finds led in the past to their identification as pit dwellings. This is now thought unlikely, and in many cases archaeological material has probably eroded into the tree-fall pit from the surrounding area. However, such features may have been occasionally adapted to provide a temporary shelter, and deliberate occupation should not be entirely ruled out in every case.

In addition to over 2,500 microliths, mostly of narrow-blade, or late Mesolithic, types, the assemblage included 100 axes or adzes and tree felling, to create clearings and obtain raw materials and fuel, must have been a regular activity. The assemblage also includes nearly 600 scrapers and over 200 burins, indicating the usual range of maintenance activities expected at a home base. The excavated shelter would have been sufficient to accommodate a single family only, but the settlement may have included several such structures. The relatively substantial nature of the shelter might indicate winter occupation and hazel-nuts are usually collected in the autumn, though they can be stored and consumed at any time. Finds of Portland chert may be an indication that during the annual cycle at least some of the Broom Hill band got as far as the south coast.

HUNTING IN THE UPLANDS: THE SOUTHERN PENNINES

Although a number of caves on the fringes of the Pennines were occasionally visited during the Lateglacial, there is no extensive evidence for hunting in the uplands until the early Postglacial. As suggested in chapter 5, such areas became increasingly hospitable as the climate grew more temperate and rising sea levels effectively reduced their altitudinal range. A series of sites in the southern Pennines provides a glimpse of hunting in the uplands during the early Postglacial.

Deepcar

The site at Deepcar (NGR SK 292981) lies 12 km north-west of Sheffield, overlooking the valley of the River Don at an altitude of about 150 m. Opposite the site, the Don is joined by a tributary which flows down from the Derwent Moors to the north (fig. 7.15a). During the early Postglacial the 'carrland' in the bottom of the valley may have included some open water. Unfortunately no dates are available for Deepcar and there is no biological evidence. The stone tool assemblage, which included nearly 37,000 items, has been compared to those from Star Carr and Thatcham, and accordingly Deepcar is considered to date from the mid-tenth millennium also.

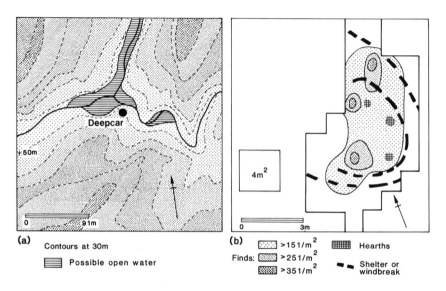

Figure 7.15 Deepcar: (a) location and (b) density distribution of stone tools and outline of putative structure (redrawn with modifications from Radley and Mellars 1964).

The main interest of Deepcar, apart from its rich flint assemblage, lies in what appear to be the remains of a small oval shelter defined by two concentric arcs of stone (fig. 7.15b). The inner arc defines an area 3.7 m by 4.6 m and includes traces of three small hearths. The outer arc is incomplete but defines an area at least 6.4 m by 8.2 m. It is not known whether these features were contemporary, but the inner arc alone would have made a very small structure whereas the outer enclosed an area of 52 m^2, just about sufficient for a single family or a party of hunters.

Most of the stone tools were found within the area of the shelter, and three clusters were identified, each about 1 m across. Only 0.4 per cent of the assemblage consisted of retouched pieces and nearly half these were microliths, while 25 per cent were scrapers. The majority of the material is debris from flint working and if the assemblage and the shelter are contemporary, the flint working evidently took place inside. The large number of finds at Deepcar implies either a stay of some duration, or repeated short-term use, and the concentration on microlith manufacture suggests that Deepcar may have been a hunting camp which acted as a temporary base for forays into the surrounding uplands.

Smaller sites

Evidence for such forays is provided by a series of small sites at altitudes above 350 m. These usually consist of concentrations of stone tools, often only about 3 m^2 in extent and associated with one or more hearths. Of two such concentrations on Warcock Hill (NGR SE 030096), west of Huddersfield and at 380 m, one has a radiocarbon date of 9210 ± 340 BP, while 4 km north at Lominot (NGR SE 006123) a similar site, at 426 m, is dated to 9565 ± 470 BP. Both dates have broad ranges but none the less imply hunting in the uplands during the latter part of the tenth millennium BP. Artefacts were quite numerous, 9,148 and 714 from the Warcock Hill sites and 3,525 at Lominot, though in each case several distinct concentrations were represented. The proportion of 'tools' was small, 1.1 per cent, 5.3 per cent and 2.3 per cent respectively, the majority of them microliths. These sites probably mark the overnight camps of hunting parties.

This pattern of upland hunting, once established, was of long duration. Site number 5 on Broomhead Moor (NGR SK 224951), dated to *c.* 8570, provides a later example of an upland hunting camp. A total of 1,652 stone artefacts, including many geometric microliths (fig. 7.16c), was found in two clusters, each about a metre across and just under 3 m apart. There was also a pattern of stakeholes which makes no sense as a shelter, but may have been a wind-break (fig. 7.16a). Pollen analyses suggest that the area was dominated by hazel scrub, while oak, alder, elm, birch, pine and lime were also growing in the area (fig. 7.16b). Open-country plants accounted for less than 30 per cent and ground up to about 500 m may have been lightly wooded.

Hunting at above 300 m is likely to have been always a summer or autumn activity and it is a pity that animal remains have not survived on any of these sites. Reindeer may still have been present in the southern Pennines in the late tenth millennium BP but the main quarry was almost certainly red deer, and this species is known to make small-scale altitudinal migrations in summer in search of food and to avoid insects. Late summer and autumn is also the time when game birds may be taken. The discovery of charcoal at some of these sites has led to the suggestion that fire may have been used in hunting, either to drive animals towards the hunters or to stimulate new growth in areas where prey could be easily ambushed. Such fires could easily get out of control and Mesolithic hunters, by initiating widespread deforestation, may have started a programme of environmental degradation of which the upland peat and heather moors familiar today are the end product.

The upland sites were part of an annual cycle which would have included a diverse range of habitats. Of the raw materials used at Deepcar 95 per cent came from sources in East Yorkshire, 80 km to the north-east. This provides some indication of the scale of operations of the Deepcar hunters

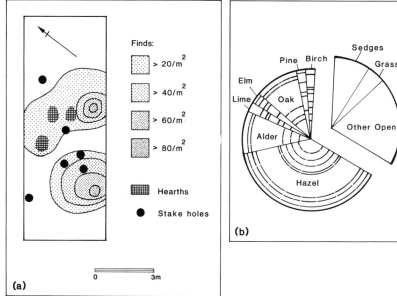

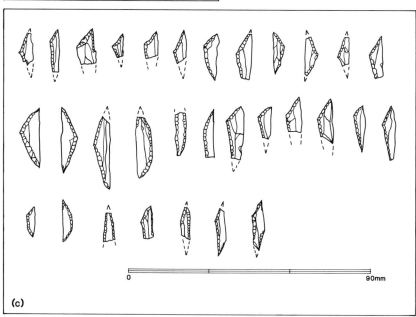

Figure 7.16 Broomhead Moor Site V: (a) density distribution of stone tools (redrawn with modifications from Radley *et al.* 1974), (b) pollen chart for sample at 0.70–0.80 mm (based on data in ibid.), (c) geometric microliths (redrawn from ibid.).

and the other groups foraging in the Pennines from the tenth millennium BP.

SPECIALIZED ACTIVITIES

In chapter 6, in addition to looking at locations which may have been home bases or hunting camps we also examined briefly several examples where the evidence suggested rather more specialized activities. In two cases, the Poulton elk and the Flixton horses, the evidence still related to economic activity but the behaviour at Kendrick's Cave had a more ritual character. Although caves continued to be occupied during the early Postglacial, albeit on a reduced scale compared to the Lateglacial, the incidence of cave burial increased and many caves where Mesolithic artefacts have been found have also contained human remains in varying degrees of completeness. The best known early Postglacial cave burial is that of the 'Cheddar Man', who was found virtually complete in a side chamber of Gough's Cave at the beginning of the century. This skeleton has recently been dated to c. 9100 BP.

The largest early Postglacial cemetery known in the British Isles was also located in a cave in the Mendip Hills. Aveline's Hole in Burrington Comb (NGR ST 476587) is believed at one time to have contained the remains of over seventy individuals. The majority were found more than 150 years ago and very little is known about them. Even those recovered between 1919 and 1933 were destroyed by enemy action during the Second World War along with the excavation records. The most completely recorded burials were discovered in 1924 when two skeletons were found crushed by a rock fall. They were slightly tinged with red ochre and associated with grave goods, the most notable of which was a group of pig and red deer incisors. Some had been pierced for suspension, while a horse incisor had its root decorated with parallel incisions similar to the specimens found at Kendrick's Cave (fig. 6.17b). A few surviving human fragments have been dated to c. 9000 BP while a modified animal bone dated to c. 12,400 BP hints at a phase of occupation in the cave during the Lateglacial Interstadial. Although few details of the burials are known, the presence of such a large number suggests that the cave was used as a cemetery over many generations.

ADDITIONAL READING

All the sites considered in this chapter have made a contribution to the study of stone tool typology. Readers interested in this topic are referred to the general works mentioned at the end of chapter 1 and to Jacobi's summary of the British Mesolithic sequence (1976).

The original excavations at Star Carr were published by Clark in 1954 and reprinted in 1971, while his reassessment appeared in 1972. The different aspects of what has become known as 'the Star Carr debate' are summarized by Legge and Rowley-Conwy (1988). The recent excavations at Seamer are yet to be published but interim summaries have been provided by Schadla-Hall (1987, 1989) while the Flixton 1 site was published by Moore (1950). In addition to the contribution of Walker and Godwin in the original Star Carr report, palaeoenvironmental studies of Lake Pickering have been published by Cloutman (1988) and Cloutman and Smith (1988). The fauna from Star Carr was originally studied by Fraser and King (1971), while the most recent account, with references to other work, is provided by Legge and Rowley-Conwy (1988). Wheeler published his views on the absence of fish in 1978 (1978a). Microwear analysis of stone tools from Star Carr has been undertaken by Dumont (1988, 1989). The dating of Star Carr has been reviewed by Day and Mellars (1995).

The original excavations at Thatcham were published by Wymer (1962), palaeoenvironmental investigations by Churchill (1962) and a study of the fauna by King (1962). More recent work at the site has been published by Healey *et al.* (1992). Details of Mesolithic huts in northern Europe are from Clark (1952, 1975), Newell (1981) and Gron (1983, 1989).

The Mount Sandel excavations are described in full by Woodman (1985), and this report includes contributions from Hamilton *et al.* on pollen from the site and from Garry Bog, van Wijngaarden-Bakker on faunal remains, and Dumont on microwear analysis. Faunal remains from Lough Boora are described by van Wijngaarden-Bakker (1989) while the site was initially published by Ryan (1980).

Interim statements on the excavations at Broom Hill have been published by O'Malley and Jacobi (1978) and Selkirk (1978), while the issue of tree-falls versus pit dwellings has been dealt with by Newell (1981) and Woodman (1985). Examples of 'pit dwellings' were described by Clark (1934), Clark and Rankine (1939) and Leakey (1951).

Examples of Mesolithic sites in the southern Pennines and adjoining upland areas are provided by Radley and Mellars (1964), Radley *et al.* (1974) and Jacobi (1978). The evidence for fire as a cause of deforestation in the Mesolithic has recently been reviewed in detail by Simmons (1996) who provides a full set of references to earlier work on this interesting topic. The development of moorlands and upland mires is dealt with by Moore (1988).

The discoveries at Aveline's Hole were described in a series of papers by J. A. Davies published between 1921 and 1925 in volumes 1 and 2 of the *Proceedings of the University of Bristol Spelaeological Society*. Summaries have been published by Garrod (1926) and more recently by Jacobi (1987). The accelerator dates appear in *Archaeometry* Datelist 4.

8 Case studies III: Coastal adaptations

In the two previous chapters we have considered a series of examples in which bands of hunters were mainly concerned with the exploitation of terrestrial prey, chiefly large grazing and browsing animals. There has been some evidence that birds were taken and, at least in the case of Mount Sandel, fishing was also important. In the deciduous woodlands, a wide range of plant foods was available but, apart from hazel-nuts, there is little direct evidence that such resources made a significant contribution to subsistence. A feature of the archaeological record from about 8000 BP is unequivocal evidence for the exploitation of marine resources. This evidence is usually in the form of accumulations of the shells of marine molluscs, sometimes in their millions, in features known as shell middens. However, it is unlikely that shellfish were often a major subsistence item, and the shells are simply the most conspicuous element in a range of food debris which usually also includes fish bones, the remains of sea birds and marine mammals and occasional, but by no means common, bones of terrestrial prey. In this chapter we shall look at some examples of coastal exploitation as represented by shell middens. Both of the case studies are taken from sites in northern Britain, where evidence for coastal exploitation is particularly well preserved and has been studied in detail. The activities at Morton appear to have included some deep-sea fishing while the sites on Oronsay could only be reached by a sea crossing of several kilometres. In both cases the use of boats is implied.

CANOES AND SKIN BOATS

The hunters of the Lateglacial arrived in Britain dryshod by walking across the land bridge from the Continent and there is little evidence that they took much interest in marine resources. Rivers had occasionally to be crossed but this need imply nothing more elaborate than a floating log. The early Postglacial sites of Thatcham and Star Carr were both situated beside lakes, and this has led to the assumption that the occupants employed some form of water craft. At Star Carr Clark found what he took to be a paddle and, on the assumption that the surrounding birch forests would not include trees of sufficient size for dugout canoes, argued in favour of the use of skin boats. Birch-bark canoes might be considered an alternative, and enigmatic rolls of birch bark found at Star Carr might have been primitive puncture kits. However, birches of the kind used by North American Indians did not grow in early Postglacial Britain, and it might be doubted whether our native birch trees ever produced sheets of bark of sufficient size for canoe manufacture to be practicable.

The earliest unequivocal evidence for water craft dates from the ninth millennium BP when the settlement of the Inner Hebrides and Ireland began. These developments will be looked at in more detail in chapter 9, but neither would have been possible without an effective means of marine transport. In the context of the British Isles in the early Postglacial, the choice appears to have been between skin boats or logboats.

Skin boats leave few archaeological traces, but their use can be inferred from a number of factors. In the first place, a skin-working technology of the level required in boat building had existed since at least the Lateglacial. People were regularly wearing skin clothing and, in addition to the ubiquitous flint scrapers, the presence of awls and needles suggests that such clothing might have become quite elaborate in its tailoring and fastenings. It is also assumed that tents and other temporary shelters were usually roofed with hides stretched over a timber frame. In many respects a skin boat is very like an inverted and scaled-down version of such a shelter, and it is intriguing that skin boats are usually built upside-down. Skin boats are very seaworthy and are capable of long voyages, such as the journeys made by Irish monks to Iceland in the early Middle Ages. Skin boats are still regularly in use on the west coast of Ireland, where curraghs are employed in inshore fishing and provide transport between the mainland and offshore islands, while there are numerous parallels with the Eskimo umiak, used for transport, fishing and the hunting of marine mammals (plate xiiia).

It seems likely that the settlement of Ireland and the Inner Hebrides was accomplished with skin boats not unlike the curragh or umiak. Although no archaeological traces of these craft survive in Britain, Stone Age rock carvings from western Norway perhaps provide some indication of what they were like (fig. 8.1).

Most people's idea of a primitive boat is a dugout canoe, but it would have been a rash person who ventured far in such a craft in the cold, stormy waters around the British Isles and the tidal surges of the Inner Hebrides and St George's Channel. The use of dugout canoes must have been mainly confined to rivers and lakes.

Dugout canoes belong to the logboat family which is thought to have been ancestral to most of the plank-built craft familiar today. It is simply its most basic form, and before metal tools led to developments in carpentry in the fourth millennium BP most dugouts were little more than hollowed-out tree trunks. Indeed the difficulty of doing even this with stone tools must have been considerable and time consuming, though the judicious use

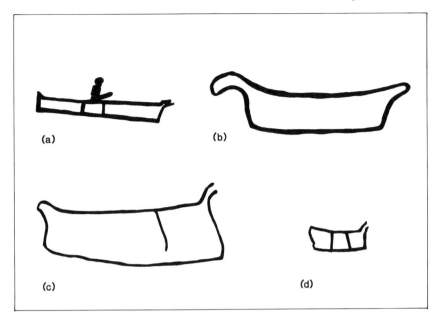

Figure 8.1 Norwegian Stone Age rock carvings of skin boats: (a) Rodoy (b) Forselv (c) and (d) Evenlus (after Clark 1952 plate IV(b) and Johnstone 1980 figs 9.1, 9.3).

of fire would speed up the process. The first requirement, of course, is suitable trees. Clark felt that this was unlikely in the early Postglacial boreal forests, but contemporary birch and pine woods may give a poor indication of what these earlier forests were like and, by the eighth millennium, with the spread of deciduous woodland, suitable trees would have been plentiful. Examples are recorded of immense oak and pine trees recovered from peat deposits which must have stood 30 m before the first branch, while the largest British logboat, the third-millennium BP example from Brigg, was only about 15 m long.

Logboats are not uncommon finds, several hundred being known from the British Isles, though few survive today. Of the surviving examples which have been securely dated, none are earlier than the fourth millennium BP and, were it not for evidence from Denmark, there might be some doubt that Late Stone Age hunters used craft of this kind. The best example of a Mesolithic logboat is the dugout canoe recently found at Tybrind Vig, in the Little Belt in Denmark. This craft (fig. 8.2) is fashioned out of a single log of lime. It is 9 m long, about 0.65 m wide, with sides at least 0.2 m high, though two planks found in the hull might have been used to raise the freeboard to about 0.4 m. It had a boulder near the stern, which it is assumed was used to provide ballast. Right at the stern were remains of a fireplace on a pad of clay. The stern itself was missing, but appears to have consisted of a board which was held in place by pegs, or tenons mortised into the hull. The Tybrind Vig boat has a radiocarbon date

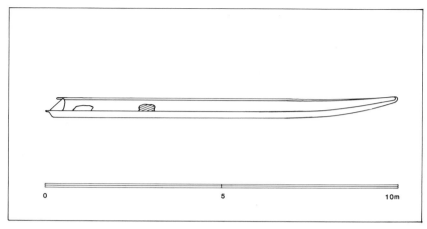

0   5   10m

Figure 8.2 Reconstruction drawing of the sixth-millennium BP dugout canoe from Tybrind Vig, Denmark (redrawn from Anderson 1985).

of *c.* 5260 BP while a similar lime log dugout from Praestelyngen, also in Denmark, has a date of *c.* 5000 BP. A very similar logboat from Toome on the north shore of Lough Neagh in Northern Ireland has been described by Peter Woodman. This was made from oak, and was just over 6 m long, about 0.75 m wide and 0.25m deep. Like the Tybrind Vig boat it had a boulder near the stern, but whether these weights were intended for ballast or just to stop the boats from floating away is unclear. The Toome boat is undated but a late Mesolithic Bann Flake was found in the hull and other stone tools collected nearby suggest a Mesolithic or Neolithic date.

For long considered to be the best example of a Mesolithic logboat from Britain is the example from the Friarton Brick works, Perth, found in about 1880 but no longer surviving. This consisted of a log of pine about 4.5 m long, from which had been hollowed out a cavity 1.8 m long and 0.6 m deep. Traces of charring suggest that this had been accomplished by the use of fire. Its dating to the early Postglacial rests on the fact that it is reported to have been found below deposits laid down at the time of the Main Postglacial Transgression, which in the Firth of Tay occurred during the seventh millennium BP. However, these stratigraphical relationships were not fully recorded at the time of the discovery, and, as Sean McGrail has pointed out, the dating of the Friarton boat is by no means secure. From the description, this craft seems to have been similar to one found at Pesse in the Netherlands. This was also made from pine and has been dated to *c.* 8300 BP (plate XIIIb). But it is by no means certain that the Pesse find was indeed a boat, rather than a trough or coffin, and the same doubts also apply to the Friarton boat, in view of the small size of the cavity compared with the overall length of the log.

The existence of unequivocal logboats in southern Scandinavia in the sixth millennium BP makes their use in Britain at the same time very likely.

Their use much earlier than this is more open to question. If skin boats were used at sea they could also be used on inland waters and the Welsh coracle may offer a contemporary analogy similar to that provided by the Irish curragh.

MORTON

Situated about 4 km from the present coast, during the seventh millennium BP the sites at Morton (NGR NO 467257) (figs 8.3a and 9.7c no. 2) may have occupied a small island joined to the mainland at low tide (fig. 8.3b). Traces of human activity have been studied at two locations on the former island, Morton A and Morton B (fig. 8.3c), the former consisting of a cluster of hearths, stakehole arrangements and stone tools, the latter a midden.

Radiocarbon dates are available from both areas, but four of the seven dates from Site A were obtained from composite samples and should be disregarded. The remaining three, two from Hearth T53.1 and one from a burnt stake in cutting T42, form a tight group with a mean value of *c.* 6380 BP. Three dates were obtained from the midden, and although the mean value of *c.* 6200 BP is a little later than the dates from Site A, the samples were taken from various levels within the midden. The lowest, and presumably the earliest, of the midden samples gave a date of *c.* 6380 BP and we may assume that the midden began to accumulate while hunters camped around the hearths on Site A.

An aspect of the material from Morton which has attracted comment is the presence in the stone tool assemblage of a range of microlith types normally considered to be of early Mesolithic date (fig. 8.4). Did these socalled 'early' types survive late on the east coast of Scotland or was Morton occupied much earlier than the dates suggest? This problem cannot be resolved at present, but there is evidence elsewhere in Scotland for occupation during the ninth millennium BP when early Mesolithic assemblages would not seem so out of place. The seventh-millennium BP occupations at Morton are well dated and it is on these that we shall focus.

The Main Postglacial Transgression reached its maximum extent on the east coast of Scotland early in the seventh millennium BP and by the time hunters began to camp regularly at Morton, and dump their rubbish on the beach, sea levels were already falling. Apart from the presence of hazelnut shells and charcoal we know little about the vegetation, though a recent study of land snails identified mainly species of shady woodland environments and fallen timber. The regional picture is one of open deciduous woodland with oak, elm and hazel predominant and it has been suggested that the immediate vicinity of the site included areas of salt marsh and intertidal mudflats (figs 8.3b and 9.9).

The midden, which was an elongated feature 30 m by 3.5 m and up to 0.75 thick, was mainly composed of shellfish remains, of which cockle

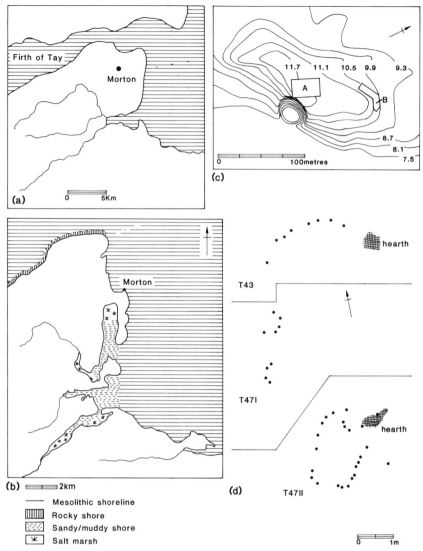

Figure 8.3 Morton, Fife: (a) location (b) the seventh-millennium BP environment (redrawn with modifications from Deith 1986) (c) Sites A and B (the hollow on the south side is a disused andesite quarry), (d) windbreaks and other shelters at Morton A (figs (c) and (d) are redrawn from Coles 1971).

(*Cerastoderma edule*) and Baltic tellin (*Macoma balthica*) were the most abundant. These are both bivalves and typical of a sandy foreshore. Thirty-eight other species were identified, and although these may indicate catholic tastes and a willingness to range widely, they are present in small numbers only.

A total of 1,818 animal bones was found during the excavation of the

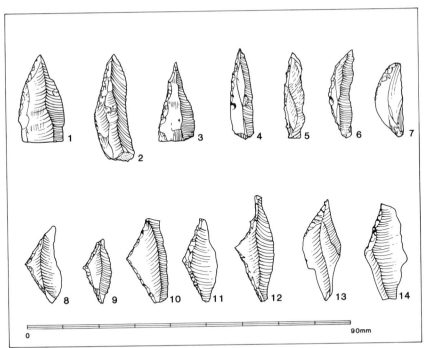

Figure 8.4 A selection of microliths from Morton A including two obliquely blunted points (nos 13 and 14) (after Coles 1971).

midden but only 9 per cent could be identified beyond the mammal/bird/ fish level. Of the 325 mammal bones 22 were identified to species. These include remains of two red deer, one roe, two wild cattle, a wild pig and a hedgehog.

Eleven species of birds were identified among the 217 bird bones, of which the most common were guillemot (*Uria aalge*), gannet (*Sula bassana*), cormorant (*Phalacrocorax carbo*) and razorbill (*Alca torda*). During the spring and early summer these birds nest on the ledges of rocky cliffs, and can be caught by a skilled climber. Suitable sites lay within 10 km of Morton along the southern shore of the Firth of Tay and it seems likely that sea birds may have played an important part in the diet.

Fish bones were the most numerous, nearly 1,000 being recognized, 10 per cent of which could be identified. Over 90 per cent of the identifiable bones were of cod, and, as both heads and caudal vertebrae were present, it appears that whole fish were being processed. Cod enter inshore waters during the autumn and winter. As they are difficult to catch from the shore, their presence in such large numbers must imply the use of boats. Cod can reach up to 50 kg in weight and average 11 kg, but this is put into perspective by the remains of a single sturgeon (*Acipenser sturio*), which may have been 3 m long and weighed 250 kg! The taking of such a large fish from a skin boat is vividly evocative of the hazards that had occasionally to be faced by the Morton hunters.

The archaeological remains at Site A consisted of a series of hearths, groups of stakeholes (fig. 8.3d), and scatters of discarded artefacts, typically about 1.5 m across. The stakehole settings suggest very insubstantial structures, more like wind-breaks than shelters and some, situated close to hearths, may mark the positions of racks for drying cod. Remains excavated in cutting T53 consisted of a hearth represented by charcoal, burnt bone, fired sand and pebbles. Of the 690 artefacts found, 77 were in a dense cluster within 0.5 m of the hearth. Types included cores and knapping debris, utilized flakes and blades and retouched pieces which made up about 5 per cent of the assemblage. Most of the retouched pieces were microliths, though scrapers and burins were also present. John Coles, the excavator, thought the hearth had been used on just two or three occasions.

The midden at Site B rested on the shingle of a raised beach dating from the Main Postglacial Transgression and we should not forget that earlier deposits may have been removed by the rising sea level. However, the earliest levels of the midden appear to be contemporary with the dated occupations at Site A. The development of the midden was intermittent, a number of distinct weathering horizons being noted when there was a temporary cessation of accumulation. The midden probably formed part of the area peripheral to the occupations which took place at Site A, but was itself also the scene of occupation on a similar scale. This activity is represented by areas of deliberate levelling and settings of stone which may mark the positions of hearths or supports for light structures. Most produced very few artefacts and are thought to represent stays of short duration. Typical assemblages are those from cuttings T50 and T59, which formed a single area. One consisted of a couple of heavy-duty stone tools, called by Coles 'bashed lumps', a core, six flakes, a burin and a microlith. Animal remains included mammals, cod, sea birds and shellfish. Another occupation extended over an area of 3 m by 2.5 m and was focused around a stone-built hearth. Finds included six chopping tools, a core, twenty-five flakes, four segments of bone with polished ends and a range of animal remains. The area immediately around the hearth had been kept clear of stone and bone debris.

Several interesting points emerge from a comparison of these two sites. The first to note is the contrast in the quantity of material recovered. Over 13,000 stone artefacts were found on Site A and 372 on Site B. This discrepancy may have arisen because Site A was occupied for a longer period, but there may also have been some segregation of activities at Morton, stone working mainly taking place on Site A. That the latter was the case is implied by the distribution of different types. For example, on Site A 1.7 per cent of the stone artefacts found were microliths, whereas only a single example (0.2%) was found on Site B. Whatever activities took place on the midden they did not seem to involve the use or manufacture of microliths. The survival of animal remains on Site B and their virtual absence from Site A is partly due to contrasting soil conditions, but can also be attributed to the habit of the Morton people of dumping their food waste on the midden.

The small scale and intermittent nature of the occupation at Morton raises the question of whether the site was favoured at a particular time of the year. While cod is most likely to have been fished during the autumn and winter, nesting sea birds could have been caught during the spring and early summer. Studies of incremental shell growth in cockles indicate that shellfish gathering took place in both the summer and the winter, with the emphasis on the latter season. If the acquisition of any particular resource was the reason for people to visit Morton, this was clearly available in more than one season. One such resource is raw material for stone working and Morton is notable for the variety of materials used. Most of these outcrop naturally within a radius of about 50 km of the site but many can also be conveniently collected as pebbles on the beaches around the site.

During the late seventh millennium BP the main focus of interest at Morton appears to have been the availability of raw materials. When visits were made during the summer, sea birds were taken from the cliffs and during the autumn and winter there was the possibility of fishing for cod. Shellfish were available all year round, but may have been collected as much for bait as for human consumption. Some terrestrial mammals were also consumed, but they were probably brought to the site already jointed. Looked at within our interpretative framework, Morton appears more like a field camp than a home base. The scale of occupation is what we would expect if visits were made by a task group only, rather than the whole band. An inference to be drawn from this is that a hitherto undiscovered home base lies somewhere within the general area.

CNOC COIG

The Cnoc Coig shell midden is one of a group of five such sites on the small Hebridean island of Oronsay (NGR NR 361885) (figs 8.5 and 9.7d no. 4; plate xva). These sites have been known to archaeologists for over a century and in the 1970s were the subject of a detailed study by Paul Mellars, who excavated in several of the middens. Cnoc Coig is the most completely studied of the middens.

Radiocarbon dates from all five sites indicate that the middens were accumulating between *c.* 6100 BP and *c.* 5400 BP, though individual sites were in use at different times during this period, with Cnoc Coig being one of the latest. Today the middens stand more than 10 m above the high-tide mark but sea level was about 9 m higher at the time they began to form and in his 1913 excavations at Cnoc Sligeach, Henderson Bishop recorded that the lower levels of the midden were interstratified with storm-beach

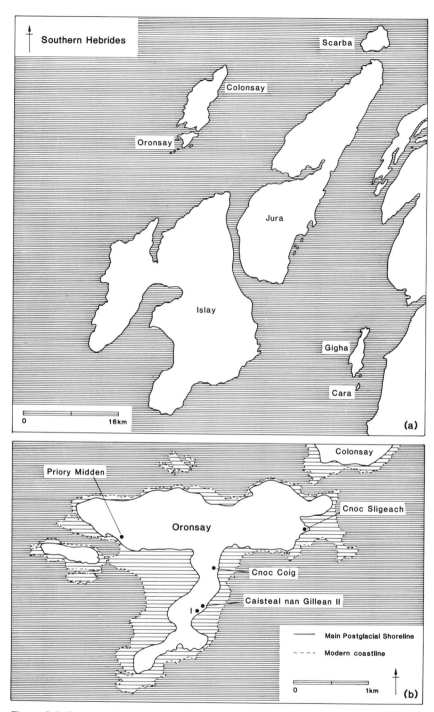

Figure 8.5 Oronsay: (a) location, (b) shell midden sites and coastline at the time of the Main Postglacial Transgression (redrawn from Mellars 1987).

deposits. It appears that it was important for the middens to be situated as close as possible to the water's edge. In some cases their occupants were in danger of being struck by flying shingle during storms. Such an exposed position would offer at least one distinct advantage, namely some relief from the ravages of biting insects, especially the Highland Midge (*Culicoides impunctatus*) whose activities are severely restricted once wind speeds exceed 5.5 m.p.h. As anyone who has undertaken fieldwork in the Highlands during the summer or even attempted to spend a holiday there knows, a beach in a strong breeze can often be the only place where survival seems possible!

In western Scotland sea level at the time of the Maximum Postglacial Transgression, in the mid-seventh millennium BP, was higher than at any time since the Lateglacial and earlier middens are likely to have been destroyed by rising sea levels. With sea levels this high Oronsay was considerably reduced in size, and may have been wholly separated from the neighbouring island of Colonsay, which today can be reached dryshod at low tide.

At the time the middens were accumulating Oronsay was cloaked in a mantle of birch–hazel scrub, a very different situation from the treeless, windswept landscape of today. There is also some evidence that gales may have been less frequent and the passage to Oronsay from the larger islands of Islay or Jura, or even the mainland, would have been less hazardous.

The islands of Oronsay and Colonsay are surrounded by deep waters and their terrestrial mammalian fauna, apart from the otter (*Lutra lutra*), is virtually non-existent. Other, larger, animals such as deer and wild pig had simply not spread as far as this by the time the islands were cut off towards the end of the Lateglacial. However, the offshore islets and skerries are important breeding and moulting sites for grey seals, the waters are rich in fish, especially saithe, and the extensive rocky foreshore abounds in limpets. This situation is reflected in a surprisingly precise fashion in the faunal remains recovered from the middens.

Terrestrial mammals are represented by red deer and wild pig. In both cases the skeletal parts present are mostly not those that would be expected if animals were being butchered on site, or even consumed there. The main meat-yielding bones and the usual butchery waste are both missing (fig. 8.6). Instead there is a highly selective assemblage of bones and antlers, mainly of the types used in the manufacture of artefacts, principally the ubiquitous 'limpet scoops', but including harpoons and, in the case of the red deer antlers, mattocks (fig. 8.7). It seems likely that the deer and wild pig remains were brought to Oronsay as raw materials for use in tool manufacture. These imports may have included the occasional meaty joint, but the evidence for this is rare and these species were mostly consumed elsewhere.

Remains of six or seven otters were found at Cnoc Coig, and the evidence of the bones identified indicates that whole carcasses were being

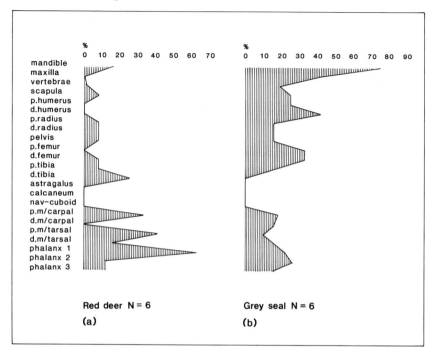

Figure 8.6 Skeletal-part analyses for six red deer and six adult grey seals from the Cnoc Coig midden, Oronsay (based on data from Grigson in Mellars 1987; for the method of calculation see Legge and Rowley-Conwy 1988): compare with figs 7.6 and 7.8 (pp. 120 and 123).

processed. Concentrations of otter bones might represent whole animals and the absence of evidence for butchery suggests that otters may have been principally taken for their pelts. Otters are common on the island today and were perhaps caught in traps, a procedure which would minimize damage to their pelts.

Remains of grey seals constitute about 60 per cent of the fauna recovered at Cnoc Coig and, unlike red deer and wild pig, skeletal-part representation is such as to suggest that whole animals were being butchered at the midden (fig. 8.6). A minimum of at least nine or ten individuals is represented, including both pups and adults. The assemblage also includes three bones of common or harbour seal and some vertebrae and ribs from a dolphin or porpoise. Grey seals are represented in all the Oronsay middens while dolphin or porpoise is also reported from the Cnoc Sligeach midden (NGR NR 371889). Bones of a large cetacean, probably a common rorqual, were found during the recent excavations at Priory Midden (NGR NR 359889) and there is a nineteenth-century record of a similar find from the Caisteal nan Gillean I midden (NGR NR 359879).

The taking of marine mammals was obviously an important activity for

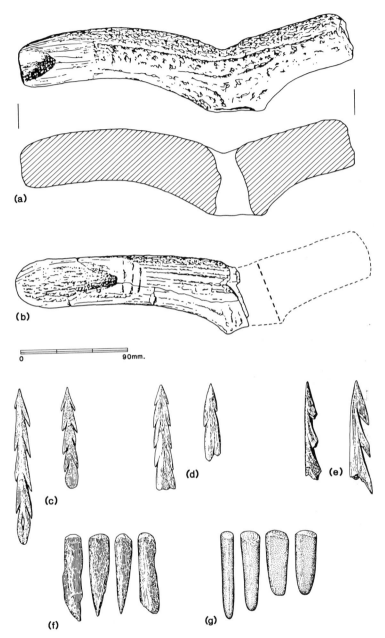

Figure 8.7 Artefacts regarded as typical of the 'Obanian' culture from various sites: (a) and (b) mattocks made from the beams of red deer antlers; (c) and (d) biserial bone or antler harpoons; (e) uniserial bone or antler harpoons; (f) bone or antler 'limpet scoops'; (g) stone 'limpet scoops' ((a) Meiklewood; (b) Risga; (c) MacArthur Cave; (d), (f) and (g) Caisteal nan Gillean I; (e) Druimvargie Rock Shelter) (redrawn from Clark 1956, Lacaille 1954 and Mellars 1987).

the Oronsay hunters. Grey seals could have been harpooned or clubbed while out of the water during their moulting or breeding seasons and the dolphins, porpoises and rorquals may have been driven ashore, or taken advantage of when stranded. However, in view of the long period of time over which the middens were accumulating, the number of individual animals involved is small. Activity at Cnoc Coig spanned a period of at least 150 years, and even if allowance is made for the 30 per cent of the midden not excavated, a total of perhaps a dozen grey seals is a small harvest.

If hunting grey seals was not the main objective what else could have been the *raison d'être* for the intensive activity on this small island 6,000 years ago? The middens are composed mainly of the shells of limpets, millions per midden, and we might therefore assume that people came to Oronsay to collect limpets. This is unlikely. Of the wide range of shellfish available around the coasts of the British Isles limpets are one of most unpalatable, and in the recorded past have generally been consumed only in emergencies when most other foods have failed. Limpets are also ubiquitous on rocky shores and it would not be necessary to make the dangerous journey to Oronsay to secure virtually infinite supplies.

As is the case with all shell middens, the shellfish remains are simply the most conspicuous element. Far less conspicuous, but probably of much greater importance in delineating major areas of economic activity, are fish bones. Although a detailed study of the fish remains from the Oronsay middens is yet to be published, it has been estimated that the total meat weight represented by fish remains in certain levels of the middens was equivalent to that of limpets, and fish are, of course, of far greater food value. Saithe account for 95 per cent of the fish remains recovered from Cnoc Coig and it seems that one of the main incentives for coming to Oronsay was to fish for saithe in the inshore waters. Indeed, the reason for gathering limpets may have been to provide bait, either for lines or to scatter on the surface like bread crumbs so that the fish could then be netted or caught in fish traps by the falling tide. In the nineteenth century, shellfish were regularly used as bait by Scottish fishermen and the quantity of the bait used could be equivalent, in terms of weight, to that of the fish caught. The fish remains at Cnoc Coig were found in distinct concentrations and may represent the processing of individual catches.

Other animals represented in the midden include thirty species of bird, details of which are not yet available, and various crustaceans including crabs, which could have been a seasonally important source of food. Plant foods are represented, as usual, by the ubiquitous shells of hazel-nuts, which may have been abundant on the island.

Although strictly speaking part of the faunal assemblage, the small numbers of human bones from the Oronsay middens exhibit no traces of butchery and are unlikely to be food waste. Neither are they likely to be formal burials, the range of bones represented being very restricted and consisting mostly of fingers and toes. It is difficult to offer a satisfactory explanation for the presence of these human remains but one possibility is that funerary rituals may have included a stage during which corpses were exposed on scaffolds while decomposition took place. The clean bones may then have been bagged for burial elsewhere, and in the process small bones of the kind found in the middens could have been lost.

Cnoc Coig lies on the eastern side of the island and formed in the lee of an outcrop of solid rock, while surrounding sand dunes may have provided further protection. About 70 per cent of the midden has been examined and it is clear that it consists of a number of distinct accumulations of shellfish remains up to 0.65 m deep (fig. 8.8a). At least two of the major heaps were associated with the remains of oval shelters represented by arcs of stakeholes. Each structure was about 3.5 m across and had a central hearth. In addition, other hearths were found throughout the midden, but particularly along the northern side where some shelter was offered by the rock outcrop (fig. 8.8b). Within the make-up of the midden, lenses of burnt material were frequently encountered, suggesting that from time to time hearths were raked out, and surplus ash and debris dumped to one side. The whole site appears to have been the scene of intense activity, each successive phase taking place partly on the debris of previous phases and ultimately leading to the formation of the midden as a distinct topographical feature. Occasional lenses of dune sand confirm that this activity was intermittent.

Details of the artefacts recovered during the recent excavations have not been published but it is reported that they are much the same as those found during earlier work on the middens in the late nineteenth and early twentieth centuries. The most numerous finds from all the excavations consist of small, elongated pebbles or slivers of bone or antler carefully bevelled at one or both ends (fig. 8.7f and g). It has been suggested that they were used for gouging limpets from their shells, and they are often referred to as 'limpet scoops'. However, limpets are easily enough evicted, particularly if heated, without the need for a specialized tool, and these implements are more likely to have been used for some other purpose – skin working has been suggested. Rather larger pebbles with battered ends are described as 'limpet hammers', which seems plausible given the difficulty of gathering these animals, unless they can be taken by surprise. A swift lateral blow with a suitable pebble is usually found to be effective. More specialized implements consist of barbed points of bone or antler, probably harpoons (fig. 8.7c, d and e) and heavy-duty tools made of red deer antler and referred to as mattocks (fig. 8.7a and b). These are well suited to both digging and dismembering carcasses: and a well-known example from Meiklewood in the Royal Museum of Scotland (fig. 8.7a) was found with the remains of a stranded whale. The only ornaments found are numerous perforated cowrie-shells, probably worn in necklaces.

Similar finds were recovered from a midden on the island of Risga in

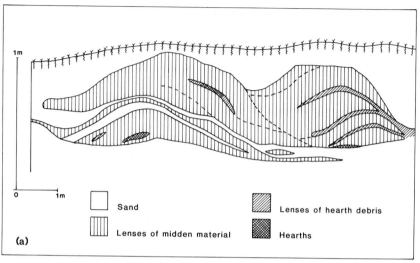

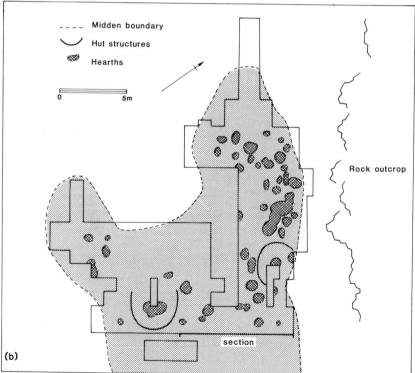

Figure 8.8 Cnoc Coig midden, Oronsay: (a) schematic section (note vertical exaggeration) (b) plan showing structures within midden and hearth areas (redrawn with modifications from Mellars 1987).

Loch Sunart (NGR NM 610602) and from middens in two natural shelters at Oban, the Druimvargie Rock Shelter (NGR NN 855295) and MacArthur Cave (NGR NN 860300) (fig. 8.7a–e). These finds are thought to be broadly contemporary, and are grouped together by archaeologists as the 'Obanian' culture, a specifically late Mesolithic manifestation orientated towards coastal exploitation. Although chipped stone tools are found in the middens, examples of familiar Mesolithic types such as microliths are notably lacking. Assemblages with microliths are known from the Inner Hebridean islands of Islay, Jura and Rhum but the radiocarbon dates place these assemblages rather earlier than most of the shell middens.

It was noted above that the Oronsay middens were situated close to what must have been the high-tide mark. Sea level had been rising for the previous 2,000 years and any earlier middens, perhaps contemporary with the microlithic assemblages on Jura and Islay, would have been destroyed. In addition, recently obtained radiocarbon dates of *c.* 7800 BP for a barbed point from the Druimvargie Rock Shelter and *c.* 7660 BP for a newly discovered midden at the Ulva Cave, Mull (NGR NM 431384) (plate xic) demonstrate at least some overlap between the middens and the microlithic assemblages. It now seems likely that both are facets of a single way of life which developed in the Inner Hebrides once people became established there, the lack of early shell middens being due to their destruction by rising sea levels.

If this suggestion is correct, and fishing for saithe and hunting marine mammals was just one aspect of a wider pattern of subsistence, we might expect some evidence that the Oronsay middens were occupied on a seasonal, or at least intermittent, basis. Saithe, like most fish, spawn at a regular time of the year and initially grow rapidly. This growth is particularly well recorded in their otoliths, small bones found in the ear, and measurements of otoliths from contemporary saithe show that it is possible to distinguish the age of the fish and the season in which they were caught (fig. 8.9a and b). Similar measurements of over a thousand saithe otoliths from Cnoc Coig (fig. 8.9c) indicate that most of these fish were caught during the autumn. This accords well with other indications of autumnal occupation such as the shells of hazel-nuts and the bones of grey seal pups.

Otoliths from the other middens have also been measured and indicate activity at other seasons, such as summer and winter. However, in these cases only a small part of each midden has been examined and it is not known whether the results are representative of the sites as a whole. Although most of the fishing at Cnoc Coig took place during the autumn, there is evidence for brief episodes during the summer and winter, and the high proportion of bull grey seal remains might indicate sealing during the spring when these animals are moulting and can be easily caught while hauled out on rocky skerries.

If activity on Oronsay represents only part of an annual cycle, do we have any indication of what other areas were regularly visited? I am

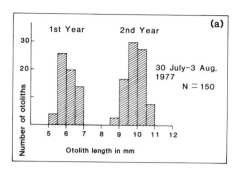

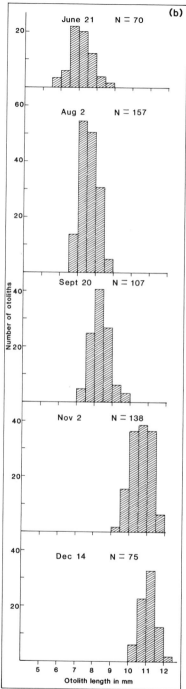

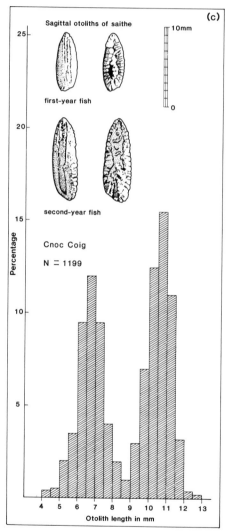

Figure 8.9 Saithe otoliths and the seasonality of activity at Cnoc Coig midden: (a) fish caught in the Inner Hebrides between 30 July and 3 August 1977 belong to two clear size categories which may be equated with their age in years; (b) the mean size of second-year fish caught on five different dates during the second half of 1978 can be seen to increase in a systematic fashion; (c) otoliths collected from the Cnoc Coig midden indicate that both first- and second-year fish were caught; comparison with 8.9(b) implies that most fishing at Cnoc Coig took place in the autumn (redrawn from Mellars and Wilkinson 1980).

inclined to accept the views that the microlithic assemblages on Jura and Islay reflect another facet of this way of life, but as the sites in question do not have faunal assemblages, seasonality data are lacking. The Oronsay hunters clearly had access to herds of red deer and wild pig, whose remains they brought to the island for industrial purposes. There were probably herds of these animals on Jura or Islay, where the annual round of the Oronsay hunters may have included one or more seasons devoted to the exploitation of terrestrial, as opposed to marine, prey.

Lastly, it would be interesting to establish whether the people who regularly travelled to Oronsay from the larger islands were entire families or bands rather than members of specialist task groups. The human bones found in several of the middens include the remains of men, women and children and it would appear that entire families made the seasonal move to Oronsay.

From *c.* 7000 BP sea levels fell intermittently until the present level was reached about 500 years later. As a consequence shell middens post-dating the Main Postglacial Transgression have not been subject to destruction by wave action, and numerous examples survive from later periods, though not on Oronsay. The exploitation of coastal resources continued throughout prehistory and elements of a way of life followed by the 'Obanian' Late Stone Age hunters continued until quite recent times. But from about 5500 BP this was within the context of a regional economy in which food production, or farming, was becoming increasingly important. The complex interrelationships between wild and domesticated resources and between hunters and farmers lie beyond the scope of this book.

ADDITIONAL READING

The development of marine transport has received a good deal of attention and authoritative accounts have been published by Greenhill (1976), Johnstone (1980) and McGrail (1987). Details of the Tybrind Vig and Toome boats are taken from Anderson (1985) and Woodman (1978) respectively, while Anderson (1994) has recently published details of additional finds from Denmark. Data on the stature of ancient trees are from Rackham (1980).

The excavations at Morton have been published by Coles (1971, 1983), while problems of the dating of the artefacts have been discussed in a group of papers by Bonsall, Clarke and Wickham-Jones, Myers, and Woodman, published in *Scottish Archaeological Review* 1988. The seasonality of the occupations at Morton has been dealt with by Deith (1983, 1986, 1989).

The recent excavations on the island of Oronsay have yet to be published in full, but the monograph edited by Mellars (1987) provides comprehensive details of the ecological aspects of the project. In particular, I have used contributions to the monograph by Jardine (coastal change), Andrews *et al.* (past and present vegetation), Switsur and Mellars (radiocarbon dating), Grigson and Mellars (mammalian remains) and Meiklejohn and Denston (human remains). Stratigraphical details of the excavations at Cnoc Coig are taken from Mellars' own contributions. Preliminary results of seasonality studies have been published by Mellars (1978b) and Mellars and Wilkinson (1980). Grigson (1989) has commented on the Oronsay birds and data on the wind tolerance of the Highland Midge are from Hendry (1989). Henderson Bishop's excavations on Oronsay were published in 1914 and details of Risga, MacArthur Cave and Druimvargie Rock Shelter are from Lacaille (1954). Clark (1956) provides a useful description of 'Obanian' artefacts. The radiocarbon dates from Druimvargie Rock Shelter and Ulva Cave were published by Bonsall and Smith (1989) and Bonsall *et al.* (1989) respectively.

The 'Obanian' of south western Scotland has been placed in a wider context by Wickham-Jones (1994) and by the work *The Southern Hebrides Mesolithic Project* (Mithen and Lake 1996). A European context for coastal adaptations in the Postglacial is provided by papers published in Fischer (1995).

9 The Lateglacial and early Postglacial settlement of the British Isles

In the preceding chapters we have examined the archaeological record of the Late Stone Age hunters of the British Isles in some detail, and seen that it is possible to gain a number of revealing insights into their way of life. It is now time to increase the scale of observation and consider the region as a whole. The maps in figures 9.4 and 9.7 show the distribution of settlement by 10 km squares of the National Grid at 1,000-year intervals on the basis of 304 radiocarbon dates with standard deviations of less than 251 years. The maps appear to provide a graphic illustration of the spread of settlement across the British Isles during the period between 13,000 BP and 5000 BP. But how valid is this pattern, given that we know of over 3,500 sites from the period in question?

The validity of the pattern can be checked both intuitively and objectively. First, does it make sense? I believe it offers a convincing picture but readers may decide for themselves. A more objective assessment is provided by comparing the distribution of all records for late Upper Palaeolithic activity with the distribution of radiocarbon dates earlier than 9999 BP. The late Upper Palaeolithic period is conventionally dated to between c. 13,000 and 10,000 BP and there are 126 sites which have produced archaeological material thought to belong to this period. These are plotted in figure 9.1. If the radiocarbon dates provide an accurate record of settlement at this time all sites, dated by whatever means, should lie within the area known to have been settled by 10,000 BP. Figure 9.1 shows that this is indeed largely the case, the only potentially significant anomalies being five records from Scotland, four of which are isolated finds.

Single flint tanged points have been found on the islands of Tiree (fig. 9.1 no. 1) and Jura (fig. 9.1 no. 2). These are thought to be of a late Upper Palaeolithic type, but one which was still current on the Continent after 10,000 BP. A barbed bone point from Glen Avon, Banffshire (fig. 9.1 no. 3) is another possible late Upper Palaeolithic artefact, although again the date range of this type extends to well after 10,000 BP. The fourth isolated find is a single worked flint recovered from the bed of the North Sea by an oil drilling platform between Shetland and Norway. The sea is 140 m deep

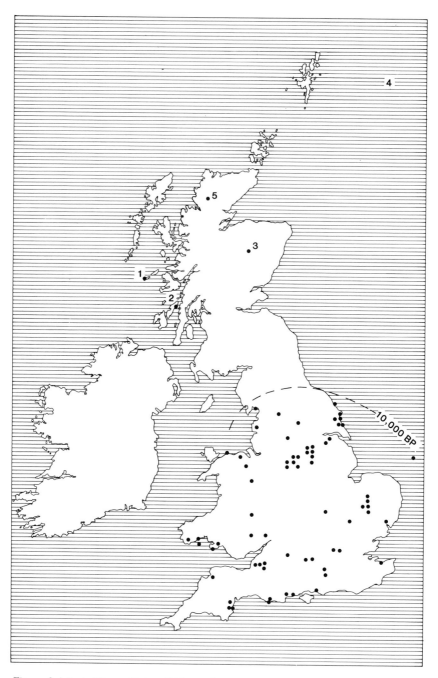

Figure 9.1 Late Upper Palaeolithic settlement recorded by radiocarbon dates and artefacts, and the 10,000 BP isochron (for numbered locations see text).

at this point and can only have been dry land when sea levels were low at the time of the glacial maximum. However, the flint is quite undiagnostic and could have arrived on the sea bed at any time, either through being lost overboard or during the course of a shipwreck. Potentially more convincing than any of these undated finds is the radiocarbon date of *c.* 10,000 BP for a portion of unmodified reindeer antler found in a cave at Inchnadamph (fig. 9.1 no. 5). The interest of this site lies in the fact that the dated specimen is part of a substantial assemblage of antlers that may be the residue of a cache accumulated by a band of hunters operating in the area. This interpretation is yet to be established beyond doubt and the remoteness of Inchnadamph from other areas of Lateglacial settlement urges caution until the date and status of the assemblage have been confirmed.

It can be seen that these anomalies do not, as yet, present a serious challenge to the validity of the settlement pattern revealed by the radiocarbon dates. I expect that as the number of dates increases some adjustments will be called for, but it will take more than a few ambiguous records to invalidate the pattern as a whole and if it provides a stimulus to further research it will have served its purpose.

The resettlement of the British Isles was not simply a matter of a spread of occupation from adjoining areas of northern Europe northwards and westwards until the seemingly limitless expanse of the Atlantic Ocean was confronted. While bands of hunters and gatherers extended their ranges into hitherto unexplored areas, the density of settlement in areas already occupied was consolidated, both through population growth and as a consequence of the continued immigration of peoples from the flooded North Sea Lowlands. Simultaneously, there was a movement into the uplands, which were becoming increasingly less hostile as rising sea levels led to climatic amelioration. The details of this pattern are as yet poorly understood, but its general outlines seem reasonably clear.

THE GRASSLANDS OF THE LATEGLACIAL TUNDRA

Although humans may have made occasional visits to the ice-free areas of southern Britain during the glacial maximum there is no evidence that they did, and the earliest radiocarbon-dated records of Lateglacial human settlement date from around 12,600 BP. It appears, therefore, that the reoccupation of Britain only became a practical proposition with the arrival of relatively mild conditions during the Lateglacial Interstadial. The vegetation of the British Isles and the North Sea Lowlands at this time was one of open tundra and scrub but within this regional uniformity lay a great deal of local variability. In chapter 5 we saw that tundra can be composed of a community of plants including open-country species and trees and shrubs, which vary in importance both temporally and spatially. During the Lateglacial Interstadial tree species probably became more important, at least in southern Britain, only to recede again at the time of the Loch

Lomond Readvance. Similarly, the contrast between the maritime west and the continental east was especially marked. Altitudinal variation remains marked even to the present day.

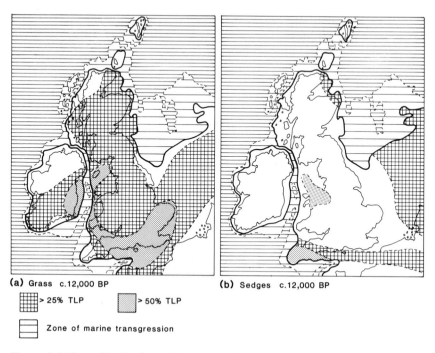

(a) Grass c.12,000 BP   **(b)** Sedges c.12,000 BP

> 25% TLP   > 50% TLP

Zone of marine transgression

Figure 9.2 Plant distributions (after Huntley and Birks 1983) and contemporary coastline *c.* 12,000 BP.

Figures 9.2 and 9.3 show the distribution of some typical plants at *c.* 12,000 BP. Tundra is an open environment with trees contributing less than 50 per cent of the total land pollen (TLP), and the distribution of grasses (fig. 9.2a) provides a good indication of the extent of open conditions, with values greater than 25 per cent indicative of predominantly treeless vegetation. The sedges (fig. 9.2b) tell a similar story. They are plants of wet or damp ground and high values are confined to the maritime areas of western and southern England and the North Sea Lowlands.

A range of shrubs and trees was also to be found, which might be locally important, even dominant, components of the vegetation. The crowberry (fig 9.3a) is a small, heather-like shrub with black berries which does not produce much pollen and has poor dispersal. Values of even 1 per cent can indicate that it is common and at *c.* 12,000 BP this was the case throughout most of Britain and the North Sea Lowlands. Juniper (fig 9.3b) occurs mainly as a shrub, but can grow into a small tree. Values of greater than 5 per cent TLP indicate that it was abundant.

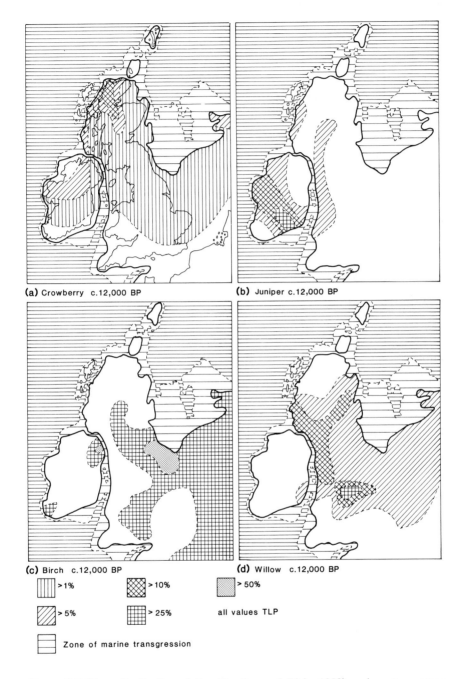

(a) Crowberry c.12,000 BP

(b) Juniper c.12,000 BP

(c) Birch c.12,000 BP

(d) Willow c.12,000 BP

>1%	>10%	>50%
>5%	>25%	all values TLP
Zone of marine transgression		

Figure 9.3 Plant distributions (after Huntley and Birks 1983) and contemporary coastline *c.* 12,000 BP.

The two most common trees were birch and willow. Birch pollen presents particular problems because few palynologists have felt able to distinguish dwarf birch (*Betula nana*) from the various tree forms such as the silver birch (*B. pendula*) and the brown or downy birch (*B. pubescens*). Dwarf birch is a low shrub whereas the tree forms can grow up to 30 m in height and form genuine woodland stands. It seems that dwarf birch was mainly a shrub of cool episodes, whereas in the Lateglacial Interstadial tree birches were probably dominant. All birch produce a lot of pollen, but TLP values greater than 25 per cent can be taken to indicate local stands and where the values exceed 50 per cent birch-dominated woodland covered the landscape (fig. 9.3c). Other shrubs of birch woodland are crowberry and several varieties of *Vaccinium* such as bilberry, cranberry and cowberry.

Sixty-nine species of willow (*Salix* spp.) are known from Europe, including a range of dwarf varieties, larger shrubs and small trees. Willows are plants of damp conditions and shrub and tree forms are often found growing on fen carr and river banks, whereas dwarf willows are plants of damp tundra soils. Willows do not generally form woodland though they may contribute to the understorey (fig. 9.3d).

The landscapes of the Lateglacial Interstadial were predominantly open, though in some regions birch and birch/willow woodland was important while small stands of trees and shrubs could be found almost anywhere where conditions were suitable. These landscapes produced little apart from berries and firewood that human groups could use directly. They were, however, rich in herds of grazing and browsing animals, and it was in pursuit of these, rather than on berry-picking expeditions, that people returned after an absence of many millennia. The variety of animals to be found is striking and without contemporary parallel. It included species associated with a wide range of rather differing habitats, from tundra grassland to deciduous woodland, and further emphasizes the unique character of Britain's ecology. This uniqueness effectively rules out any attempt to reconstruct the fauna of the Lateglacial Interstadial by analogy, and we must interpret the evidence we have as best we can.

This evidence is admittedly biased. It mostly comes from caves, and in many instances consists of animal remains accumulated by cave-using humans. What we see is evidence for the animals in which humans were interested. But such evidence does at least provide a minimal picture.

The case studies in chapter 6 made it clear that the most commonly preyed-upon species was the wild horse, though red deer, wild cattle and hares were also important. Very occasionally reindeer were taken, but they do not seem to have been a major subsistence item at this time. There are hints that there may have been some scavenging of mammoth and woolly rhino which had died from natural causes. Where there is evidence, the picture is always of a broad range of animals being hunted.

The radiocarbon dates for the period between 13,000 BP and 12,000 BP give the impression that the resettlement of the southern half of Britain was rapid. Dates from the Creswell Crags in Derbyshire and from Cheddar Gorge in Somerset are statistically indistinguishable. The climatic amelioration after 13,000 BP is thought to have been rapid and a rapid response to the new opportunities it offered can be expected from both humans and other animals. But for all its apparent rapidity we should not view it as a single event.

In areas where population density is low, ethnographers have recorded many cases where hunting bands have adjusted their home ranges according to opportunity or necessity. Since such home ranges can be several hundred kilometres in extent, the spread of humans across the 400 km from eastern England to Torbay, or the rather shorter distance to Morecambe, could have been accomplished by piecemeal adjustments over just a few generations.

The most striking feature of figure 9.4a is the fact that the records are distributed between two widely separated groups, one of which extends through the north Midlands to Morecambe Bay, the other from the south coast to the lower Wye Valley. The former group includes Creswell Crags (fig. 9.4a no. 1), the latter the Cheddar Gorge caves (fig. 9.4a no. 2) and Kent's Cavern (fig. 9.4a no. 3). Most records come from caves, and it might be argued that the pattern observed has less to do with human geography than geology, in that it is only in caves that the earliest evidence survives. However, there are plenty of records from non-cave sites later than 12,000 BP and it is difficult to see why the forces of destruction should selectively erase sites of one millennium but not another. It is also the case that the most north-westerly record, the Poulton elk kill site (fig. 9.4a no. 4), does not come from a cave but from a lake deposit. Similarly, the open encampment at Hengistbury Head (fig. 9.4a no. 5), although not dated by radiocarbon, also appears to belong to this period. Accordingly, the pattern depicted in figure 9.4a, while likely to be incomplete, may approximate to the actual distribution of settlement during this early period.

The explanation of a pattern based on such limited and incomplete evidence is very difficult, but I feel we may have evidence for two distinct movements into Britain during the Lateglacial Interstadial, one from the North Sea Lowlands through the north Midlands and towards the Irish Sea, the other along the broad coastal plain that was to become the English Channel and into south-west England. In each case we can envisage groups of hunters gradually extending the range of their annual movements westward and northward. The intervening, unoccupied, zone appears to have been dominated by birch and willow scrub (fig. 9.3c and d) and may have had less to offer than the areas to the north and south. These bands of hunters must have come from adjoining parts of Europe, and archaeologists have attempted to identify their areas of origin by looking for similarities in material equipment which might imply a shared technological tradition. However, this approach has yet to produce results of much

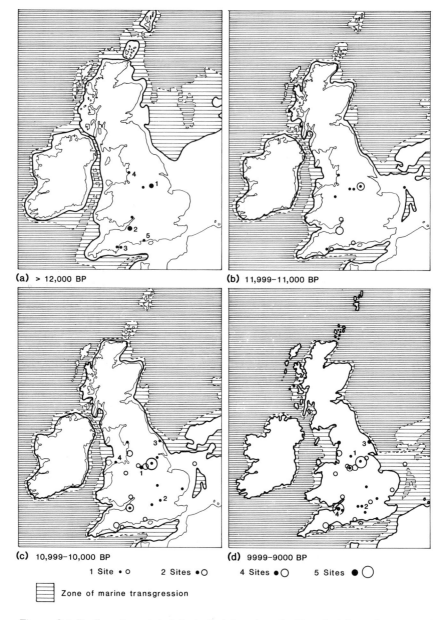

(a) > 12,000 BP

(b) 11,999–11,000 BP

(c) 10,999–10,000 BP

(d) 9999–9000 BP

1 Site • ○   2 Sites •○   4 Sites ●○   5 Sites ● ○

Zone of marine transgression

Figure 9.4 Radiocarbon-dated Lateglacial and early Postglacial settlement and coastlines before 9000 BP; solid dots = new records, open circles = records carried forward from previous phases (for numbered locations see text).

use in the present context, and in any case lies outside the scope of this book.

In each of the case studies in chapter 6, we appeared to be looking at the activities of small groups, perhaps extended families. The unspecialized nature of most of the assemblages accords with our expectations of a home base and, where there were biological remains, there is a hint that occupation was seasonal. The hunters of the Lateglacial Interstadial may have followed a pattern of residential foraging, in which the whole band moved on as resources became depleted. It is possible that the population amounted to no more than a handful of such family groups and that only occasionally did they come together to form slightly larger aggregations. Creswell Crags may have provided a focus for such gatherings among the northern group while the caves in Cheddar Gorge could have provided a similar focus for the more southerly group. We know from their selection of raw materials that the band which used Gough's Cave ranged over quite a wide area.

It is impossible to say anything conclusive about social organization during this period. We can expect that the authority of senior members was acknowledged within the band and a higher level of authority among members of the same kin or lineage may have transcended band organization. The rare items of ornament that have survived may have been explicit or implicit statements of personal identity or status, and the same may have applied in the few cases where individuals were afforded funerary rites. But this is all very speculative.

Temperatures were dropping again by 12,000 BP and did not return to the levels reached at *c.* 13,000 BP until the early Postglacial. As was noted in chapter 5, the phase of ice accumulation which led to the Loch Lomond Readvance had begun by 12,000 BP. Throughout most of this period ice sheets and glaciers were confined to the Highlands of Scotland, though after about 11,400 BP corrie glaciers had begun to form in Snowdonia and the Lake District while elsewhere in the uplands snow lie became prolonged and extensive. Sea levels remained low and most of the southern North Sea was dry land. The land bridges to Orkney and Shetland had been cut by 13,000 BP but Ireland remained connected to south-west Scotland by a narrow isthmus of glacial moraines. The Polar Front which lay far to the north at 12,000 BP swept south to the latitude of Portugal by 11,000 BP but retreated again to the latitude of western Scotland by 10,200 BP. At 13,000 BP the mean temperature for the warmest month was around 17°C but that for the coldest remained at 0°C. Between 12,000 BP and 11,400 BP these temperatures dropped from 15°C to 10°C and from −9°C to −20°C respectively. The pattern of precipitation is more difficult to reconstruct but after a dry, rather continental episode around 12,000 BP increases in precipitation appear to be reflected in ice accumulation.

It is difficult to document at the regional scale the changes in the vegetation that must have taken place during the period of falling temperatures between 12,000 BP and the maximum of the Loch Lomond Readvance at *c*. 10,800 BP. These must have involved an increase in the extent of fully open conditions at the expense of scrub and woodland. Corresponding adjustments in the fauna can also be expected, with open-country species such as wild horse and reindeer being favoured, while red deer and wild cattle suffered loss of habitat.

The distribution of radiocarbon-dated records for the period between 11,999 and 11,000 BP is shown in figure 9.4b. Only eleven dates are available for this period, distributed between seven sites. Interpretation of such slender evidence is hazardous, but there does seem to be a hint of an overall decline in activity during this period which is especially marked in the area formerly occupied by the southern group. I have suggested that during the Lateglacial Interstadial south-western Britain may have lain within the annual cycle of one or more bands who entered the area from the south-east via what was to become the English Channel, but was at that time a broad coastal plain. Rising sea level was leading to the progressive inundation of this plain, the effect of which was the increasing isolation of south-west Britain, which in turn may have led to the area being temporarily abandoned. This situation appears to have persisted throughout the eleventh millennium (fig. 9.4c).

In northern Britain the frontier of settlement advanced less than 100 km in the period between 12,000 and 10,000 BP and this is very likely due to the fact that throughout most of this period Britain was experiencing a final episode of harsh climate. But there does seem to have been some consolidation of settlement in areas occupied previously, especially in the southeast.

With the exception of Thatcham, none of the sites examined as case studies dates from the period between 12,000 and 10,000 BP, and Thatcham was cited as an example of hunters adapting to forest conditions. However, two additional cases may be referred to briefly. At Ossum's Cave in Staffordshire (fig. 9.4c no. 1) an assemblage of reindeer bone associated with artefacts has been dated to *c*. 10,700 BP and an assemblage including reindeer and horse found at Uxbridge (fig. 9.4c no. 2) has dates of *c*. 10,300 and 10,000 BP. The prominence of these open-country forms may be attributed to the harsh conditions prevailing during the Loch Lomond Readvance, and we should not forget the dates of *c*. 10,400 and *c*. 10,000 BP obtained for horse remains from Flixton Site 2 (fig. 9.4c no. 3) and from Kendrick's Cave (fig. 9.4c no. 4).

A LAND OF LAKES AND FORESTS

Compared with the period between 13,000 and 10,000 BP, that down to 9000 BP was one of rapid change. The ice sheets and glaciers of the Loch Lomond Readvance had completely melted by 10,000 BP and sea levels rose from −50 m to −35 m OD, the effect of which was to turn the Dogger

Bank into a large island and the Straits of Dover into a broad inlet (fig. 9.5a). Ireland became separated from the rest of Britain but the mainland remained joined to the Continent by a narrow land bridge extending from southern Yorkshire to the German Bight. The Polar Front had retreated northwards and by 9500 BP the waters of the North Atlantic Drift again washed the shores of northern Britain. Temperatures rose rapidly, with those for the warmest and coldest months averaging 16°C and 2°C respectively by 10,000 BP. Precipitation was lower than during the period of ice advance and, although inundation increased rapidly, the North Sea remained a relatively shallow lagoon and eastern Britain continued to be subjected to dry, continental influences.

The early Postglacial landscape was dotted with lakes, a legacy of the melting glaciers which gradually disappeared as falling sea levels improved drainage and vegetation began to colonize lake margins, initiating a sequence which led from reed swamp to the development of peat and ultimately fen woodland. The early forests of Britain were dominated by birch, which contributed over 50 per cent of the total tree and shrub pollen (TTSP). Pine also began to be locally important, while willow, which had been a significant component of the tundra vegetation, declined to less than 10 per cent. At 10,000 BP birch forests covered the North Sea Lowlands and most of mainland Britain, except for the west and far north, which remained more open (fig. 9.5a), and the south, where mixed deciduous woodland was already becoming established.

The understorey of birch forests varies according to latitude, altitude and soil status. Today, gorse (*Ulex europaeus*) and bracken (*Pteridium aquilinum*) are common, but so also are a range of berry-bearing shrubs such as bilberry, blackberry (*Rubus fruticosus*), cranberry, cowberry and crowberry. Locally, these may have been abundant and constituted seasonally important food sources for birds, animals and humans. Animal prey included elk, wild cattle and red deer, familiar from the Lateglacial, and woodland species such as roe deer and wild pig.

Radiocarbon records for settlement in the period between 9999 and 9000 BP document further consolidation but little movement north of the areas reached by the end of the Lateglacial (fig. 9.4d). The caves in the Mendips were once more visited regularly but the groups involved are more likely to have come from the north or east, rather than the south, where the coastal plain had disappeared under the rising sea level. A date of *c.* 9300 BP from Waystone Edge (fig. 9.4d no. 1) in Yorkshire records movement into the uplands. Other tenth-millennium dates from Lominot Site 3 (NGR SE 000130) and Warcock Hill South (NGR SE 030097), both in the southern Pennines, may tell a similar story, though with standard deviations greater than 300 years I have considered them too imprecise to use.

The sites at Thatcham (fig. 9.4d no. 2) and Star Carr (fig. 9.4d no. 3) provide good examples of home bases situated beside lakes in clearings made in the forest. At Thatcham both the residential area and the peripheral

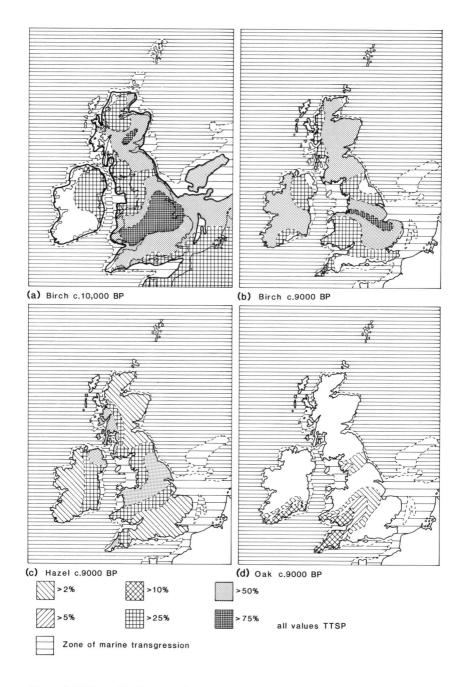

(a) Birch c.10,000 BP

(b) Birch c.9000 BP

(c) Hazel c.9000 BP

(d) Oak c.9000 BP

>2%	>10%	>50%
>5%	>25%	>75%
Zone of marine transgression		all values TTSP

Figure 9.5 Plant distributions (after Huntley and Birks 1983) and contemporary coastline *c.* 10,000–9000 BP.

zone were examined, whereas only the latter was excavated at Star Carr, though recent work in the area is leading to a more balanced picture. The upland case studies, Deepcar and the sites at Lominot and on Warcock Hill, had more limited ranges of material and can be regarded as field camps. These distinctions hint at a pattern of logistic foraging, in which specialist task groups ranged widely in search of prey while other members of the band remained at the home base. Activity continued to be organized on a seasonal basis, and during the course of an annual cycle considerable distances may have been covered. The groups hunting in the southern Pennines obtained their supplies of flint in East Yorkshire, up to 80 km to the north-east.

Again, the most intangible aspect of hunter-gatherer life is its social organization, but there is little to suggest that this differed significantly from Lateglacial times and indications of personal status remain rare. A possibly new development is the emergence of cemeteries. While human remains are known from Lateglacial contexts at both Gough's Cave and Pinhole, the seventy or more formal interments at Aveline's Hole (fig. 9.4d no. 4) are a new departure. Although very little is known about these burials, they do have some interesting implications. In normal circumstances, it would take many generations for a family-sized band to accumulate such a large number of burials. They must either result from an extraordinarily persistent pattern of funerary behaviour, or have been drawn from a larger population, perhaps encompassing several bands. The latter is the more likely, and may be the earliest evidence we have of a level of social organization transcending that of the co-residential band.

WOODS AND RIVERS, COASTS AND ISLANDS

Mixed deciduous woodland had begun to establish itself in southern England before the end of the Lateglacial and by 9000 BP had spread throughout the British Isles, apart from the far north where tundra persisted. Unlike the preceding birch forests which came and went within a period of hardly a thousand years, the deciduous woods belong to a period of relative stability. When major changes did occur, from about 5000 BP onwards, these were not brought about by the climate, but by Neolithic farmers who started to fell the trees and clear the land for cultivation. However, it would be a mistake to view this long period as one of total stability and unvarying uniformity.

Summer temperatures had risen to present levels (16°C) by 9500 BP and exceeded them by several degrees (18.5°C) by 8000 BP. These high levels were maintained until well after 6000 BP and the period between 8000 and 6000 BP is often referred to as the Postglacial climatic optimum. By 8500 BP the North Sea land bridge was finally breached and Britain became an island. The establishment of fully maritime conditions led to a rise in precipitation, but at first the zone of open water was narrow and continental influences predominated in eastern Britain. Sea levels continued to rise for a further 2,000 years and by about 6500 BP the British Isles had assumed their familiar shape.

Deciduous woodland established itself in southern England and spread northwards at the expense of the birch forests, though birches remained an important component of the northern woods (fig. 9.5b). Similarly, the distinction between the predominantly maritime west and the continental east also led to variability. If we add variability due to altitude, with woodland extending to above 300 m, we can see that the mixed deciduous woods of the early Postglacial were far from uniform, either spatially or temporally.

A local presence of oak is reflected by TTSP values in excess of 2 per cent whereas those greater than 10 per cent indicate areas where oaks are a significant component of the vegetation (fig. 9.5d). The pattern strongly suggests a diffusion of oak into Britain from the south-west and emphasizes the preference of oaks for broadly maritime conditions. Elms (*Ulmus*) have the same preference, and their distribution at 9000 BP is strikingly similar to that of oaks (fig. 9.6a). Hazel (*Corylus*) was also an important component of these woods and was present as an understorey shrub throughout the British Isles. Values greater than 25 per cent TTSP suggest woods in which hazel forms a major part of the canopy, the case through-out central and northern England, western Scotland and eastern Ireland (fig. 9.5c). At 9000 BP pine (*Pinus*) also became briefly important in southern England with values in excess of 50 per cent TTSP indicating the dominance of pine woods and those greater than 25 per cent implying small stands of pine in an otherwise forested landscape (fig. 9.6b).

Radiocarbon-dated records of human settlement between 8999 and 8000 BP are plotted in figure 9.7a. The main development during this period is the spread of settlement up the west coast as far as Kinloch, on the island of Rhum (fig. 9.7a no. 1) and to Mount Sandel (fig. 9.7a no. 2) and Lough Boora (fig. 9.7a no. 3) in Ireland. No such movement is recorded in eastern Britain, the most northerly site dating from before 8000 BP being Filpoke Beacon in County Durham (fig. 9.7a no. 4). The explosive settlement of north-western Britain and Ireland merits special attention. Why, when settlement had hardly advanced for three millennia, should there be this spectacular movement over just a few centuries?

The productivity of the sea varies with temperature, and whereas the plankton biomass of the North Atlantic Drift exceeds 300 mg/m^3, in the cooler waters to the north it can be less than half this. This variability in productivity is reflected all the way up the food chain and must have had a bearing on the extent to which the early inhabitants of the British Isles looked to the sea for sustenance. During much of the Lateglacial the coasts of Britain were washed by cool polar waters which are unlikely to have been as productive as those which became established during the tenth millennium as the Polar Front made its final retreat northwards. I think it is

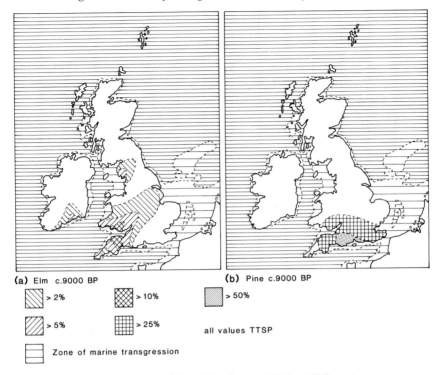

(a) Elm c.9000 BP

(b) Pine c.9000 BP

⧄ > 2%	⧇ > 10%	▦ > 50%
⧄ > 5%	⊞ > 25%	all values TTSP
☐ Zone of marine transgression		

Figure 9.6 Plant distributions (after Huntley and Birks 1983) and contemporary coastline *c.* 9000 BP.

no coincidence that the colonization of western Scotland, the Inner Hebrides and Ireland began at a time when both quantitative and qualitative increases in the marine biomass are likely to have encouraged interest in the exploitation of coastal and marine resources. It seems inconceivable that such movements could have taken place except within the context of a partly maritime-orientated economy.

Mount Sandel provides a good example of a seasonally occupied home base in a major river valley. It is important to realize that in the forests and woods, rivers and their valleys provided major arteries for communication, either on foot or by boat (fig. 9.8). Mount Sandel, with its unequivocal structural remains, provides the first objective evidence for the size of a co-residential group. With about 30 m² of floor space its shelter could not have accommodated more than a single family, and there appears never to have been more than one or two such shelters in use at a time. A similarly sized structure was excavated at Broom Hill (fig. 9.7a no. 5) and archaeologists have so far failed to identify evidence for larger aggregations of population. These probably did occur, but on a temporary basis, and most of the time people seem to have lived in small, isolated groups.

The development of the settlement pattern of mainland Britain between

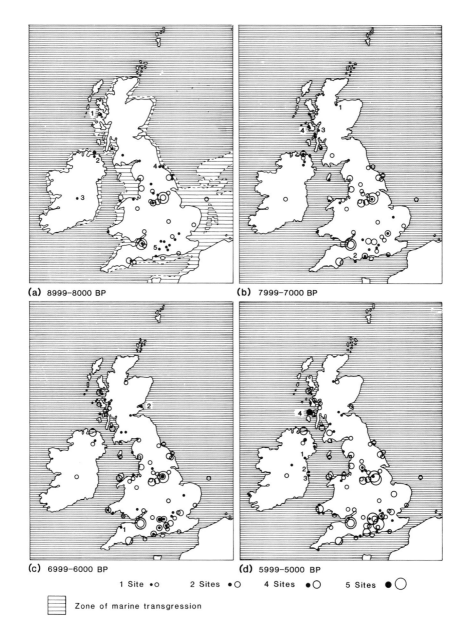

(a) 8999–8000 BP

(b) 7999–7000 BP

(c) 6999–6000 BP

(d) 5999–5000 BP

1 Site •o   2 Sites •○   4 Sites •○   5 Sites ●○

Zone of marine transgression

Figure 9.7 Radiocarbon-dated Postglacial settlement between 8999 and 5000 BP omitting records regarded as Neolithic; solid dots = new records, open circles = records carried forward from previous phases (for numbered locations see text).

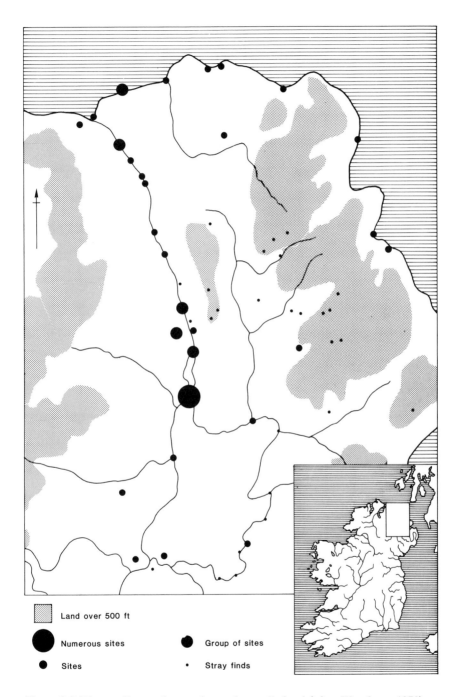

Land over 500 ft

Numerous sites

Group of sites

Sites

Stray finds

Figure 9.8 River valley settlement in north-east Ireland (after Woodman 1978).

7999 and 7000 BP (fig. 9.7b) was mainly one of consolidation in existing areas, though this period does have the first dated records from the Isle of Man and from north-east Scotland. The latter consists of two dates, *c.* 7800 and 7300 BP from features associated with Mesolithic finds at Castle Street, Inverness (fig. 9.7b no. 1). As there is no firmly dated evidence for settlement in eastern Scotland before 7000 BP, this may be evidence for movement up the Great Glen or around the north coast. Dated records are similarly in short supply in Ireland but the available evidence indicates a period of consolidation rather than further rapid spread.

The vegetation of the British Isles at 7000 BP was a mosaic of tree and shrub communities with comparatively little open ground apart from in the far north, on exposed summits, along the coasts and on river flood plains. Oak (fig. 9.9a) and hazel (fig. 9.9b) were to be found virtually everywhere but the other components of the woodland varied from region to region. Elm (fig. 9.9c), from its limited distribution at 9000 BP, had become much more widespread. Pine (fig. 9.9d), which had an almost exclusively southern distribution at 9000 BP, was important in central and northern Scotland, where the last remnants of the formerly extensive birch forests were also still to be found. Elm and pine were both important in Ireland.

Two species not recorded at 9000 BP had become significant by 7000. The linden or lime (*Tilia*) is notoriously underrepresented in pollen diagrams because of its poor pollen dispersal and values as low as 1 per cent TTSP are regarded as indicating the local presence of this tree (fig. 9.10a). The other new arrival is alder (*Alnus*), a high pollen producer with a preference for wet sites such as river banks and lake sides. Values in excess of 10 per cent TTSP are thought to indicate the presence of alder-dominated woodland in the area (fig. 9.10b). The widespread occurrence of this tree in England and Wales may be partly due to the establishment of fully maritime conditions with the inundation of the North Sea land bridge.

Although the deciduous woodlands are more familiar than the birch forests of the early Postglacial and the Lateglacial tundras, today's woods are a poor reflection of those of 7,000 years ago. Not only did these earlier woods extend for hundreds of kilometres with little open space, they also included some massive trees, examples of which are occasionally exhumed during peat-digging operations. Oliver Rackham has drawn attention to a group of such 'bog oaks' from near Ely in the Fens, some of which, when standing, rose to nearly 30 m before the first branch, while pines of similar stature are also recorded. These tell us, more eloquently than any number of pollen diagrams, what the mixed deciduous woods of lowland Britain actually looked like to the hunters and gatherers who so successfully exploited them for several thousand years. Throughout the period from 8000 BP there are persistent indications of disturbance of these woods by humans, usually in the form of clearance episodes recognized in pollen diagrams and accompanied by lenses of charcoal indicative of forest fires. It has been suggested that much of this was deliberate and intended to

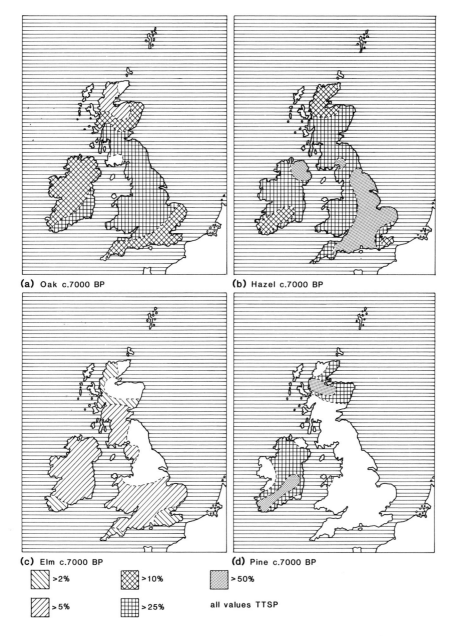

(a) Oak c.7000 BP

(b) Hazel c.7000 BP

(c) Elm c.7000 BP

(d) Pine c.7000 BP

>2%	>10%	>50%
>5%	>25%	all values TTSP

Figure 9.9 Plant distributions *c.* 7000 BP (after Huntley and Birks 1983).

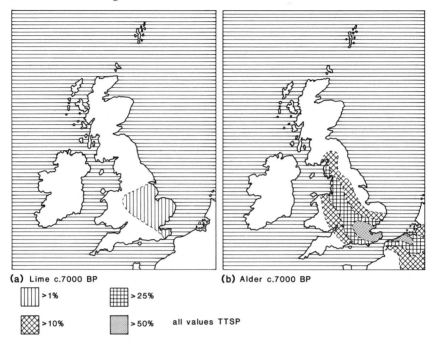

(a) Lime c.7000 BP   **(b)** Alder c.7000 BP

▦ >1%	⊞ >25%		
▨ >10%	▩ >50%	all values TTSP	

Figure 9.10 Plant distributions *c.* 7000 BP (after Huntley and Birks 1983).

promote new growth attractive to game. However, it is very difficult to prove intention in these circumstances, and some of the fires may have started by accident or, if deliberate, were intended to drive game rather than as an act of early land management. Most of this evidence comes from the uplands and it is doubtful that the widespread use of fire would ever have been possible in the damp oak and lime woods of the lowlands.

Figure 9.7c and d documents the distribution of dated records for the periods between 6999 and 6000 BP, and 5999 and 5000 BP, though the latter map specifically excludes sites regarded as Neolithic on botanical, faunal or artefactual grounds. The settlement of the mainland had largely been accomplished by 6000 BP and the same process was completed in Ireland within the following 500 years.

A feature of the archaeological record for north-west Britain during the sixth millennium is evidence for the exploitation of coastal resources as indicated by the 'Obanian' group of shell middens, of which Cnoc Coig provided an example in chapter 8. In the past it was assumed that hunters only turned their attention in these directions as a response to diminishing yields from terrestrial species, and this was taken to account for the relatively late date of most hunter-gatherer coastal sites in Britain. This seems unlikely, and earlier shell middens are widespread in the British Isles, extending from the south coast and Bristol Channel where sites at Culver Well, Portland (fig. 9.7b no. 2), and Westward Ho! in Devon (fig.

9.7c no. 1) have produced dates of *c*. 7100 BP and *c*. 6580 BP respectively, to northern Britain where middens at the Druimvargie Rock Shelter (fig. 9.7b no. 3) and Ulva Cave (fig. 9.7b no. 4) have been dated to *c*. 7800 and 7700 BP. It is evident that the exploitation of coastal resources was well under way by the middle of the eighth millennium BP. In any case, as we have seen, the settlement of the Inner Hebrides and Ireland had begun before the end of the ninth millennium and this is unlikely to have happened except within the context of a partly maritime economy.

A further point to consider in assessing the potential of marine and coastal resources is the increase in their overall abundance due to rising sea level and the concomitant lengthening of the coastline. When the ice sheets were at their maximum extent the unglaciated portion of Britain had a coastline of approximately 1,500 km. By the time of the Main Postglacial Transgression this had increased to 8,000 km and gave rise to a massive expansion of inshore fishing grounds and shellfish beds. This is a point of major importance to the role of coastal exploitation in the lives of the Late Stone Age hunters and gatherers of the British Isles. Opportunities simply became far more numerous as time passed.

From about 7000 BP sea levels fell intermittently until the present level was reached about 500 years later. As a consequence shell middens post-dating the Main Postglacial Transgression have not been subjected to destruction by wave action, and numerous examples survive from later periods. The exploitation of coastal resources continued throughout pre-history and elements of a way of life followed by the 'Obanian' Late Stone Age hunters continued until quite recent times. But from about 5500 BP this was within the context of a regional economy in which food pro-duction, or farming, was becoming increasingly important. This transition is particularly well documented by the finds from a group of shell middens on the east coast of Ireland. The middens at Rock Marshall, Sutton and Dalkey Island (fig. 9.7d nos 1, 2 and 3) all have radiocarbon dates around the middle of the sixth millennium BP. In addition to marine molluscs and fish, the faunas recorded include grey seal, small cetaceans and terrestrial mammals such as red deer and wild pig. At Dalkey Island a new com-ponent was added in the form of domesticated cattle and sheep, while a second midden, dated to *c*. 4300 BP, also included pottery, which in Britain is usually taken to indicate a Neolithic date. But the complex interrelation-ships between wild and domesticated resources and between hunters and farmers lie beyond the scope of this book.

Throughout the Lateglacial and early Postglacial there is little evidence that social organization developed far beyond the level of the band which gathered, hunted and lived together. Wider social relations must have existed in order to maintain a genetically healthy population, but these were probably only manifest when, periodically, several bands came together. The use of cemeteries may hint at this wider level of social organization, the members of several interrelated bands being buried together. This development is usually considered to be a feature of the late Mesolithic and throughout northern Europe, from Brittany to southern Scandinavia and the Baltic, cemeteries become a feature of the archaeological record in the centuries immediately preceding the adoption of farming. The use of cemeteries is thought to coincide with the adoption of a more sedentary way of life made possible by widening the range of resources taken and perhaps necessitated in some areas by population growth, which constrained the extent to which any group could range freely and hunt and gather at will.

These developments do not appear to have taken place in the British Isles. To begin with, Aveline's Hole provides the best example of a Mesolithic cemetery in Britain, but the burials here date from the tenth millennium BP, a time when sedentism is unlikely. Second, coastal sites exhibit the widest range of resources but many of these are markedly seasonal and seasonal movements between areas must have continued to be necessary. In fact mobility, perhaps on a seasonal basis, remained a feature of life for a substantial part of the population of the British Isles long after the widespread adoption of farming. But this is another fascinating subject which lies beyond the scope of the present study.

ADDITIONAL READING

Lists of late Upper Palaeolithic and Mesolithic settlements in England and Wales have been published by Campbell (1977), Wymer and Bonsall (1977), and in Ireland by Woodman (1978). There is at present no comprehensive coverage for Scotland. Radiocarbon dates have been taken from the *Radiocarbon Index* published by the Council for British Archaeology and, for dates from the mid-1980s onwards, from *Radiocarbon*. Since 1985 dates produced by the Oxford University Radiocarbon Accelerator have been listed in *Archaeometry*. The dating of the Lateglacial resettlement of Britain has been reviewed in papers by Charles and Jacobi (1994), Cook and Jacobi (1995) and Barton and Roberts (1996) while a potential problem in the use of radiocarbon dates in the early Postglacial has been highlighted by Day and Mellars (1995). The debate about the Lateglacial settlement of Scotland has been continued by Wickham-Jones (1990, 1994) and Edwards and Mithen (1995), though conclusive evidence is still lacking. Further radiocarbon dates from the Inchnadamph caves have been published by Murray *et al.* (1993). Green and Zvelebil (1990) have reviewed the evidence from Ireland. These developments can now be placed in a northwest European context by reference to Barton *et al.* (1991), Fischer (1995) and Larsson (1996). Details of plant distributions are from Huntley and Birks (1983), while Rackham (1980) paints a vivid picture of the ancient woods and forests of the British Isles. The deliberate use of fire in woodland and game management has been reviewed in detail by Simmons (1996).

Epilogue

The reoccupation of the British Isles from about 12,500 BP marks the beginning of an episode of settlement and landuse that has continued to the present day. For the first 7,000 years of this episode, people lived the lives of hunters and gatherers, the common inheritance of the human race for millions of years. In this book I have tried to throw some light on the details of their way of life. I have also tried to show that the most complete understanding we can hope to attain can only be achieved by seeing the evidence within its context, particularly that of the environment and the social and ecological frameworks which structured human life at all its levels.

Hunters and gatherers are still to be found in small numbers in many parts of the world, though it is to be wondered for how much longer, and elements of this way of life survive in the British Isles. But throughout the past 5,000 years subsistence has become increasingly based on the direct production of food through farming.

The widespread adoption of food production is the most significant event in the history of the British Isles between the initial recolonization by humans in the wake of the retreating ice sheets and the Industrial Revolution. The manner in which farming was introduced is a subject of much interest and debate. The familiar suite of plants and animals, wheat, barley and sheep, were not to be found in the native flora and fauna and must have been introduced from outside. Similarly, the earliest domestic cattle and pigs are very different from their wild contemporaries and are unlikely to have been derived directly from British stock. How were these introductions effected? By Neolithic farming colonists from northern Europe migrating to Britain or by British Mesolithic fishermen trading and raiding among such communities in their home areas and bringing home the proverbial bacon? Whatever the answer to these questions, the fact that the first clear evidence for farming dates from the centuries immediately before 5000 BP means that there was evidently a period during which hunter-gatherers and farmers co-existed with varying degrees of amity or enmity.

I have deliberately avoiding treating the related subjects of the introduction of farming and the survival of hunting and gathering. This book has been about Late Stone Age hunters and gatherers, and these additional topics are more appropriately treated elsewhere. The first small bands of hunters who wandered this way in search of migratory herds of horse and reindeer, or later hunted deer around the shores of Lake Pickering or fished for salmon in the River Bann, or later still hunted seals and caught saithe among the Inner Hebrides, made their own distinct and unique contribution to the culture, life and landscape of the British Isles, a contribution which we can still perceive, and of which we are the inheritors.

Saturday June 9th 1990

Appendix: Radiocarbon dates for hunter-gatherer sites in the British Isles between 13,000 BP and 5000 BP

(dates with standard deviations greater than 251 Radiocarbon Years are omitted)

Laboratory Codes: **BM** British Museum; **Birm** Department of Geological Sciences, University of Birmingham; **CAR** Department of Plant Science, University College, Cardiff; **D** Department of Botany, Trinity College, Dublin; **F** Davy-Faraday Laboratory, Royal Institution; **GrN** Isotopes Physics Laboratory, University of Groningen; **GU** Department of Chemistry, University of Glasgow; **GX** Geochron Laboratories, Cambridge, Mass.; **GaK** Gakushuin University, Tokyo; **HAR** Atomic Energy Research Establishment, Harwell; **I** Teledyne Isotopes, New Jersey; **NZ** New Zealand Institute of Nuclear Sciences; **OxA** Oxford University Accelerator; **Q** Godwin Laboratory, Cambridge; **SRR** Scottish Universities Research and Reactor Centre, East Kilbride; **St** Laboratory for Isotope Geology, Stockholm; **UB** Palaeoecology Laboratory, Queen's University, Belfast; **Y** Department of Geology and Geophysics, Yale University.

NGR		Name	Lab code	Mean	±
NR	369888	Cnoc Sligeach, Oronsay	GX–1903	5015	210
NR	518798	Glenbatrick Waterhole	GX–2564	5045	215
SH	982572	Brenig Valley (BG 5328)	HAR–1436	5120	100
O	26 39	Sutton Midden	I–5067	5250	100
NR	373889	Cnoc Sligeach	Birm–465	5255	155
SU	389676	Wawcott Farm	BM–0449	5260	130
H	992982	Newferry Site 4	D–36	5290	170
SS	094985	Lydstep	OxA–1412	5300	100
O	279262	Dalkey Island	D–38	5300	170
H	992982	Newferry	UB–503	5310	85
TQ	030715	Staines	OxA–1158	5350	100
N	39 69	Lough Derravaragh	I–4234	5360	110
SE	137010	Dunford Bridge 'B'	Q–0799	5380	80
J	523654	Ringneill	Q–770	5380	120

Q	30 00	Ferriter's Cove Site 1	BM–2227R	5400	220
H	992982	Newferry Site 3 Zone 3	UB–489	5415	90
Q	30 00	Ferriter's Cove Site 1	BM–2227AR	5420	150
SY	955805	Blashenwell	BM–1258	5425	150
NR	371889	Cnoc Sligeach	BM–0670	5426	159
NR	361885	Cnoc Coig	Q–1352	5430	130
NR	359879	Caisteal nan Gillean II	Birm–347	5450	140
NR	359880	Caisteal nan Gillean II	Q–1355	5460	65
NR	345888	Priory Midden	Q–3004	5470	50
NX	635918	Smittons Site T3	OxA–1594	5470	80
SW	705120	Windmill Farm, Lizard	HAR–5668	5470	130
J	12 07	Rockmarshall Midden	I–5323	5470	110
SD	085916	Williamson's Moss	UB–2713	5480	90
Q	30 00	Ferriter's Cove Site 3	BM–2229R	5490	160
NR	361885	Cnoc Coig	Q–1351	5495	75
SD	085916	Williamson's Moss	GU–1664	5500	70
Q	30 00	Ferriter's Cove Site 3	BM–2229AR	5500	130
SD	085916	Williamson's Moss	UB–2712	5520	85
SM	883346	Abermawr Bog Clearance	OxA–1377	5520	150
NR	361885	Cnoc Coig	Q–1354	5535	140
TQ	076942	Tolpits Lane	BM–1676R	5540	110
SD	085816	Williamson's Moss	UB–2545	5555	40
NH	650453	Muirtown, Inverness	GU–1473	5635	65
NR	361885	Cnoc Coig	Q–1353	5645	80
TQ	553563	High Rocks	BM–0040	5660	150
SK	529794	Thorpe Common Rock Shelter	Q–1118	5680	150
SU	727091	Wakeford Copse	HAR–0233	5680	120
NM	431384	Ulva Cave	GU–2602	5690	60
H	992982	Newferry Site 3 Zone 3	UB–630	5705	90
TQ	553563	High Rocks	BM–0091	5730	150
SY	955805	Blashenwell	BM–1257	5750	140
Q	30 00	Ferriter's Cove Site 2	BM–2228R	5750	140
NR	369888	Cnoc Sligeach, Oronsay	GX–1904	5755	180
H	992982	Newferry	UB–508	5795	105
SE	03 09	Rocher Moss South Site II	Q–1190	5830	100
NS	335337	Shewalton	OxA–1947	5840	80
SE	008128	March Hill II	Q–0788	5850	80
NR	373889	Cnoc Sligeach	Birm–462	5850	140
Q	30 00	Ferriter's Cove Site 2	BM–2228AR	5850	130
NR	345888	Priory Midden	Q–3001	5870	50
SP	960015	Stratford's Yard *Bos prim.*	BM–2404	5890	100
NS	726956	Meiklewood	OxA–1159	5920	80
NS	951798	Inveravon	GX–2334	5955	180
SM	882997	Freshwater West	Q–0530	5960	120
TQ	016879	Misbourne Viaduct	OxA–0618	5970	100
NX	343421	Barsalloch	GaK–1601	6000	110
NM	610602	Risga antler mattock	OxA–2023	6000	90
NS	951798	Inveravon	GX–2331	6010	180
SE	008128	March Hill II	Q–1188	6020	220
SU	400680	Wawcott Site XXIII	BM–0826	6079	113
NM	431384	Ulva Cave Midden	GU–2602	6090	50
TQ	016879	Misbourne Viaduct	OxA–0619	6100	120
NO	467257	Morton T 50/59	Q–0928	6115	110
SU	400680	Wawcott Site III	BM–0767	6120	134

NO	467257	Morton T 50.1/3	Q–0988	6147	90
SS	094985	Lydstep	OxA–1378	6150	120
TQ	016879	Misbourne Viaduct	OxA–0601	6190	90
SM	791110	Nab Head	OxA–0861	6210	90
H	992982	Newferry Site 3 Zone 4	UB–490	6215	100
NX	483938	Starr 1	OxA–1596	6230	80
NX	635918	Smittons Site T1	OxA–1595	6260	80
SU	774354	Oakhanger Warren	F–67	6300	110
NO	467257	Morton T 42	GaK–2404	6300	150
TQ	087945	Tolpits Lane	Q–1099	6330	80
SU	774354	Oakhanger Warren	F–68	6380	115
NO	467257	Morton T 50.5, T 57.2	Q–0981	6382	120
NO	467257	Morton T 53.1	NZ–1193	6400	125
SK	529794	Thorpe Common Rock Shelter	Q–1116	6433	115
H	992982	Newferry Site 3 Zone 5	UB–653	6440	185
NO	467257	Morton T 53.1	Q–0989	6450	80
SY	951805	Blashenwell	BM–0089	6450	150
SU	384259	Broom Hill	Q–1128	6534	125
SU	503667	Thatcham Site III	OxA–0940	6550	130
SJ	020825	Splash Point, Rhyl	OxA–1009	6560	80
SS	430290	Westward Ho!	HAR–5632	6580	150
SS	43 29	Westward Ho!	Q–0672	6585	130
H	992982	Newferry Site 3 Zone 6	UB–890	6590	60
H	992982	Newferry Site 3 Zone 5	UB–505	6605	170
SK	529794	Thorpe Common Rock Shelter	Q–1117	6616	220
TL	616838	Peacock's Fm, Shippea Hill	Q–586	6685	150
NM	860300	MacArthur Cave	OxA–1949	6700	80
SK	536743	Mother Grundy's Parlour	Q–0554	6705	140
NO	467257	Morton	Q–0948	6735	180
SD	089925	Monk Moors	BM–1216	6750	155
NO	467257	Morton T 47/55/56.1/2/3	NZ–1192	6790	150
SS	435295	Westward Ho!	Q–1212	6810	140
SK	536743	Mother Grundy's Parlour	Q–0553	6815	140
S0	211192	Gwernvale pit F308	CAR–118	6900	80
NR	373889	Cnoc Sligeach	Birm–464	6910	160
H	992982	Newferry Site 3 Zone 7	UB–886	6915	60
SS	435295	Westward Ho!	Q–1211	6955	140
H	992982	Newferry Site 3 Zone 7	UB–516	6955	60
C	85 30	Mount Sandel Upper	UB–2358	6980	135
H	992982	Newferry Site 3 Zone 7	UB–887	6980	115
H	992982	Newferry Site 3 Zone 7	UB–885	7075	120
SY	685694	Culver Well	BM–0960	7101	97
SY	685694	Culver Well	BM–0473	7150	135
H	992982	Newferry Site 3 Zone 6	UB–514	7175	105
SS	437859	Paviland Cave	OxA–0681	7190	80
H	992982	Newferry Site 3 Zone 7	UB–517	7190	110
SU	384259	Broom Hill	Q–1191	7220	120
SU	031701	Cherhill	BM–0447	7230	140
TL	379081	Broxbourne	OxA–0593	7230	150
NH	665453	Castle Street, Inverness	GU–1376	7275	235
SH	984572	Brenig 53	HAR–1135	7300	100
NR	995247	Auchareoch, I.o.Arran	OxA–1599	7300	90
N0	467257	Morton T 43.44.46	NZ–1302	7330	200
SM	791110	Nab Head	OxA–0860	7360	90

NR	685939	North Carn	SRR–161	7414	80
H	992982	Newferry Site 3 Zone 7	UB–496	7485	115
NM	404999	Kinloch	GU–2149	7570	50
TL	616838	Peacock's Fm, Shippea Hill	Q–587	7600	150
SK	536743	Mother Grundy's Parlour	Q–0552	7602	140
SC	295688	Cass ny Hawin	UB–2658	7640	80
SH	977572	Brenig 40	HAR–0656	7650	80
SC	295688	Cass ny Hawin	UB–2659	7660	100
NM	431384	Ulva Cave	GU–2600	7660	60
D	24 32	Cushendun	I–5134	7670	140
H	981903	Toome	Y–95	7680	110
SZ	178904	Hengistbury Head	OxA–0411	7690	110
SC	295688	Cass ny Hawin	UB–2660	7695	95
NH	665453	Castle Street, Inverness	GU–1377	7800	85
NM	855295	Druimvargie Rock Shelter	OxA–1948	7810	90
SU	384259	Broom Hill	Q–1460	7830	120
NM	404999	Kinloch	GU–2145	7850	50
SU	760350	Oakhanger Warren Site V	BM–0221	7869	104
NR	995247	Auchareoch, I.o.Arran	OxA–1600	7870	90
NM	404999	Kinloch	GU–2147	7880	70
C	85 30	Mount Sandel Upper	UB–2359	7885	120
NM	404999	Kinloch	GU–2039	7925	65
NY	300651	Redkirk Point Hearth	UB–2470	7935	110
SU	880400	Kettlebury Site 103	OxA–0379	7940	120
NR	644874	Lussa Wood I	SRR–159	7963	200
SH	352679	Trwyn Ddu	HAR–1193	7980	140
NX	483928	Loch Doon SW flint site	OxA–1598	8000	100
NY	300651	Redkirk Point hearth	UB–2445	8000	65
NR	995247	Aurchareoch, I.o.Arran	OxA–1601	8060	90
NM	431384	Ulva Cave midden	GU–2600	8060	50
SX	935641	Kent's Cavern Vestibule	OxA–1786	8070	90
SM	791110	Nab Head	OxA–1497	8070	80
NM	404999	Kinloch	GU–2146	8080	50
SU	502668	Thatcham Site 2 layer 2	BM–0065	8100	180
NZ	50 32	West Hartlepool Sub.Forest	BM–0090	8100	180
SD	959406	Ickornshaw Moor	Q–0707	8100	150
NZ	50 32	West Hartlepool Sub.Forest	BM–0083	8110	180
TL	379082	Broxbourne Site 106E	Birm–419	8120	160
SZ	178904	Hengistbury Head	OxA–0412	8140	120
SU	474676	Greenham Dairy Farm	OxA–0956	8160	100
NZ	475375	Filpoke Beacon	GrN–6382	8210	50
TA	033820	Seamer Carr arrow shaft	HAR–6498	8210	150
TQ	087945	Tolpits Lane	Q–1147	8260	120
SU	880440	Kettlebury Site 103	OxA–0378	8270	120
NM	404999	Kinloch	GU–2150	8310	150
SU	384259	Broom Hill	Q–1383	8315	150
N	15 18	Lough Boora	UB–6400	8350	70
N	15 18	Lough Boora	UB–2200	8350	70
C	85 30	Mount Sandel Lower	UB–532	8370	200
C	85 30	Mount Sandel Upper	GRN–10470	8380	50
C	85 30	Mount Sandel Upper	GRN–10471	8430	60
C	85 30	Mount Sandel Upper	UB–2008	8440	65
N	15 18	Lough Boora	UB–2267	8450	70
N	15 18	Lough Boora	UB–2199	8475	75

SU	384259	Broom Hill	Q–1528	8515	150
NM	404999	Kinloch	GU–1874	8515	190
SJ	025779	Rhuddlan	BM–0822	8528	73
SU	384259	Broom Hill	Q–1192	8540	150
C	85 30	Mount Sandel Upper	UB–2361	8545	165
C	85 30	Mount Sandel Upper	UB–913	8555	70
NM	404999	Kinloch	GU–2040	8560	75
C	85 29	Castleroe	UB–2172	8560	75
SK	224951	Broomhead Moor Site 5	Q–0800	8573	110
SU	503668	Thatcham Site II	Q–1130	8580	100
SH	352679	Trwyn Ddu	HAR–1194	8590	90
NM	404999	Kinloch	GU–1873	8590	95
SZ	178904	Hengistbury Head	OxA–0398	8590	120
NZ	475375	Filpoke Beacon	GrN–6373	8593	45
SE	032098	Warcock Hill III	Q–0789	8606	110
SH	352679	Trwyn Ddu	Q–1385	8640	150
C	85 30	Mount Sandel Upper	UB–2360	8670	100
NZ	50 32	West Hartlepool Sub.Forest	BM–0081	8680	180
NZ	50 32	West Hartlepool Sub.Forest	BM–0080	8700	180
TL	379081	Broxbourne Site 105	Birm–343	8700	170
C	85 30	Mount Sandel Upper	UB–912	8725	115
SJ	025779	Rhuddlan	BM–0691	8739	86
ST	476587	Aveline's Hole	OxA–1070	8740	100
C	85 29	Castleroe	UB–2171	8755	135
NZ	475375	Filpoke Beacon	Q–1474	8760	140
SU	787298	Longmoor	OxA–0377	8760	110
C	85 30	Mount Sandel Upper	UB–2356	8765	135
SU	474676	Greenham Dairy Farm	Q–0973	8779	110
C	85 30	Mount Sandel Upper	UB–951	8790	185
C	85 30	Mount Sandel Upper	UB–2007	8795	135
TQ	190778	Kew Bridge	OxA–1160	8820	100
SK	096563	Wetton Mill Minor	Q–1127	8847	210
ST	476587	Aveline's Hole	OxA–0800	8860	100
SU	777357	Oakhanger Warren Site VII	Q–1494	8885	160
H	992982	Newferry Site 3 Zone 7	UB–637	8895	125
SU	787298	Longmoor	OxA–0376	8930	100
C	85 30	Mount Sandel Upper	UB–2357	8955	185
C	85 30	Mount Sandel Upper	UB–952	8960	70
SU	777357	Oakhanger Warren Site VII	Q–1492	8975	160
C	85 30	Mount Sandel Upper	UB–2362	8990	80
SU	777357	Oakhanger Warren Site VII	Q–1490	8995	160
SK	097548	Elder Bush Cave	OxA–0812	9000	130
TA	028810	Star Carr VP85A	CAR–923	9030	100
SU	777357	Oakhanger Warren Site VII	Q–1493	9040	160
ST	532479	Badger Hole I	OxA–0679	9060	130
ST	467539	Gough's Cave	BM–0525	9080	150
ST	476586	Aveline's Hole	Q–1485	9090	110
SU	777357	Oakhanger Warren Site VII	Q–1491	9100	160
ST	467539	Gough's New Cave	OxA–0814	9100	100
ST	476587	Aveline's Hole	OxA–0799	9100	100
SM	791110	Nab Head	OxA–1496	9110	80
ST	477587	Aveline's Hole	BM–0471	9114	110
SM	791110	Nab Head	OxA–1495	9210	80
SU	777357	Oakhanger Warren Site VII	Q–1489	9225	170

SP	875625	Earls Barton	OxA–0500	9240	160
TA	034819	Seamer Carr sample 2157	CAR–197	9260	90
SU	420672	Marsh Benham	Q–1129	9300	150
ST	533479	Badger Hole 2	OxA–1459	9360	100
TA	028810	Star Carr VP85A	CAR–921	9360	110
SE	018142	Waystone Edge	Q–1300	9396	210
SU	502668	Thatcham Site 5 no.1	Q–0652	9480	160
SU	503667	Thatcham	OxA–0894	9490	110
TA	028810	Star Carr VP85A	OxA–1154	9500	120
TA	027810	Star Carr	Q–0014	9557	210
SU	502668	Thatcham Site 5 no.2	Q–0650	9670	160
SU	420672	Marsh Benham	Q–1380	9690	240
TA	028810	Star Carr VP85A	OxA–1176	9700	160
SU	503667	Thatcham	OxA–0732	9760	120
SU	502668	Thatcham Site 5 no.4	Q–0677	9780	160
TL	377026	Waltham Abbey B–Point	OxA–1427	9790	100
TA	030835	Seamer Carr *Equus ferus*	BM–2350	9790	180
SU	502668	Thatcham Site 5 no.3	Q–0651	9840	160
SK	529834	Anston Stones Cave	BM–0439	9850	115
SK	529834	Anston Stones Cave	BM–0440a	9940	115
SH	780828	Kendrick's Cave mandible	OxA–0111	10000	200
TQ	055850	Three Ways Wharf, Uxbridge	OxA–1902	10010	120
SU	502668	Thatcham Site 3 no.1	Q–0658	10030	170
NC	268170	Inchnadamph	SRR–1788	10080	70
TQ	055850	Three Ways Wharf, Uxbridge	OxA–1778	10270	100
SE	89 04	Messingham	Birm–349	10280	120
SP	875625	Earl's Barton	OxA–0803	10320	150
SU	502668	Thatcham Site 3 no.2	Q–0659	10365	170
SK	534742	Robin Hood's Cave	BM–0603	10390	90
TA	034812	Flixton Site 2	Q–0066	10413	210
SK	534742	Robin Hood's Cave	BM–0604	10590	90
SK	096556	Ossom's Cave	GrN–7400	10590	70
SK	097548	Elder Bush Cave	OxA–0811	10600	110
SD	391756	Kirkhead Cave	HAR–1059	10700	200
TM	134443	Sproughton	OxA–0518	10700	160
TM	134443	Sproughton	OxA–0517	10910	150
SK	536743	Mother Grundy's Parlour	Q–1459	11160	170
SK	075676	Dowel Hall Cave	OxA–1463	11200	120
SK	536743	Mother Grundy's Parlour	Q–1483	11285	180
SK	536743	Mother Grundy's Parlour	Q–1484	11320	230
SJ	259233	Porth y Waen	OxA–1946	11390	120
SX	814675	Three Holes Cave	OxA–1501	11520	150
SD	331387	Poulton elk context	St–3836	11665	140
TG	700700	Leman and Ower Banks point	OxA–195O	11740	150
SK	100663	Fox Hole Cave	OxA–1493	11970	120
SX	814675	Three Holes Cave	OxA–1499	11970	150
SK	100663	Fox Hole Cave	OxA–1494	12000	120
SK	536743	Mother Grundy's Parlour	OxA–0733	12060	160
SO	546156	King Arthur's Cave	OxA–1562	12120	120
SX	934641	Kent's Cavern	GrN–6204	12180	100
SK	536743	Mother Grundy's Parlour	OxA–0734	12190	140
SD	331387	Poulton elk context	St–3832	12200	160
ST	467541	Sun Hole	OxA–0535	12210	160
SO	546156	King Arthur's Cave	OxA–1563	12210	120

SK	534741	Church Hole Cave	OxA–0735	12240	150
ST	467539	Gough's New Cave	BM–2184R	12250	160
ST	467539	Gough's New Cave	OxA–0591	12260	160
SK	534742	Robin Hood's Cave	OxA–1670	12290	120
ST	467539	Gough's New Cave	OxA–1071	12300	180
ST	467539	Gough's New Cave	BM–2187R	12300	200
SX	935641	Kent's Cavern black band	OxA–1789	12320	130
ST	467539	Gough's New Cave	OxA–0589	12340	150
SK	533741	Pin Hole Cave	OxA–1467	12350	120
SX	814675	Three Holes Cave	OxA–1500	12350	160
ST	467539	Gough's New Cave	BM–2183R	12350	160
ST	467539	Gough's New Cave	OxA–0590	12370	150
ST	467541	Sun Hole	BM–0524	12378	150
ST	476587	Aveline's Hole	OxA–1121	12380	130
SK	534742	Robin Hood's Cave	OxA–1617	12420	200
SK	534742	Robin Hood's Cave	OxA–1619	12450	150
SK	534742	Robin Hood's Cave	OxA–1618	12480	170
ST	467539	Gough's New Cave	OxA–0592	12500	160
ST	467539	Gough's Old Cave	OxA–0587	12530	150
SK	534742	Robin Hood's Cave	OxA–1616	12600	170

References

Aitken, M. J. 1990 *Science-based Dating in Archaeology*, London.

Anderson, Soren H. 1985 'Tybrind Vig, A preliminary report on a submerged Ertebølle settlement on the west coast of Fyn', *Journal of Danish Archaeology* 4: 52–69.

—— 1994 'New finds of Mesolithic logboats in Denmark', in Christer Westerdahl (ed.) *Crossroads in Ancient Shipbuilding*, Oxbow Monograph 40, Oxford, 1–10.

Armstrong, A. L. 1924 'Excavations at Mother Grundy's Parlour, Creswell Crags', *Journal of the Royal Anthropological Institute* 5: 146–78.

Barth, Edvard K. 1983 'Trapping reindeer in south Norway', *Antiquity* 57: 109–15.

Barton, N., Roberts, A. J. and Roe, D. A. (eds) 1991 *The Late Glacial in North-west Europe: Human Adaptation and Environmental Change at the End of the Pleistocene*, CBA Research Report no. 77.

Barton, R. N. E. 1992 *Hengistbury Head, Dorset, Volume 2: The Late Upper Palaeolithic and Early Mesolithic Sites*, Oxford University Committee for Archaeology, Monograph no. 34, Oxford.

Barton, R. N. E. and Roberts, A. J. 1996 'Reviewing the British Late Upper Palaeolithic: new evidence for chronological patterning in the Lateglacial record', *Oxford Journal of Archaeology* 15(3): 245–65.

Beasley, M. J. 1987 'A preliminary report on incremental banding as an indicator of seasonality in mammal teeth from Gough's Cave, Cheddar, Somerset', *Proceedings University of Bristol Spelaeological Society* 18(1): 116–28.

Behrensmeyer, A. K. and Hill, A. P. (eds) 1980 *Fossils in the Making: Vertebrate Taphonomy and Paleoecology*, Chicago.

Beltran, Antonio 1982 *Rock Art of the Spanish Levant*, Cambridge.

Bergman, C. A. and Barton R. N. E. 1986 'The Upper Palaeolithic site of Hengistbury Head, Dorset, England', in S. N. Collcutt (ed.) *The Palaeolithic of Britain and its Nearest Neighbours: Recent Trends*, Sheffield, 69–72.

Bettinger, Robert L. 1991 *Hunter-Gatherers: Archaeological and Evolutionary Theory*, London and New York.

Binford, L. R. 1978a *Nunamiut Ethnoarchaeology*, New York.

—— 1978b 'Dimensional analysis of behaviour and site structure: learning from an Eskimo hunting stand', *American Antiquity* 43: 330–61.

—— 1980 'Willow smoke and dogs' tails: hunter-gatherer settlement systems and archaeological site formation', *American Antiquity* 45(1): 4–20.

—— 1981 *Bones: Ancient Men and Modern Myths*, New York.

—— 1983 *In Pursuit of the Past: Decoding the Archaeological Record*, New York.

—— 1989 *Debating Archaeology*, London.

Bintliff, John 1991 'Post-modernism, rhetoric and scholasticism at TAG: the current state of British archaeological theory', *Antiquity* 65: 274–8.

Bishop, A. H. 1914 'An Oronsay shell-mound – a Scottish pre-Neolithic site', *Proceedings of the Society of Antiquaries of Scotland* 48 (1913–14): 52–108.

Bonsall, Clive 1981 'The coastal factor in the Mesolithic settlement of north-west England', in B. Gramsch (ed.) *The Mesolithic in Europe*, Potsdam, 451–72.

—— 1988 'Morton and Lussa Wood: the case for early Flandrian settlement of Scotland: comment on Myers', *Scottish Archaeological Review* 5: 30–3.

—— (ed.) 1989 *The Mesolithic in Europe*, Edinburgh.

Bonsall, Clive and Smith, Christopher 1989 'Late Palaeolithic and Mesolithic bone and antler artefacts from the British Isles: first reactions to accelerator dates', *Mesolithic Miscellany* 10(1): 33–8.

—— 1990 'Bone and antler technology in the British late Upper Palaeolithic and Mesolithic: the impact of accelerator dating', in Pierre M. Vermeersch and Philip van Peer (eds) *Contributions to the Mesolithic in Europe*, Leuven, 359–68.

Bonsall, C., Sutherland, D. G., Lawson, T. J., Russell, N. J. and Barnetson, L. 1989 *Ulva Cave: Excavation Report No. 2*, Edinburgh.

Bowman, S. 1990 *Radiocarbon Dating*, London.

Bramwell, D. 1960 'Some research into bird distribution in Britain during the Late Glacial and Post-Glacial periods', *Bird Report 1959–60 of Merseyside Naturalists Association*, 51–8.

Burch, E. S. 1972 'The caribou/wild reindeer as a human resource', *American Antiquity* 37(3): 339–68.

Burleigh, R. 1986 'Radiocarbon dates for human and animal bones from Mendip caves', *Proceedings University of Bristol Spelaeological Society* 17(3): 267–74.

Campbell, John B. 1977 *The Upper Palaeolithic of Britain* Vols I and II, Oxford.

—— 1986 'Hiatus and continuity in the British Upper Palaeolithic: a view from the Antipodes', in Derek A. Roe (ed.) *Studies in the Upper Palaeolithic of Britain and Northwest Europe*, BAR S296, Oxford, 7–42.

Chaplin, R. E. 1975 'The ecology and behaviour of deer in relation to their impact on the environment of prehistoric Britain', in J. G. Evans, Susan Limbrey and Henry Cleere (eds) *The Effect of Man on the Landscape: The Highland Zone*, CBA Research Report 11, London, 40–2.

Charles, R. and Jacobi, R. M. 1994 'The lateglacial fauna from the Robin Hood Cave, Creswell Crags: a re-assessment', *Oxford Journal of Archaeology* 13(1): 1–32.

Churchill, D. M. 1962 'The stratigraphy of the Mesolithic sites III and V at Thatcham, Berkshire, England', *Proceedings of the Prehistoric Society* 28: 362–70.

Clark, J. G. D. 1934 'A late Mesolithic settlement at Selmeston, Sussex', *Antiquaries Journal* 14: 134–58.

—— 1946 'Seal-hunting in the stone age of North-western Europe: study in economic prehistory', *Proceedings of the Prehistoric Society* 12: 12–48.

—— 1947 'Whales as an economic factor in prehistoric Europe', *Antiquity* 21: 84–104.

—— 1952 *Prehistoric Europe: The Economic Basis*, London.

—— 1956 'Notes on the Obanian with special reference to antler- and bone-work', *Proceedings of the Society of Antiquaries of Scotland* 89 (1955–6): 91–106.

—— 1971 *Excavations at Star Carr* (2nd edition), Cambridge.

—— 1972 *Star Carr: A Case Study in Bioarchaeology,* Reading, Mass.

—— 1975 *The Earlier Stone Age Settlement of Scandinavia,* Cambridge.

Clark, J. G. D. and Godwin, H. 1956 'A Maglemosian site at Brandesburton, Holderness, Yorkshire', *Proceedings of the Prehistoric Society* 22: 6–22.

Clark, J. G. D. and Rankine, W. F. 1939 'Excavations at Farnham, Surrey, 1937–38', *Proceedings of the Prehistoric Society* 5: 61–118.

Clarke, A. and Wickham-Jones, C. R. 1988 'The ghost of Morton revisited: comment on Myers', *Scottish Archaeological Review* 5: 35–7.

Clarke. D. L. 1976 'Mesolithic Europe: the economic basis', in G. de G. Sieveking, I. H. Longworth and K. E. Wilson (eds) *Problems in Economic and Social Archaeology*, London, 449–82.

Cloutman, E. W. 1988 'Palaeoenvironments in the Vale of Pickering. Part 1: Stratigraphy and palaeogeography of Seamer Carr, Star Carr and Flixton Carr', and 'Palaeoenvironments in the Vale of Pickering. Part 2: Environmental history at Seamer Carr', *Proceedings of the Prehistoric Society* 54: 1–20 and 21–36.

Cloutman, E. W. and Smith, A. G. 1988 'Palaeoenvironments in the Vale of Pickering. Part 3: Environmental history at Star Carr', *Proceedings of the Prehistoric Society* 54: 37–58.

Cohen, M. N. 1977 *The Food Crisis in Prehistory*, New Haven.

Cohen, M. N. and Armelagos, G. J. 1984 *Palaeopathology at the Origins of Agriculture*, London.

Coles, J. M. 1971 'The early settlement of Scotland: excavations at Morton, Fife', *Proceedings of the Prehistoric Society* 37: 28–366.

—— 1983 'Morton revisted', in A. O'Connor and D. V. Clarke (eds) *From the Stone Age to the 'Forty-Five'*, Edinburgh, 9–18.

Collcutt, S. N. 1985 'Analysis of sediments in Gough's Cave, Cheddar, Somerset, and their bearing on Palaeolithic archaeology', *Proceedings University of Bristol Spelaeological Society* 17(2): 129–40.

Conolly, Ann P. and Dahl, Eilif 1970 'Maximum summer temperature in relation to the modern and Quaternary distributions of certain arctic–montane species in the British Isles', in D. Walker and R. G. West (eds) *Studies in the Vegetational History of the British Isles*, Cambridge, 159–223.

Constandse-Westermann, T. S. and Newell, R. R. 1988 'Patterns of extraterritorial ornaments dispersion: an approach to the measurement of Mesolithic exogamy', *Rivista di Antropologia*, Rome, supplement to vol. 66: 75–126.

—— 1989 'Social and biological aspects of the western European Mesolithic population structure: a comparison with the demography of North American Indians', in Clive Bonsall (ed.) *The Mesolithic in Europe*, Edinburgh, 106–15.

Cook, Jill 1986 'Marked human bones from Gough's Cave, Somerset', *Proceedings University of Bristol Spelaeological Society* 17(3): 275–8.

Cook, Jill and Jacobi, Roger 1995 'A reindeer antler or "Lyngby" axe from Northamptonshire and its context in the British Late Glacial', *Proceedings of the Prehistoric Society* 60: 75–84.

Coon, Carleton S. 1972 *The Hunting Peoples*, London.

Crane, Eva 1983 *The Archaeology of Beekeeping*, London.

Currant, A. P. 1986 'The Lateglacial mammal fauna of Gough's Cave, Cheddar, Somerset', *Proceedings University of Bristol Spelaeological Society* 17(3): 286–304.

—— 1987 'Late Pleistocene saiga antelope *Saiga tatarica* on Mendip', *Proceedings University of Bristol Spelaeological Society* 18(1): 74–80.

Currant, A. P., Jacobi, R. M. and Stringer, C. B. 1989 'Excavations at Gough's Cave, Somerset 1986–7', *Antiquity* 63: 131–6.

Cziesla, Erwin 1992 *Jager und Sammler: Die mittlere Steinzeit im Landkries Pirmasens,* Bruhl.

Day, S. P. and Mellars, P. A. 1995 ' "Absolute" dating of Mesolithic human activity at Star Carr, Yorkshire: new Palaeoecological studies and identification of the 9600 BP radiocarbon "Plateau" ', *Proceedings of the Prehistoric Society* 60: 417–22.

Degerbol, M. 1961 'On the find of a preboreal dog (*Canis familiaris*) from Star Carr, Yorkshire with remains of other Mesolithic dogs', *Proceedings of the Prehistoric Society* 27: 35–65.

Deith, M. R. 1983 'Molluscan calendars: the use of growth-line analysis to establish seasonality of shellfish collection at the Mesolithic site of Morton, Fife', *Journal of Archaeological Science* 10: 423–40.

—— 1986 'Subsistence strategies at a Mesolithic camp site: evidence from stable isotope analysis of shells', *Journal of Archaeological Science* 13: 61–78.

—— 1989 'Clams and salmonberries: interpreting seasonality data from shells', in Clive Bonsall (ed.) *The Mesolithic in Europe,* Edinburgh, 73–9.

Dennell, Robin 1983 *European Economic Prehistory: A New Approach,* London.

Dumont, J. V. 1988 *A Microwear Analysis of Selected Artefact Types from the Mesolithic Sites of Star Carr and Mount Sandel,* BAR 187, Oxford.

—— 1989 'Star Carr: the results of a micro-wear study', in Clive Bonsall (ed.) *The Mesolithic in Europe,* Edinburgh, 231–40.

Edwards, Kevin J. and Mithen, Steven 1995 'The colonization of the Hebridean Islands of Western Scotland: evidence from the palynological and archaeological records', *World Archaeology* 26(3): 348–64.

Fischer, A. 1989 'Hunting with flint-tipped arrows: results and experiences from practical experiments', in Clive Bonsall (ed.) *The Mesolithic in Europe,* Edinburgh, 29–39.

—— (ed.) 1995 *Man and Sea in the Mesolithic,* Oxford.

Foley, Robert 1981 'A model of regional archaeological structure', *Proceedings of the Prehistoric Society* 47: 1–18.

Forsberg, L. L. 1985 *Site Variability and Settlement Patterns,* Umea.

Fraser, F. C. and King, J. E. 1971 'Faunal remains', in J. G. D. Clark *Excavations at Star Carr* (2nd edition), Cambridge, 70–95.

Gamble, Clive 1986 *The Palaeolithic Settlement of Europe,* Cambridge.

Garrod, D. A. E. 1926 *The Upper Palaeolithic Age in Britain,* Oxford.

Gendel, P. A. 1984 *Mesolithic Social Territories in Northwestern Europe,* BAR S218, Oxford.

—— 1989 'The analysis of lithic styles through distributional profiles of variation: examples from the western European Mesolithic', in Clive Bonsall (ed.) *The Mesolithic in Europe,* Edinburgh, 40–7.

Gentles, D. S. and Smithson, P. A. 1986 'Fires in caves: effects on temperature and airflow', *Proceedings University of Bristol Spelaeological Society* 17(3): 205–17.

Green, S. W. and Zvelebil, M. 1990 'The Mesolithic colonization and agricultural transition of South-east Ireland', *Proceedings of the Prehistoric Society* 56: 57–88.

Greenhill, B. 1976 *The Archaeology of the Boat: A New Introductory Study*, London.

Grigson, Caroline 1978 'The Late Glacial and Early Flandrian ungulates of England and Wales – an interim review', in Susan Limbrey and J. G. Evans (eds) *The Effect of Man on the Landscape: the Lowland Zone*, CBA Research Report 21, London, 46–56.

—— 1989 'Bird-foraging patterns in the Mesolithic', in Clive Bonsall (ed.) *The Mesolithic in Europe*, Edinburgh, 60–72.

Grøn, O. 1983 'Social behaviour and settlement structure: preliminary results of a distribution analysis on sites of the Maglemose culture', *Journal of Danish Archaeology* 2: 32–42.

—— 1989 'General spatial behaviour in small dwellings: a preliminary study in ethnoarchaeology and social psychology', in Clive Bonsall (ed.) *The Mesolithic in Europe*, Edinburgh, 99–105.

Hallam, J. S., Edwards, B. J. N., Barnes, B. and Stuart, A. J. 1973 'A Late Glacial elk associated with barbed points from High Furlong, Lancashire', *Proceedings of the Prehistoric Society* 39: 100–28.

Harrison, C. J. O. 1986 'Bird remains from Gough's Cave, Cheddar, Somerset', *Proceedings University of Bristol Spelaeological Society* 17(3): 305–10.

—— 1987 'Pleistocene and prehistoric birds of south-west Britain', *Proceedings University of Bristol Spelaeological Society* 18(1): 81–104.

—— 1988 'Bird bones from Soldier's Hole, Cheddar, Somerset', *Proceedings University of Bristol Spelaeological Society* 18(2): 258–64.

—— 1989 'Bird remains from Gough's Old Cave, Cheddar, Somerset', and 'Bird remains from Chelm's Combe Shelter, Cheddar, Somerset', *Proceedings University of Bristol Spelaeological Society* 18(3): 490–11 and 412–14.

Hassan, F. 1979 *Demographic Archaeology*, New York.

Healey, F., Heaton, M. and Lobb, S. J. 1992 'Excavations at the Mesolithic site at Thatcham, Berkshire', *Proceedings of the Prehistoric Society* 58: 41–76.

Hendry, George 1989 *Midges in Scotland,* Aberdeen.

Houtsma, P., Kramer, E., Newell, R. R. and Smit, J. L. 1996 *The Late Palaeolithic Habitation of Haule V*, Assen.

Huntley, B. and Birks, H. J. B. 1983 *An Atlas of Past and Present Pollen Maps for Europe: 0–13000 Years Ago*, Cambridge.

Ingold, Tim 1988 *Hunters, Pastoralists and Ranchers*, Cambridge.

Innes, J. B. and Simmons, I. G. 1988 'Disturbance and diversity: floristic changes associated with pre-elm decline woodland recession in north east Yorkshire', in M. Jones (ed.) *Archaeology and Flora of the British Isles*, Oxford, 7–20.

Jacobi. R. M. 1976 'Britain inside and outside Mesolithic Europe', *Proceedings of the Prehistoric Society* 42: 67–84.

—— 1978 'Northern England in the eighth millennium bc: an essay', in P. A. Mellars (ed.) *The Early Postglacial Settlement of Northern Europe*, London, 295–332 .

—— 1980 'The Upper Palaeolithic in Britain, with special reference to Wales', in J. A. Taylor (ed.) *Culture and Environment in Prehistoric Wales*, BAR 76, Oxford, 15–99.

—— 1985 'The history and literature of Pleistocene discoveries at Gough's Cave, Cheddar, Somerset', *Proceedings University of Bristol Spelaeological Society* 17(2): 102–15.

—— 1986a 'The Lateglacial archaeology of Gough's Cave at Cheddar', in S. N. Collcutt (ed.) *The Palaeolithic of Britain and its Nearest Neighbours: Recent Trends*, Sheffield, 75–9.

—— 1986b 'A.M.S. results from Cheddar Gorge – trodden and untrodden "lifeways" ', in J. A. J. Gowlett and R. E. M. Hedges (eds) *Archaeological Results from Accelerator Dating*, Oxford, 81–6.

—— 1987 'Misanthropic miscellany: musings on British early Flandrian archaeology and other flights of fancy', in P. Rowley-Conwy, M. Zvelebil and H. P. Blankholm (eds) *Mesolithic Northwest Europe: Recent Trends*, Sheffield, 163–8.

Jenkinson, R. D. S. 1984a *Creswell Crags*, BAR 122, Oxford.

—— 1984b 'A rapid but short lived colonisation of the British Isles by the Northern Lynx', in R. D. S. Jenkinson and D. D. Gilbertson (eds) *In the Shadow of Extinction*, Sheffield, 111–15.

Jenkinson, R. D. S. and Gilbertson, D. D. (eds) 1984 *In the Shadow of Extinction: A Quaternary Archaeology and Palaeoecology of the Lake, Fissures and Caves at Creswell Crags SSSI*, Sheffield.

Jenkinson, R. D. S., Gilbertson, D. D. and Bramwell, D. 1984 'The birds of Britain – When did they arrive?', in R. D. S. Jenkinson and D. D. Gilbertson (eds) *In the Shadow of Extinction*, Sheffield, 89–99.

Jensen, Helle Juel 1988 'Functional analysis of prehistoric flint tools by high power microscopy: a review of West European research', *Journal of World Prehistory* 2(1): 53–88.

Jochim, M. A. 1976 *Hunter-Gatherer Settlement and Subsistence*, New York.

Johnstone, Paul 1980 *The Sea-craft of Prehistory*, London.

Jones, M. (ed.) 1988 *Archaeology and Flora of the British Isles*, Oxford.

Jones, R. L. and Keen, D. H. 1993 *Pleistocene Environments of the British Isles,* London.

Keeley, L. H. 1974 'Technique and methodology in microwear studies: a critical review', *World Archaeology* 5: 323–36.

—— 1980 *Experimental Determination of Stone Tool Uses*, Chicago.

Kidson, C. and Tooley, M. J. 1977 *The Quaternary History of the Irish Sea*, Liverpool.

King, Judith 1962 'Report on animal bones', in J. J. Wymer 'Excavations at the Maglemosian sites at Thatcham, Berkshire', *Proceedings of the Prehistoric Society* 28: 355–61.

Lacaille, A. D. 1954 *The Stone Age in Scotland*, Oxford.

Lamb, Hubert H. 1985 'Climate and landscape in the British Isles', in S. R. J. Woodell (ed.) *The English Landscape: Past, Present and Future*, Oxford, 148–67.

Larsson, Lars (ed.) (1996) *The Earliest Settlement of Scandinavia*, Stockholm.

Leakey, L. S. B. 1951 'Preliminary excavations of a Mesolithic site at Abinger Common, Surrey', *Surrey Archaeological Society Research Paper* No. 3.

Legge, A. J. and Rowley-Conwy, P. A. 1988 *Star Carr Revisited*, London.

Leroi-Gourhan, A. 1984 *Pincevent: campement magdalenien de chasseurs de rennes*, Paris.

—— 1985 'Pollen analysis of sediment samples from Gough's Cave, Cheddar', *Proceedings University of Bristol Spelaeological Society* 17(2): 141–4.

Leroi-Gourhan, A. and Brezillon, M. 1966 'L'habitation magdalénienne no. I de Pincevent (Seine-et-Marne)', *Gallia Préhistoire* 9: 263–385.

—— 1972 'Fouilles de Pincevent: essai d'analyse ethnographique d'un habitat magdalénian', *Gallia Préhistoire* Supplement 7.

Lieth, H. and Whittaker, R. H. 1975 *Primary Productivity of the Biosphere*, Berlin.

Limbrey, Susan and Evans, J. G. 1978 *The Effects of Man on the Landscape: The Lowland Zone*, CBA Research Report 21, London.

Long, D., Wickham-Jones, C. R. and Ruckley, N. A. 1986 A flint artefact from the northern North Sea', in Derek A. Roe (ed.) *Studies in the Upper Palaeolithic of Britain and Northwest Europe*, BAR S296, Oxford, 55–62.

Louwe Kooijmans, L. P. 1971 'Mesolithic bone and antler implements from the North Sea and from the Netherlands', *Berichten van de Rijksdienst voor bet Oudheidkundig. Bodenmonderz*, Jaargang 20–1 (1970–1): 97–73.

—— 1985 *Sporen in het land: De Nederlandse delta in de prehistorie*, Amsterdam.

Lowe, J. J. and Walker, M. J. C. 1987 *Reconstructing Quaternary Environments*, Harlow.

McBurney, Charles 1959 'Report on the first season's fieldwork on British Upper Palaeolithic cave deposits', *Proceedings of the Prehistoric Society* 25: 260–9.

Mace, Angela 1959 'The excavation of a late Upper Palaeolithic open-site on Hengistbury Head, Christchurch, Dorset', *Proceedings of the Prehistoric Society* 25: 233–59.

McGrail, S. 1978 *Logboats of England and Wales*, BAR 51, Oxford.

—— 1987 *Ancient Boats in N.W. Europe*, London.

Mellars, P. A. 1975 'Ungulate populations, economic patterns and the Mesolithic landscape', in J. G. Evans, Susan Limbrey and Henry Cleere (eds) *The Effect of Man on the Landscape: The Highland Zone*, CBA Research Report 11, London, 49–56.

—— (ed.) 1978a *The Early Postglacial Settlement of Northern Europe*, London.

—— 1978b 'Excavation and economic analysis of Mesolithic shell middens on the island of Oronsay (Inner Hebrides)', in P. A. Mellars (ed.) *The Early Postglacial Settlement of Northern Europe*, London, 371–96.

—— 1987 *Excavations on Oronsay*, Edinburgh.

Mellars, P. A. and Wilkinson, M. R. 1980 'Fish otoliths as evidence of seasonality in prehistoric shell middens: the evidence from Oronsay (Inner Hebrides)', *Proceedings of the Prehistoric Society* 46: 19–44.

Mercer, John 1980 'Lussa Wood 1: the Late-glacial and early Post-glacial occupation of Jura', *Proceedings of the Society of Antiquaries of Scotland* 110 (1978–80): 1–32.

Mithen, Steven 1989 'Evolutionary theory and post-processual archaeology', *Antiquity* 63: 483–94.

Mithen, Steven and Lake, Mark 1996 'The Southern Hebrides Mesolithic Project: reconstructing Mesolithic settlement in Western Scotland', in Tony Pollard and Alex Morrison (eds) *The Early Prehistory of Scotland*, Edinburgh, 123–51.

Moore, John W. 1950 'Mesolithic sites in the neighbourhood of Flixton, north-east Yorkshire', *Proceedings of the Prehistoric Society* 16: 101–8.

—— 1954 'Excavations at Flixton, Site 2', in J. G. D. Clark (ed.) *Excavations at Star Carr* (2nd edition, 1971), Cambridge, 192–4.

Moore, P. D. 1988 'The development of moorlands and upland mires', in M. Jones (ed.) *Archaeology and Flora of the British Isles*, Oxford, 116–22.

Morner, N. A. and Wallin, B. 1977 '10000 year temperature record from Gotland, Sweden', *Palaeogeography, Palaeoclimatology, Palaeoecology* 21: 113–38.

Morrison, Alex 1982 'Man in the early Scottish environment: comment on Price', *Scottish Archaeological Review* 1(2): 73–7.

Morrison, Alex and Bonsall, Clive 1989 'The early Post-glacial settlement of Scotland: a review', in Clive Bonsall (ed.) *The Mesolithic in Europe*, Edinburgh, 134–42.

Murray, N. A., Bonsall, C., Sutherland, D. G., Lawson, T. J. and Kitchener, A. C. 1993 'Further radiocarbon determinations on reindeer remains of Middle and Late Devensian Age from the Creag Nan Uamh Caves, Assysnt, N.W. Scotland', *Quaternary Newsletter* 70 (June): 1–10.

Myers, A. M. 1988 'Scotland inside and outside the British mainland Mesolithic', *Scottish Archaeological Review* 5: 23–9.

—— 1989 'Reliablc and maintainable technological strategies in the Mesolithic of mainland Britain', in Robin Torrence (ed.) *Time, Energy and Stone Tools*, Cambridge, 78–91.

Newcomer, M. H. and Sieveking, G. de G. 1980 'Experimental flake scatter-patterns: a new interpretative technique', *Journal of Field Archaeology* 7: 345–52.

Newell, R. R. 1981 'Mesolithic dwelling structures: fact and fantasy', in B. Gramsch (ed.) *The Mesolithic in Europe*, Potsdam, 235–85.

Newell, Raymond R. and Constandse-Westermann, Trinette S. 1986 'Testing an ethnographic analogue of Mesolithic social structure and the archaeological resolution of Mesolithic ethnic groups and breeding populations', *Proceedings of the Koninklijke Nederlandse Akademie nab Wetenschappen* Series B, 89(3): 243–310.

Noe-Nygaard, N. 1974 'Mesolithic hunting in Denmark illustrated by bone injuries caused by human weapons', *Journal of Archaeological Science* 1: 217–48.

—— 1975 'Two shoulder blades with healed lesions from Star Carr', *Proceedings of the Prehistoric Society* 41: 10–16.

—— 1977 'Butchering and marrow fracturing as a taphonomic factor in archaeological deposits', *Paleobiology* 3: 218–37.

—— 1987 'Taphonomy in archaeology with special reference to man as biasing factor', *Journal of Danish Archaeology* 6: 7–62.

Oele, E., Schuttenhelm, R. T. E. and Wiggers, A. J. 1979 *The Quaternary History of the North Sea*, Symposia Universitatis Upsaliensis Annum Quingentesium Celebrantis 2, Uppsala.

O'Malley, M. and Jacobi, R. M. 1978 'The excavation of a Mesolithic occupation site at Broom Hill, Braishfield, Hampshire, *Rescue Archaeology in Hampshire* 4: 16–39.

Palmer, S. 1976 'The Mesolithic habitation site at Culver Well, Portland, Dorset: interim note', *Proceedings of the Prehistoric Society* 49: 324–6.

—— 1989 'Mesolithic sites of Portland and their significance', in Clive Bonsall (ed.) *The Mesolithic in Europe*, Edinburgh, 254–7.

Parkin, R. A., Rowley-Conwy, P. and Serjeantson, Dale 1986 'Late Palaeolithic exploitation of horse and red deer at Gough's Cave, Cheddar, Somerset, *Proceedings University of Bristol Spelaeological Society* 17(3): 311–30.

Pitts, M. W. and Jacobi, R. M. 1979 'Some aspects of change in flaked stone of the Mesolithic and Neolithic in southern England', *Journal of Archaeological Science* 6: 163–77.

Pollard, Tony and Morrison, Alex (eds) (1996) *The Early Prehistory of Scotland*, Edinburgh.

Price, R. J. 1982 'The magnitude and frequency of late Quaternary environmental changes in Scotland: implications for human occupation', *Scottish Archaeological Review* 1(2): 61–72.

Price, T. Douglas 1978 'Mesolithic settlement systems in the Netherlands', in P. A. Mellars (ed.) *The Early Postglacial Settlement of Northern Europe*, London, 81–114.

—— 1983 'The European Mesolithic', *American Antiquity* 48(4): 761–78.

—— 1987 'The Mesolithic of western Europe', *Journal of World Prehistory* 1: 225–305.

—— (ed.) 1989a *The Chemistry of Prehistoric Human Bone*, Cambridge.

—— 1989b 'The reconstruction of Mesolithic diets', in Clive Bonsall (ed.) *The Mesolithic in Europe*, Edinburgh, 48–59.

Price, T. Douglas and Brown, James A. (eds) 1985 *Prehistoric Hunter-Gatherers: The Emergence of Cultural Complexity*, New York.

Rackham, O. 1980 *Ancient Woodland*, London.

Radley, J. and Mellars, P. 1964 'A Mesolithic structure at Deepcar, Yorkshire, England and the affinities of its associated flint industries', *Proceedings of the Prehistoric Society* 30: 1–24.

Radley, J., Tallis, J. H. and Switsur, V. R. 1974 'The excavation of three "narrow blade" Mesolithic sites in the southern Pennines, England', *Proceedings of the Prehistoric Society* 40: 1–19.

Rosenfeld, A. 1964 'Excavations in the Torbryan Caves, Devonshire. II Three Holes Cave', *Transactions of the Devon Archaeological Exploration Society* 22: 3–26.

Ryan, M. 1980 'An early Mesolithic site in the Irish Midlands', *Antiquity* 54: 46–7.

Schadla-Hall, R. T. 1987 'Recent investigations of the early Mesolithic landscape and settlement in the Vale of Pickering, North Yorkshire', in P. Rowley-Conwy, M. Zvelebil and H. P. Blankholm (eds) *Mesolithic Northwest Europe: Recent Trends*, Sheffield, 46–54.

—— 1989 'The Vale of Pickering in the early Mesolithic in context', in Clive Bonsall (ed.) *The Mesolithic in Europe*, Edinburgh, 218–24.

Schiffer, M. B. 1976 *Behavioral Archaeology*, London.

—— 1989 *Archaeological Method and Theory*, Tucson.

Selkirk, A. 1978 'Broom Hill, Braishfield: Mesolithic dwelling', *Current Archaeology* 63: 117–20.

Semenov, S. A. 1964 *Prehistoric Technology*, London.

Sieveking, G. de G. 1971 'The Kendrick's Cave mandible', *British Museum Quarterly* 35: 230–50.

Simmons, I. G. 1996 *The Environmental Impact of Later Mesolithic Cultures*, Edinburgh.

Simmons, Ian and Tooley, Michael 1981 *The Environment in British Prehistory*, London.

Smith, C. and Bonsall, C. 1991 'Late Upper Palaeolithic and Mesolithic chronology: points of interest from recent research', *Proceedings of the Symposium on 'Late Glacial North-West Europe'*, Oxford, 1989.

Spiess, A. E. 1979 *Reindeer and Caribou Hunters: An Archaeological Study*, New York.

Stringer, C. B. 1985 'The hominid remains from Gough's Cave', *Proceedings University of Bristol Spelaeological Society* 17(2): 145–52.

Stuart, A. J. 1976 'The nature of the lesions on the elk skeleton from High Furlong, near Blackpool, Lancashire', *Proceedings of the Prehistoric Society* 42: 323–4.

—— 1982 *Pleistocene Vertebrates in the British Isles*, London.

Tauber, H. 1981 '¹³C evidence for dietary habits of prehistoric man in Denmark', *Nature* 2292: 332–3.

Thorburn, Archibald 1984 *Thorburn's Mammals*, New York.

Tooley, M. J. 1974 'Sea-level changes during the last 9,000 years in north-west England', *Geographical Journal* 140: 18–42.

—— 1978 S*ea-level Changes in North-West England during the Flandrian Stage*, Oxford.

Torrence, Robin (ed.) 1989 *Time, Energy and Stone Tools*, Cambridge.

van Andel, T. H. 1989 'Late Quaternary sea-level changes and archaeology', *Antiquity* 63: 733–45.

—— 1990 'Addendum to "Late Quaternary sea-level changes and archaeology" ', *Antiquity* 64: 151–2.

van Wijngaarden-Bakker, Louise H. 1985 'The faunal remains', in P. C. Woodman (ed.) *Excavations at Mount Sandel 1973–77*, Belfast, 71–6.

—— 1989 'Faunal remains and the Irish Mesolithic', in Clive Bonsall (ed.) *The Mesolithic in Europe*, Edinburgh, 125–33.

Vermeersch, Pierre M. and van Peer, Philip 1990 *Contributions to the Mesolithic in Europe*, Leuven.

Whallon, R. Jr 1978 'The spatial analysis of Mesolithic occupation floors: a reappraisal', in P. A. Mellars (ed.) *The Early Postglacial Settlement of Northern Europe*, London, 27–35.

Wheeler, A. 1978a 'Why were there no fish remains at Star Carr?', *Journal of Archaeological Science* 5: 85–9.

—— 1978b *Key to the Fishes of Northern Europe*, London.

Wickham-Jones, C. R. 1990 *Rhum. Mesolithic and Later Sites at Kinloch: Excavations 1984–86*, Edinburgh.

—— 1994 *Scotland's First Settlers*, London.

Wing, E. S. and Brown, A. B. 1979 *Palaeonutrition: Method and Theory in Prehistoric Foodways*, London.

Winterhalder, Bruce and Smith, Eric Alden 1981 *Hunter-Gatherer Foraging Strategies*, Chicago.

Wobst, H. M. 1974 'Boundary conditions for Palaeolithic social systems: a simulation approach', *American Antiquity* 39: 147–78.

—— 1976 'Locational relationships in Palaeolithic society', *Journal of Human Evolution* 5: 49–58.

Woodell, S. R. J. (ed.) 1985 *The English Landscape*, Oxford.

Woodman, P. C. 1978 *The Mesolithic in Ireland*, BAR 58, Oxford.

—— 1985 *Excavations at Mount Sandel 1973–77*, Belfast.

—— 1988 'Comment on Myers', *Scottish Archaeological Review* 5: 34–5.

—— 1990 'A review of the Scottish Mesolithic: a plea for normality', *Proceedings of the Society of Antiquaries of Scotland*: 1–32.

Wymer, J. J. 1962 'Excavations at the Maglemosian sites at Thatcham, Berkshire, England', *Proceedings of the Prehistoric Society* 28: 329–61.

Wymer, J. J. and Bonsall, C. J. (eds) 1977 *Gazetteer of Mesolithic Sites in England and Wales with a Gazetteer of Upper Palaeolithic Sites in England and Wales*, CBA Research Report 20, Norwich.

Wymer, J. J., Jacobi, R. M. and Rose, J. 1975 'Late Devensian and early Flandrian barbed points from Sproughton, Suffolk', *Proceedings of the Prehistoric Society* 41: 235–41.

Yellen, J. E. 1977 *Archaeological Approaches to the Present: Models for Reconstructing the Past*, New York.

Zivanovic, Srboljub 1982 *Ancient Diseases*, London.

Zvelebil, Marek (ed.) 1986 *Hunters in Transition,* Cambridge.

—— 1994 'Plant use in the Mesolithic and its role in the transition to farming', *Proceedings of the Prehistoric Society* 60: 35–74.

Index

(entries in italic refer to figures)